Speech Preparation Checklist

- ❑ Who is going to be in the audience?

- ❑ How can I find out more about them?

- ❑ How does the location of the speech affect its content?

- ❑ Are there any special circumstances I must take into account?

- ❑ What is my purpose?
  - ☞ To inform?
  - ☞ To entertain?
  - ☞ To persuade?

- ❑ What organizational pattern should I use?
  - ☞ Alphabetical
  - ☞ Cause-effect
  - ☞ Chronological
  - ☞ Numerical
  - ☞ Problem-solution
  - ☞ Spatial
  - ☞ Topical

- ❑ What appeal should I use?
  - ☞ Appeal to Logic
  - ☞ Appeal to Emotion

- ❑ Have I suited my style to the audience, purpose, and occasion?
  - ☞ Diction
  - ☞ Tone
  - ☞ Figures of speech
  - ☞ Sentence length

- ❑ Is my outline complete and correct?

continued

alpha
books

❑   Do I have a good opening?

❑   Have I developed the body with supporting information?
- ☞ Anecdotes
- ☞ Comparison and contrast
- ☞ Examples
- ☞ Facts
- ☞ Statistics
- ☞ Testimony by authorities

❑   Is my conclusion complete and commanding?

❑   Have I revised and edited my speech?

❑   Is the title suitable and interesting?

❑   Have I used humor appropriately?

❑   Have I included relevant and attractive visual aids, audio-visual aids, and props?

❑   Have I rehearsed enough?

❑   Will I dress for success?

❑   Will I use my voice and body language to best advantage?

The **COMPLETE**

IDIOT'S

GUIDE TO

Speaking in Public with Confidence

by Laurie Rozakis

alpha
books

A Division of Macmillan General Reference
A Simon & Schuster Macmillan Company
1633 Broadway, New York, NY 10019

International Standard Book Number: 0-02-861038-5
Library of Congress Catalog Card Number: 95-080509

97 96 95   10 9 8 7 6 5 4 3 2 1

Interpretation of the printing code: the rightmost number of the first series of numbers is the year of the book's printing; the rightmost number of the second series of numbers is the number of the book's printing. For example, a printing code of 95-1 shows that the first printing of the book occurred in 1995.

Screen reproductions in this book were created by means of the program Collage Plus from Inner Media, Inc., Hollis, NH.

Printed in the United States of America

Publisher
Theresa H. Murtha

Editor
Lisa A. Bucki

Production Editor
Matt Hannafin

Copy Editor
Anne Owen

Cover Designers
Dan Armstrong, Barbara Kordesh

Designer
Kim Scott

Illustrator
Steve Vanderbosch

Manufacturing Coordinator
Steven Pool

Production Team Supervisor
Laurie Casey

Indexer
Jeanne Clark

Production Team
*Heather Butler, Angela Calvert,
Kim Cofer, Jennifer Eberhardt, Erika Millen*

*Special thanks to Royce E. Flood for ensuring the technical
accuracy of this book.*

Contents at a Glance

Contents

20 Nowhere to Hide: Speaking Off-the-Cuff 193

Part 5: Getting Your Act Together 201

21 Preparing Visual Aids, Audio-Visual Aids, and Props 203

Foreword

Most successful people have one thing in common: they can speak with eloquence in front of a group. In particular, they can verbalize their ideas so they are heard, understood, and acted upon.

If you are like most people, public speaking is not your favorite task (or you wouldn't need this book). But in a fast-paced, complex society like ours, which is seemingly ruled by computers, effective verbal communication is vital. We need men and women to inform, persuade, entertain, motivate, and inspire. In today's competitive job market, the person with strong communication skills has a clear advantage over tongue-tied colleagues.

Giving a speech can be one of the most nerve-wracking experiences known to man—and writing one can be just as difficult. So many a potential spellbinder remains glued to his or her seat, daunted by the prospect of facing an audience. But the good news is that jittery nerves, fear of failure, and the procrastination often associated with writing and giving a speech *can* be relieved. In my 20 years as Executive Director of the world's leading organization devoted to public speaking and leadership training, I have never met or heard of a "hopeless case." In fact, I could easily fill this book with success stories from formerly tongue-tied Toastmasters who've accomplished what they once thought impossible. I honestly believe that every person who truly wants to become a confident and eloquent public speaker can. Success or failure in this area is solely dependent upon one's attitude.

So, whether you are a novice scared to death by the thought of facing an audience, or a more seasoned speaker wanting to improve your effectiveness, this book is for you. It offers step-by-step guidance and platform-tested tips that show you how to write an effective speech and deliver it with grace, power, and eloquence. But don't expect to read this book on Sunday and become one of the nation's great orators on Monday. You have to work on accomplishing your goal. Henry Ford once said, "The great trouble today is that there are too many people looking for someone to do something for them." The secret of becoming a good speaker depends on your self-discipline and your ability to put into practice the simple rules and techniques outlined in this book.

Throughout history, events have been influenced by speakers who were able to capture the moment with their words. They did so by capturing their listeners' attention, then creating a feeling of need, satisfying that need, helping their listeners visualize that satisfaction, and finally, urging them on to action. This common thread is found in nearly all historical speeches.

Words have power. Words have altered the course of history and changed forever the destiny of individuals who spoke out. Granted, you may not aspire to change world history. But by implementing what you've learned in this book, you won't have to worry about sweaty palms and butterflies in the stomach the next time you need to brief your co-workers on a new project or chair your second-grader's Halloween party committee. You will feel in control, and be persuasive and effective. Above all, you will have learned more than the ability to coherently deliver a clear thought: You will have gained increased self-confidence from having turned obstacles and defeat into personal victory. By practicing self-discipline, you will have learned to control fear instead of letting it control you.

So if you want to become a dynamic speaker, I urge you to do two things: one, read this book; two, get on your feet and practice what you've learned. Don't worry if you don't sound like a pro at the first attempt. Stay with it, and before long, you'll be in command of a skill that can change your life.

If this book isn't enough to motivate you, I don't know what is. Go for it!

Terence J. McCann

Executive Director

Toastmasters International

Terrence J. McCann is Executive Director of Toastmasters International, the world's leading organization devoted to teaching public speaking skills. Since the nonprofit educational organization was founded in 1924, more than three million men and women have benefited from its programs. There are currently 175,000 Toastmasters in 8,000 clubs in 63 countries throughout the world. For information on finding a club near you, call 1-800-9WE-SPEAK. Or, contact Toastmasters International at P.O. Box 9052, Mission Viejo, CA 92688.

Introduction

What's as reliable as losing your quarter in a New York City telephone, as constant as dandruff, as invariable as middle-aged spread? It's the scores of students who stream into my Speech class every semester looking like they're ready to face a tax audit or a root canal. And those are the happy ones.

Gender's not a factor: the men and women seem equally wretched. It's not age, either: I've had 18-year-old freshmen and 75-year-old retirees with equally long faces and hunched shoulders. Size, shape, style: nope. They all look like someone's killed their puppy.

Every semester, I remind these woebegone men and women that *they* signed up for this class. I really didn't shanghai anyone, dragging them out of their warm beds to break rocks on the chain gang. I tell them that public speaking is not a tax audit or a root canal. It's not even a flat tire on the expressway, a missed train, or a burned casserole. I tell them that they will enjoy learning the fundamentals of public speaking and sharing their skills with the class. And yet they all look morose. Tragic, even.

By the end of the semester, the class has undergone a wondrous transformation. They're happy. Really happy. Why? They have learned that they can write and deliver a good speech. And in nearly all cases, they have actually gotten to enjoy speaking in public. And you will, too. I promise.

First of all, you'll be happy because you will discover that speaking in public is not a difficult skill—if you have the proper training. (That training part is my job.) Second, you'll acquire the tangible economic, social, and political benefits that come with mastery of public speaking. You'll feel that these rewards are well worth the time it takes to learn to speak in public. And you will discover that the intangible benefits—the pride and self-esteem that come with learning to stand up and express yourself with poise and eloquence—are even more important.

What You'll Learn in This Book

This book is divided into six sections that take you through the process of writing and delivering a speech. You will see that giving a speech involves much more than just standing at a podium and talking—that's the *easy* part! You'll discover that before the speaking event comes detailed planning, analysis, research, writing, revising, and rehearsing; and that after speaking means gathering your notes, walking to your seat, and soliciting feedback. You'll find out that *how* you say it can be every bit as important as *what* you say. Here's what the six parts of this book cover:

Part 1, Clearing Your Throat, first explores how people like you feel about public speaking. Then I discuss the importance of public speaking to both your personal and public lives. Last, you'll learn about common communication problems and get an overview of the different types of speeches you will be expected to write and deliver.

Part 2, Planning Your Speech, gets into the nitty-gritty of speech preparation: audience analysis, speaking to inform, speaking to persuade, and speaking to entertain. In this part, you'll learn how all speeches are the same—and different.

Part 3, Writing the Speech, explores speech style, as well as techniques for clearly communicating your meaning, suiting your personal speaking style to audience and purpose, and fitting with the audience and occasion. Here's where you will find out all about organization. There's a special focus on the backbone of complete speech preparation: outlining. I'll take you through the process of writing a speech from the beginning (the opening), through the middle (the body), and the close (the conclusion). Then you'll learn all about using humor in your speeches and meeting the needs of multicultural and international audiences.

Part 4, Tackling Specific Types of Speeches, provides a detailed description of informational, persuasive, and entertaining speeches. I also teach you how to master impromptu and extemporaneous speaking—the skill of thinking and speaking on your feet.

Part 5, Getting Your Act Together, helps you prepare visual aids, audio-visual aids, and props to add a fuller dimension to your speeches. This section also tells you in detail why and how you should rehearse your speech. Finally, this part describes how to use your voice and appearance to maximize your chances for success.

Part 6, The Moment of Truth, describes how to actually deliver the speech. You'll learn the importance of posture and mannerisms to a successful speech. And it's here that I take care of everyone's #1 worry: stage fright. Find out my sure-fire ways to master it. The last section explores how speaker's bureaus may suit your professional speech needs.

Lastly, there's a **Glossary** of key words and definitions and an **Appendix** containing sample speeches, both new and classic examples.

More for Your Money!

In addition to all the explanation and teaching, this book has other types of information to make it even easier for you to learn how to speak in public with confidence. Here's how you can recognize these features:

Bet You Didn't Know

Interesting, useful background information that can streamline the learning process. These are the facts that you can skip, but they're so interesting that you won't want to!

Words to the Wise

These warnings help you stay on track. They help you avoid the little pitfalls . . . and the big craters.

Tell Me About It

Use these hints to make public speaking easier—and more enjoyable!

Word Power

Like every other skill worth knowing, public speaking has its own jargon. Here's where I explain these terms so you can talk to the pros in the speechbiz like the pro that you'll become!

Acknowledgments

To my brilliant, patient, thoughtful husband, gratitude for your unflagging belief in me, the vacuuming, and the two loads of laundry you do every day. I also thank you for the comic book speech that appears in the Appendix. (While I'm here, my car needs windshield wiper fluid and the oil could stand a change.)

And to my children, whose voices will ring out gloriously through the ages.

Special Thanks to the Technical Reviewer . . .

The Complete Idiot's Guide to Speaking in Public with Confidence was reviewed by experts in the field who not only checked the technical accuracy of what you'll learn here, but also provided insight and guidance to help us ensure that this book gives you everything you need to know to begin speaking like a pro. Our special thanks are extended to:

Royce E. Flood (Ph.D., Northwestern University, 1972) has taught public speaking courses for beginners and advanced students for nearly three decades. Dr. Flood has been a member of the Speech department of Butler University (Indianapolis, IN) for 24 years. He is director of Butler's Basic Public Speaking course. He has co-authored five books on public speaking and debate, including *Public Speaking: A Rhetorical Perspective* and *Modern Competitive Debate*. Dr. Flood's other academic interests include persuasion, history, and film studies.

Part 1
Clearing Your Throat

It's like this: You've listened to scores of public speakers and said to yourself, "Hey, I can do this." You can, but you never actually have. *That's where your collar gets tight and your hands begin to shake.*

Or it's like this: You have a chance to make a speech that could make a significant difference to your career, reputation, and public profile. You don't really *have to make the speech, but it would be a shame to pass up the once-in-a-lifetime opportunity.*

Or even this: One bright Monday morning, your boss says, "By the way, Bob, I've slated you to deliver the presentation at the sales conference next week in Glassy Point, Idaho. Remember: This is our key market, so we're really counting on you." The last time you gave a speech was in 10th grade English, in 19 . . . oh, we're not going to get into that. Besides, your speech was a gobbler.

So what's your problem? Weren't you supposed to learn all about public speaking in high school and college? Sure you were, but you had your bad days and your good days. So did your teachers. The upshot is that you missed it. That's what this book is all about. So let's plunge right in and get our feet wet.

What Fresh Hell Is This?

Today, people have become pretty sophisticated about what is entertaining and what isn't. Thanks to television, John and Jean Q. Public know the secrets behind the tricks. As a result, they have little patience for inadequate presentations. They're right: listening to a dull speech is a form of torture.

According to conservative estimates, about five million speeches are delivered in the United States every year. Out of all these speeches, about one million are delivered by business people for business people. It's safe to say that out of all these speeches, only a few will be remembered for more than a few hours.

What does this mean for you? Well, first, the odds are quite good that you're going to have to listen to many speeches thanks to your professional career and personal interests. It also means that you very likely are going to have to deliver a whole stack of speeches for work, friends, relatives, hobbies, service organizations, religious groups, and civic associations. That's where this chapter comes in.

In this chapter, you learn how people feel about speaking in public. You'll discover that it's natural to approach a podium with some trepidation—and why. You'll also learn some of the excuses people give to deal with their fear about speaking in public.

Words to the Wise
"The brain starts working the moment you are born and never stops until you stand up and speak in public."—Anonymous

Finally, the information in this chapter will help empower you to take positive steps to overcome any fears you may have about public speaking. I'll give you the tools you need to realize that you *can* be an effective, powerful public speaker—that you can speak to large and small groups with confidence and skill.

You Mean I Have to Get Up and Say Something?

The former head of the New York Convention and Visitors Bureau, Charles Gillett, sets up some of his speeches with the following joke:

> The Roman emperor Nero went to the arena to see the lions do lunch with the Christians. The determined animals were munching away with their usual gusto until one Christian spoke to his lion, who listened attentively and then trotted away with its tail tucked between its legs. The same fellow continued to speak to lion after lion. Each one hurried away, as meek as it had been ferocious a few moments before. Finally, Nero could take the suspense no longer. He had the Christian brought to him. Standing the smiling fellow in front of his throne, Nero said, "If you tell me what you said to the lions, I'll set you free."
>
> The Christian replied, "I told them, 'The lion who wins this contest has to get up and say a few words to the audience.'"

Anyone who has ever had to deliver a speech can identify with the lions. For many people, being at the podium is not unlike being dangled over the fiery pit of hell. Speakers know that the audience is evaluating them not only for their ability to speak, but also for their ability to *think*.

They know that there are scores of things that can go wrong while they deliver their speech—and probably will. Nonetheless, even an idiot can learn to speak in public with confidence. And if you know what you're doing, public speaking can also be enjoyable. We're going to make it easy and fun for you. Promise.

> **Word Power**
> *Speech*: Any time you stand up in front of a group of people—no matter how small—and talk, you're giving a speech.

Our Biggest Fears

"We have nothing to fear but fear itself," Franklin Delano Roosevelt claimed. Fear is definitely a major turn-off for most of us, but a team of professional market researchers found that a lot of other things terrify us even more. Over the years, I have surveyed my students, asking each person to rank ten common situations or things that can cause fear: heights, dogs, financial problems, deep water, public speaking, and the like.

The greatest fear? Speaking before a group! Nearly half the people I surveyed were more terrified of speaking before a group than of anything else. This was followed by a fear of heights, insects, financial problems, deep water, illness, death, flying, loneliness, and dogs.

According to Daniel Goleman (the *New York Times*, December 18, 1984), nearly everyone is afraid of looking like a jerk in front of others. That's probably because half the world is composed of people who have something to say and can't—and the other half have nothing to say and keep on saying it.

Only 20 percent of Americans say they have never suffered from "stage fright" at any point in their lives. As a result, enterprising folks have developed a list of excuses to avoid public speaking. They are all listed in the next section. Take your pick now because by the time you finish this book, you won't need any excuses. You'll be too busy giving entertaining, persuasive, and informative speeches!

Top Ten Excuses People Use to Avoid Public Speaking

These are the top excuses people use to try to avoid speaking in public. After the list, I describe what you can do to make sure you don't need any of them when you're addressing groups. I also provide cross-references to later chapters of the book where you can find detailed information to overcome each excuse. See which excuses you think are most valid.

1. I don't have anything to say.

2. I'll make a fool of myself in front of (a) friends (b) family (c) community members (d) business associates.

3. I have laryngitis.

4. I didn't have time to write a speech.

5. I'm embarrassed about how I might look to others.

6. I just moved here from Bora-Bora (Tibet, Mars, New York City), and no one will understand my accent.

7. I'm too nervous. I'll drop dead from fear.

8. I just had a root canal, and my lips are numb.

9. I will forget what I have to say.

10. My killer cat ate my speech.

Extra Credit: Fill in your personal favorite excuse.

_____

_____

Let's take a look at some of these excuses.

Excuse #1: *I don't have anything to say.* You don't have anything to say? Sorry, won't work. *Everyone* has something to say. In fact, everyone has a lot to say. If you don't believe me, try this experiment.

For one day, carry around a notepad and pencil. Every hour, take out the pad and list all the people you spoke with during that hour. Next to their names, write down all the things you discussed. And don't forget telephone calls; they count, too! Part of your list might look like this:

Speech Log

7:00 AM–8:00 AM

➤ Reminded spouse about late afternoon meeting.

➤ Told kids to stop arguing over the cereal.

➤ Talked to people in deli when I got my coffee.

➤ Spoke with friends on the bus.

8:00 AM–9:00 AM

➤ Asked assistant for reports.

➤ Spoke with co-workers at coffee machine.

➤ Logged on e-mail and conversed with others.

➤ Attended 8:30 meeting and spoke with everyone.

9:00 AM–10:00 AM

➤ Visited other division and spoke to them.

➤ Met with legal department about copyrights.

➤ Called Mother to say hello.

➤ Called restaurant to make lunch reservations.

Did I make my point? Every day, you end up speaking to dozens of people about dozens of things—even if you're shy. So there goes Excuse #1.

Excuse #2: *I'll make a fool of myself in front of (a) friends (b) family (c) community members (d) business associates.* Actually, the opposite response is much more likely: people will respect you for having the courage to speak in public. This goes back to what you discovered earlier in this chapter: people would rather die, drown, or be bitten by a (rabid) pooch than give a speech. Cross this one off, too. This is covered in Chapter 3, "Common Communication Problems."

Word Power
Public Speaking: The art of delivering a speech to a group of people.

Excuse #3: *I have laryngitis.* No matter how careful you are to avoid people with colds, you *can* get sick before a speech. Ever notice that you seem to get ill most often when you're under pressure? Often it's because you're not eating right or getting enough sleep. If you're like me, you get a little run down, and then Bang! A whopper of a cold!

Unfortunately, you often can't reschedule a speech—especially if it's a crucial business presentation, awards ceremony, sales talk, or eulogy. What can you do? Follow these steps:

➤ First, recognize that preparing for and giving speeches is a pressure situation that can force you to neglect your health.

➤ If you know that you have to give an important speech on a specific day, take special care to eat properly and get sufficient sleep during the week before. This is not the time to put the pedal to the metal. If anything, it's the time to rest up for the big day.

➤ If possible, avoid people with colds and flus.

➤ Try to rest your voice as much as possible before the actual speech. This is one time I suggest that you *don't* rehearse your speech.

➤ Try to reschedule the speech. If you can't, cut your speech back to the bare bones.

➤ Be honest with your audience. Explain that you have laryngitis. People will understand, especially since many of them have been in the same situation!

➤ If possible, try to use a microphone when you speak—even if the room is small and you ordinarily wouldn't need one. This will help you put the least amount of strain on your voice. See Part 5, "Getting Your Act Together," for more information about using a microphone and other audio-visual aids.

➤ Speak briefly, but use your normal speaking voice. Don't whisper—it actually puts more stress on your voice than speaking in normal tones.

➤ Above all else, don't try to be a hero; you can end up a martyr. People can do permanent damage to their voices by straining them. If your throat is sore and your voice is gone with the wind, see a doctor. If the doctor advises you not to speak, listen to the doctor. Take a well-deserved rest!

Excuse #4: *I didn't have time to write a speech.* In Part 3, "Writing the Speech," I'll take you through the process of writing a speech, step-by-step. Writing a speech *does* take time, but it's time well spent.

Excuse #5: *I'm embarrassed about how I might look to others.* While your appearance does have an impact on how the audience receives your message, remember that the audience is coming to hear you speak, not to judge your personal appearance. When your speech is good, everything else falls into place. But just for a little extra insurance, Part 5, "Getting Your Act Together," explains how to dress for success and speech-making.

Excuse #6: *I just moved here from Bora-Bora (Tibet, Mars, New York City), and no one will understand my accent.* It's true that having a foreign accent or regional dialect can make you uneasy about speaking in public. But in most cases, people will understand you just fine and respect you even more for making the attempt. This topic is covered in Part 5, "Getting Your Act Together."

Excuse #7: *I'm too nervous. I'll drop dead from fear.* If you weren't a little nervous about public speaking, you probably wouldn't be human. But after an exhaustive search of the speech records, I've determined that no one has ever dropped dead from fear of speaking in public. Chapter 25 covers ways to deal with stage fright. You'll even learn how to make your fear work *for* you instead of *against* you. So relax.

Excuse #8: *I just had a root canal, and my lips are numb.* See Excuse #3.

Excuse #9: *I will forget what I have to say.* This is an easy one to fix. To help you always remember what you want to say, just write out your speech. This is covered in Part 3, "Writing the Speech."

Excuse #10: *My killer cat ate my speech.* First, get rid of that cat! Actually, speeches do get lost, more often than you know. Sometimes pets—and kids—eat 'em. Speeches vanish into depths of briefcases, desk drawers, and car seats. I've even accidentally thrown out a speech. Steps that you can take to make sure that you always have a copy of your speech are covered in Part 5, "Getting Your Act Together."

Why We Feel Nervous about Public Speaking

You're not alone in worrying about speaking in public; many people experience "stage fright" when they have to give a speech. In Japan, to relieve the speaker's nervous anticipation and to limit the length of the speeches, the traditional "after-dinner" speeches come before the meal. Obsessing about your performance comes with the territory. It haunts beginning and experienced speakers alike: even the most skilled public speakers battle their nerves before a big presentation. In Chapter 25, you'll find out more about stage fright.

What actually causes this sense of nervousness is a sudden rush of the hormone *adrenaline* into the nervous system; it's the "fight or flight" syndrome. When we are confronted with a threatening situation, such as an automobile swerving toward us, this adrenaline stimulates our physiological reactions so we have a better chance of defending ourselves or escaping by

> **Words to the Wise**
> Stage fright is not altogether a bad thing. You can learn to use the jitters to your advantage. For example, nervousness can make you more animated, alert, and vibrant. Find out more in Chapter 25.

running away. The adrenaline rush is nature's ingenious way of helping us save our skins.

As speakers, you can use what nature has given you to your advantage. Start by recognizing that the nervous tension we feel as we are addressing a group is a form of positive energy. Being nervous is also healthy because it shows that you really care about getting your message across. You value sounding and looking good.

The Least You Need to Know

➤ A majority of people rank public speaking as their #1 fear—before dying, diving, and dogs.

➤ People make a lot of excuses to avoid speaking in public.

➤ There are simple ways to make sure that you won't need these excuses. Some are explained here. Others are explained in detail in later chapters in this book.

➤ Speaking creates an adrenaline rush. You can harness this adrenaline and make it work for you rather than letting it make you feel nervous.

Chapter 2

The Importance of Public Speaking

In This Chapter

➤ If prepared properly, you can make public speaking like spinach: good and good for you

➤ Learn to listen

➤ Discover what makes public speakers really effective

➤ Become a regular on the rubber chicken circuit

The vice president of a large corporation buttonholed me at a social gathering a few years ago because she heard I had worked with a certain publishing firm. She was trying to decide whether to hire them to do some writing for her company. "I've seen their work, and I can tell they have been involved with some solid, successful projects," she said. "But quite honestly, I don't think the person who made the pitch could sell ice in the summer time." The firm lost the business because the representative did not understand the importance of public speaking. Very likely, a good public speaker could have snagged that contract.

The way we interact with other people—in both our personal and public lives—has very little to do with the written word. It's almost totally based on speaking. Yet very few people actually stop to consider how important the way they speak is to every aspect of their lives.

What happens when we talk to people has such a powerful effect that it can make or break relationships. When I realized the importance of improving my ability to speak in public, I turned to formal education and training. The fact that you're reading this book shows that you have reached the same conclusion I have: powerful public speakers are made, not born.

In this chapter, you will learn how important it is to speak with confidence in all areas of your life, both personal and public. You will also discover what makes a good public speaker. After you fill out the Public Speaking Inventory included in this chapter, you'll have a fuller understanding of your own personal strengths and weaknesses as a public speaker. This will enable you to concentrate your time and efforts on the places where they can best serve your interests.

So Why Do This to Yourself?

Okay, so now I know that the idea of speaking in public doesn't thrill you. I also know that you're not alone; you have a lot of company in The Public Speaking Underworld. Perhaps you're even muttering in despair, "I'll never be able to do this." But you're starting off with much more on your side than you might realize.

Speech plays an all-pervasive role in our lives. Without words and the power to voice them, it is very difficult to complete our daily routines effectively. Speaking well affects our ability to apply for a job, plan or take a trip, elect public officials, argue for a raise, or even argue in general. Knowing how to speak with power helps us tell our doctor where it hurts; dine with a friend or business associate; choose a career.

No matter what your occupation, your success depends greatly on your ability to speak well. For example, people select doctors, dentists, real estate brokers, financial advisors, and lawyers not only on the basis of their professional competence, but also on the basis of how well they "click" or relate to each other. Anyone who has to deal with the public, from salespeople to stockbrokers, servers to supervisors, has to establish rapport with the people they deal with in their jobs. And this rapport is established through speech.

The difference between success and failure is often the ability to communicate clearly and effectively. Never has this been more true than in today's competitive business climate. One of the most outstanding examples of a contemporary person who has achieved success because of his speaking skills is Lee Iacocca. Mr. Iacocca saved the Chrysler Corporation by using his considerable talent as a speaker to win the backing of the president, Congress, and the American public in the largest corporate bailout in America's history. Even Iacocca credits his professional success to his skills as a speaker. In his autobiography, Mr. Iacocca writes: "I've seen a lot of guys who are smarter than I am and a lot who know more about cars. And yet I've left most them in the smoke. Why? Because I'm tough? No. . . . You've got to know how to talk to them, plain and simple."

Public speaking affects every area of communications. It is your ability to get your ideas across and to inform and persuade your audience. And yet many people insist on separating "public speaking" from "one-on-one" speaking. They think the former is stilted and ceremonial and the latter casual and relaxed. In some circumstances, this may be the case, but truly effective speakers carry the same public speaking skills into all areas of communication. They put the power of speech to work for them whenever they communicate verbally. Remember: All the great speakers were bad speakers at first.

You know that the ability to *express* ideas is as essential as the capacity to *have* ideas. Take a closer look at *your* strengths and weaknesses as a public speaker by filling out this Public Speaking Inventory worksheet.

Tell Me About It
How can you discover the "corporate culture" to establish your compatibility with others? Talk to people to learn the unwritten rules. Listen to stories to find out who are the company heroes and what they did that made them respected.

Tell Me About It
In most instances, oral channels of communication are better than written channels for group decision making because they allow misunderstandings to be rectified much more quickly. Oral communication also seems more personal, another big advantage in businesses.

13

Public Speaking Inventory

1. List the qualities you think an effective public speaker should have.
   - ➤ _____
   - ➤ _____
   - ➤ _____
   - ➤ _____
   - ➤ _____

2. List which of these qualities you now have.
   - ➤ _____
   - ➤ _____
   - ➤ _____
   - ➤ _____
   - ➤ _____

3. What are your strengths as a public speaker?
   - ➤ _____
   - ➤ _____
   - ➤ _____
   - ➤ _____
   - ➤ _____

4. What are your weaknesses as a public speaker?
   - ➤ _____
   - ➤ _____
   - ➤ _____
   - ➤ _____
   - ➤ _____

5. When do you most often have to speak in public?
   - ➤ _____
   - ➤ _____
   - ➤ _____
   - ➤ _____
   - ➤ _____

6. What public speaking situations do you find the most difficult?
   - ➤ _____
   - ➤ _____
   - ➤ _____
   - ➤ _____
   - ➤ _____

To see where you stand, complete this worksheet. If necessary, use blank paper to provide more room.

Save this copy of your Public Speaking Inventory. When you finish the book, fill out another copy of the Inventory. Then compare the two versions to see how much you have learned about public speaking and how your feelings about it have changed.

What Makes a Good Public Speaker?

Being a good public speaker makes you visible—in business, money, re-sources, and power flow to the high achievers. Speaking in public with confidence gives you the edge. There's really no mystery about what makes someone an effective public speaker. Here's our Fab Five Plus Three List to being a good public speaker:

1. *Knowledge.* The famous American writer and humorist Mark Twain said, "It takes three weeks to prepare a good ad-lib speech." If that's the case, imagine how much time it takes to prepare a good written speech! Twain was exaggerating to make his point, but not by much. Reading widely will help you gather the information to make your speeches suc-cessful. However, you don't have to wait a long time to give a speech. One of the skills you'll learn in this book is how to get the facts you need to make your point. Various research techniques are covered in depth in Part 2, "Planning Your Speech."

2. *Self-confidence.* I've already mentioned how the impression you convey can say as much, or even more, about you as your words. Many factors determine how nervous you may feel: the people in the audience, how much sleep you got the night before, what the speech means to your career. Show your confidence.

Exhibit poise about what you have to say and your ability to say it well. Don't leave the door open for your audience to doubt you; for instance, if you cite a surprising fact, acknowledge the facts and say that you doubled-checked and verified them.

Don't apologize about what you have to say. Under no circumstances begin your speech with, "I'm not much of a public speaker, so you'll have to give me a little latitude," or "Unaccustomed as I am to public speaking. . ." . In Chapter 25, "Ways to Overcome Stage Fright," you'll learn proven ways to conquer stage fright and show your natural self-confidence.

> **Tell Me About It**
>
> *Whisper...*
>
> You know more than you think you do. Follow your instincts—and my advice—and the odds are you'll do a great job. Use your common sense and do what you feel is most comfortable.

15

3. *Enthusiasm.* A close friend of mine once gave the speech at a bridge banquet. As a nationally ranked bridge player, she knows the game inside out and is passionate about it. Few things make her happier than a championship bridge game. Yet her speech was lifeless, dull, and tedious. I was astonished because she is normally animated on the subject of bridge. I wasn't going to say anything if she didn't ask for an assessment, but ask she did. "Well," I said cautiously, "this speech lacked your usual enthusiasm." "Oh," she replied, "that's because I'm not a morning person. It takes me until noon to really wake up." Her speech reflected her sluggishness.

Along with self-confidence comes enthusiasm. Effective speakers have an intensity or involvement that helps them reach out and make contact with their audience. They possess an enthusiasm about their subject that excites the audience. Even if they're tired, powerful speakers summon the energy to inspire their audience. They convey their vitality about the subject by their words, gestures, and body language. You'll learn how to do this in Part 3, "Writing the Speech," and Part 5, "Getting Your Act Together."

4. *Preparation.* There's no substitute for doing your homework. Research. Prepare. The more background work you do, the more you will be convinced that your speech is good—and it will be. Work and rework your speech until it is entertaining, important, and meaningful. All good speech writers will tell you that there's no such thing as good writing, only rewriting.

5. *Message.* Your audience may be potential supporters at a political debate. They may be friends at a retirement dinner, students at a graduation, or executives at a corporate meeting. But whoever they are, you will either win or lose them with the speech you write and deliver. There are many things that a good speech can do. Here are a few of the most important ones.

A good speech can:

> ➤ Launch a successful campaign

> ➤ Build credibility

> ➤ Clarify the issues

> ➤ Persuade voters

> ➤ Correct misconceptions

> ➤ Forge bonds

> ➤ Motivate employees

➤ Generate publicity

➤ Rev up a sales team

➤ Position yourself

➤ Calm upset people

➤ Garner support

➤ Spark interest in a new service

Think about these points as you evaluate your message:

➤ Can I teach people something they didn't know?

➤ Can I impart some knowledge that will help people?

➤ Can I entertain the audience?

➤ Can I move people to thought or action?

➤ Can I persuade them to do something for the good of the community?

➤ Can I pay tribute to a person?

6. *Listening Skills*. Remember that speaking is a two-way process. It involves not only making contact with the audience but receiving feedback from them, as well. It's not enough to be a good speaker; you also have to be a good listener. There are three main kinds of listening:

➤ **Empathic Listening.** The purpose of this type of listening is to provide the person speaking with emotional support to help him or her come to a decision, solve a problem, or resolve a situation. As a result, this type of listening focuses more on emotions than on reason or ethics. As an empathetic listener, you can restate the issues, ask questions, and critically analyze the issues. Your intention here is not to make a decision for the person speaking. Rather, it is to support the person speaking in his or her own independent decision-making process.

You do this by providing the person speaking with the chance to express all of his or her ideas and feelings. For example, if prospective clients ask about a problem they had with your product, you might want to ask questions to bring certain facts to light. By supplying these facts, you are giving your version of events as you are allowing the clients to express their fears about future problems with the product. You can allay those fears as you provide emotional support.

17

➤ **Comprehension Listening.** With this kind of task, the listener gathers as many facts as possible. The focus is on accuracy of perception. This is the type of listening you do when members of an audience ask you questions and offer comments. It's the type of listening you need when you're first asked to speak, to make sure that you understand the task and the audience. Comprehension listening demands that you focus on specific details, distinguish between different pieces of information, and organize the information into a meaningful whole.

➤ **Critical Listening.** Here's where you weigh what has been said to see if you agree with it or not. Start the process with informational listening to make sure that you have all the facts. When you are fairly sure that you understand the issues, you can then evaluate them and make decisions based on the facts, evidence, and speaker's credibility. This type of listening is most helpful for public speakers in decision-making situations and confrontational positions.

Bet You Didn't Know

Being able to listen well is an invaluable skill for effective speakers. Each of us has bad listening habits that can be overcome with training and practice. Here are three of the most common bad-listening habits:

➤ *Pseudolistening* occurs when you only go through the motions of listening. You look like you're listening, but your mind is miles away. Correct this by really focusing on what the speaker is saying.

➤ *Self-centered listening* is when you mentally rehearse your answer while the person is still speaking. It's focusing on your own response rather than on the speaker's words. Correct this listening fault by letting the other person finish speaking before you begin to frame your answer.

➤ *Selective listening* happens when you listen to only those parts of a message that directly concern you. For instance, during a business meeting, you may let your mind drift away until you hear your name, your department's name, or some specific information that is directly relevant to your concerns. You'll be a more effective communicator if you listen to the entire message.

➤ Fatigue, boredom, and internal and external distractions can also make it difficult to focus on the speaker's words.

7. *Sense of Self.* A sense of self is the way that you look at yourself. It's a relatively unchanging set of labels that describe how you perceive yourself. It's like a long list of answers to the question "Who Am I?"

   What is the source of self concept? How does it develop? Some social scientists believe that it comes from within; others believe that it develops from what others think of us. In other words, we use feedback from others to forge our own identity, matching our interpretation of ourselves with how we perceive that others view us. These people weigh the feedback from different sources, accepting the appraisals from the people they considered most important—parents, bosses, lovers, husbands, wives—as most meaningful.

   But even before they put pen to paper, effective speakers have a clear sense of who they are. They have judged communication from various sources, sifted facts and data, and formed their own self-images. This firm sense of self is communicated to audiences as confidence, power, self-assurance. It makes their message all the more meaningful.

8. *Integrity.* More years ago than I want to count, the granddaddy of speech, the Greek philosopher Aristotle, explained what a public speaker needed in order to be successful. In *The Rhetoric,* Aristotle wrote that public speakers need more than an ample vocabulary and the good taste to pick the right words for the right occasion. They need more than intelligence, self-control, and balance. They even need more than being up-to-date on the issues—although all these accomplishments and traits are useful. Above all else, he claimed, good public speakers also have to be good people. If you want a group of people to accept your ideas, you must be respected and trusted.

   People never listen to just a speech; they focus also on the person who is speaking. This fits with what you just read about forming a strong sense of self. Of course, effective speaking calls for a mastery of basic skills and techniques. But first of all, it requires you to be respected by others and by yourself. I bet you already have integrity; this book will help you master knowledge, self-confidence, and preparation, as well.

Why You're Reading This

One of the most valuable skills in any walk of life is to be able to speak well. The ability to speak clearly and effectively pays off in everything from job interviews to being president of IBM (when Big Blue really was big). The ability to write and deliver a speech is of enormous value, partly because there aren't a whole lot of people who can do it with any skill or grace.

There's no doubt that you've seen it over and over yourself. Good speeches, with a dash of humor, a touch of class, and an entertaining approach can make the difference between winning or losing a business deal; between raising some money or collecting pots of it for your favorite worthy cause; between having your listeners on their feet, applauding with enthusiasm or just skulking for the door; between nodding in understanding or just nodding off. Remember: It's better to be looked over than overlooked.

The Least You Need to Know

➤ Everyone feels nervous about speaking in public; it's an inborn physiological reaction. It's what you do with the fear that counts.

➤ Good public speakers have knowledge, self-confidence, a strong self-image, and integrity. They convey an important message and prepare thoroughly.

➤ Effective speakers listen closely to what others are saying. They process what they have heard. They try to avoid common listening faults.

➤ The ability to speak clearly, cogently, and competently in public pays off.

➤ Any idiot can learn to speak in public with confidence, and it will be even easier for you because you're no idiot.

Chapter 3

Common Communication Problems

In This Chapter

➤ Define "communication"

➤ Explore the communication process

➤ Discover common communication fallacies

➤ Figure out what the other fella's saying so you can communicate more effectively

What do people mean by "communication" anyway? The first thing I'll tackle in this chapter is the definition of "communication." You will find out what I mean when I talk about "communication." Then, you'll learn all about the process of communicating.

"Communication" can mean different things and can be used in different ways. Fundamentally, *communication* is the process of sending and receiving messages to achieve understanding. Here's a generally accepted definition: *Communication* is the social process by which people in a specific situation construct meaning using symbolic behavior.

What Communication Is

Communication is a human process. Although scientists have shown that some animals—notably apes and dolphins—communicate in a highly complex way, in this book I'll concentrate on human communication. Humans make their needs known through verbal and nonverbal communication. Our painting, sculpture, music, dance, and other art forms also communicate our feelings. More than half our communication, however, takes place through speaking and writing. I'm going to focus on the most common type of communication: *speech.*

Communication is the process of creating meaning. Sometimes people think of communication as a series of isolated actions. Person A says one thing; person B says another. That's not how communication works. Communication involves four parts: sender, message, receiver, and response. The way we interpret speech and communicate in specific situations depends on a wide variety of variables. Some of these include our personal experiences, mood at that moment, and overall values. Communication is an ongoing process with variable conditions and outcomes.

Communication arises from context. *Context* is the time and place of the communication experience. Meaning is constructed as a social process, embedded in the context of the interchange. Context influences what we say, how we say it, and the way others understand what we say. For example, the meaning you take from a friend's praise for your new outfit depends in part on when the praise is offered. If it comes at the beginning of the day, it has one meaning. "What a nice way to start the day," you might think. But if your friend asks to borrow your car right after she compliments your outfit, you're likely to construct a different meaning. "She only said something nice to get a favor," you might think. Communication changed because of the time and circumstance.

Communication is a symbolic process. Words and actions carry symbolic overtones or meanings greater than what they appear to be. First, think about words. For example, to a person who speaks English, "pain" means aches, discomfort, suffering. To a French speaker, however, the word carries no such meaning. Instead, it means "bread." Every language has a *grammar*, or system of rules, that tells us how to use these symbols to communicate with each other. Understanding and following these rules enables us to communicate with each other.

Word Power
Communication: a human, social process whereby people in a specific situation con-struct meaning using symbolic behavior.

Actions also have symbolic meanings; the word is not the only thing to consider when we communicate. For example, making a circle by placing your thumb and forefinger together means "A-OK" in English. It's generally accepted as a symbol for agreement in the North American culture, but in the Latin America culture, it is an obscene gesture. Some of these actions are universally accepted. Scientists have discovered that people in all cultures smile and that all smiles connote happiness. But few of these actions cross cultures, which can create embarrassing and even dangerous communication problems. You can find out more about communication as a symbolic process in Chapter 16, "Writing International Speeches."

Communication skills are vital to our professional and personal lives. Communication allows us to constantly analyze what we see, feel, and hear. From this sensory input, we can form convictions, opinions, needs, likes, and strengths—the sum and substance of our personalities.

Words to the Wise
Occasionally, gestures can work alone to communicate meaning. This is especially true when traffic is stalled during rush hour, at ball games presided over by hard-of-hearing umpires, and when the ATM line stretches to Mars. However, words and actions often work in tandem to enable us to communicate. As a result, don't communicate by word or gesture alone unless your meaning will be absolutely clear.

Types of Communication

Communication can be divided into five categories: intrapersonal communication, interpersonal communication, small group communication, public communication, and mass communication. Let's take a look at each one in turn.

Tell Me About It
Don't confuse intrapersonal communication with crystals, pyramids, and past lives. We're dealing with inner voices, not inner children.

Intrapersonal communication=communicating with yourself:

➤ Evaluating feedback

➤ Constructing meaning

Interpersonal communication =communicating with people:

➤ Talking with two or more people

➤ Working as equals

Small group communication=communicating with three or more people:

➤ Stating beliefs as a group

➤ Working with others to solve problems

Public communication=large group communication:

➤ Sharing as audience and speakers

➤ Receiving less feedback

Mass communication=communicating through mass media:

➤ Communicating through TV, radio, films, and so on

➤ Separating audience and speaker and limiting feedback

How good are you at communicating? Take the Communications Quiz to find out!

Communications Quiz

Put a check next to each answer that you think is correct.

❏   **1.** Communication is always meaningful.

❏   **2.** Communication is not always valuable.

❏   **3.** If people could only communicate openly with each other, the world would be a better place.

❏   **4.** Unfortunately, there are some problems that can't be solved through communication.

❏   **5.** Miscommunication is the source of much of the world's misery.

❏   **6.** You are usually better off speaking more because then you can get your meaning across more fully.

❏   **7.** It's the quality of communication that matters, not the quantity.

❏   **8.** Many communication problems come from the idea that meaning comes entirely from words.

❏   **9.** Meaning is derived from nonverbal as well as verbal communication.

❏ **10.** Communication is like breathing—you do it naturally.

Check your responses against our answers. What does your score reveal about your *CQ*? (Communications Quotient!)

1. No. Spoken language cannot be considered a good thing in itself because it can be cruel, unethical, or misleading.

2. Yes. See #1.

3. No. Communication can't cure all the world's evils.

4. Yes. Communication can help people understand each other better, but it cannot always resolve strife or bring people together.

5. Yes. Successful communication can't cure the world's evils, but it can help keep them from happening if people achieve understanding.

6. No. Communication is more elusive than that. There are times when more speech can help, but other times just keeping quiet conveys the most effective message of all.

7. Yes. See #6.

8. Yes. Meaning comes from the emotional associations that words carry, nonverbal communication, and context—not just from words.

9. Yes. See #8.

10. No. If only it were so! Communication is neither easy nor especially natural. Speech is not the same as communication, as you'll find out in this lesson.

Score Yourself

8–10 correct	You're almost ready for tabloid TV.
6–9 correct	Not bad for a beginner!
4–8 correct	What's the frequency, Kenneth?
0–3 correct	How's that again?

Communication is such a complex process that it's no wonder a number of myths have sprung up about it. What's astonishing is the stubbornness of these myths. Some have become so enshrined that they appear to be fact. So let's take a closer look at the most common communication myths and discover why they are not valid.

Communication Is Always Valuable: It's Not

According to Article I of the Bill of Rights:

> Congress shall make no law respecting an establishment of religion, or prohibiting the free exercise thereof; or abridging the freedom of speech, or of the press; or the right of the people peaceably to assemble, and to petition the Government for a redress of grievances.

Our nation's founders believed so strongly in freedom of speech that they placed it first among our freedoms, with freedom of religion, press, and the right to petition. Unfortunately, some misguided souls have interpreted this to mean that communication is always important and helpful. It's not. Here's why.

Spoken language cannot be considered a good thing in itself. It can be used to express important ideas, to bring people together, and to share feelings. On the other hand, some words, spoken carelessly or deliberately, can distort issues, shatter relationships, and suppress emotions.

But even if communication is not unkind or unethical, it is not always appropriate or prudent. For instance, sometimes an impulse to share feelings creates anger rather than trust, resentment rather than security. You should not try to make it artificially valuable. In the same way, you shouldn't try to make some important social impact when you're just supposed to introduce a speaker at a seminar.

Communication Can Solve Everything: It Can't

Ever hear these time-honored chestnuts?

➤ "If only people could talk openly with each other, there wouldn't be so many problems."

➤ "If only countries understood each other, we could all live in peace and harmony."

Adding these clichés to trash TV and the advice of self-help gurus makes it appear that all the world's ills could be solved if only everyone could sit down and really communicate with each other.

Now, there's no doubt that better communication is a step in the right direction. But it's also undeniable that there are many problems that better communication simply cannot solve. There are some countries, cultures, groups, and people whose values are so far apart that no amount of communication can bring them together. The conflicts will remain long after the communication is completed. For example, if you are having an argument with a colleague, there are instances when you may be best off walking away until the situation stops sizzling.

Better communication can help people understand each other's problems, but it won't solve all those problems. Better communication can perhaps help countries more fully understand each other's positions, but there's no saying that it will help soften or shift those positions. There's no guarantee that better communication can make people love, or even like, each other.

More Communication Is Better: It's Not

This delusion about communication is related to the previous one. Some people believe that if a brief conversation does not make others see things your way, a longer discussion will. Sometimes, of course, your opponent will simply capitulate from exhaustion and give in to anything you say. In most cases, however, a great deal of talk has just the opposite effect.

Now, I'm not suggesting that America institute a universal gag rule (though sometimes we do have leanings in that direction). Rather, I'm suggesting that communication is more subtle than more=better. There are times when reinforcing a point can be useful. Other times, though, running off at the mouth just makes the situation more difficult. There are even times when it's best not to say anything at all. Keeping quiet can prevent people from saying things that they might later regret.

The most effective communication is a balance between knowing when to speak and when not to. Follow these guidelines:

➤ Extending communication cannot help people resolve their problems.

➤ A great deal of talk is often more productive than less talk.

➤ With communication, it's the content that's important, not the amount.

➤ Some problems can actually be made worse by too much talking.

➤ Sometimes, your best bet is to keep quiet.

Words = Meaning (Guess Again)

Communication *is* a social process of making meaning. Communication *is not* separate, isolated acts. Communication would be easy if people asked and answered questions in predictable ways. It would be even easier if every exchange was scripted in advance, and we just read from the pages.

But such is not the case. Our interpretation of words in a specific situation and the way we respond to them depend on our experiences, values, and emotions. Sometimes people use different words to mean the same thing. For example, some people call artificially flavored carbonated water "soda," and others call it "pop."

Bet You Didn't Know

OOOOH.

Many words carry loaded overtones, or *connotations*, different from their dictionary meanings or *denotations*. Study the following chart to see what I mean.

Word	Denotation	Connotation
stubborn	persistent	obstinate, pigheaded
resolute	persistent	determined
famous	well-known	celebrated
notorious	well-known	disreputable
cheap	inexpensive	tight-fisted
thrifty	inexpensive	frugal
house	residence	none
home	residence	warmth, welcome

Communication Is Simple (Ha!)

Many people believe that communication is like breathing—you're born knowing how to do it. It's not a skill you have to learn, they argue, because it comes with the total package.

It's true that speaking itself may not be difficult, but you've learned in this chapter that communication is not the same as speaking. Communication is something that can be taught and learned. Training and practice can make an enormous difference in our ability to make our meaning understood and our ability to understand what others are saying.

Communication is also influenced by what we want to perceive. In many cases, we assume that other people feel the same way that we do. As you've probably discovered the hard way, this is not always the case. We also tend to tune out messages that are unpleasant, threatening, or disturbing. Instead, we understand messages that reinforce our sense of well-being or tell us what we want to hear.

Take the "Are You a Responsible Communicator?" test to see how sensitive you are in communicating.

Are You a Responsible Communicator?

Put a check next to each answer that you think is correct.

❑ 1. It is important to treat other people in the situation as unique individuals.

❑ 2. Avoid thinking of people as typical or stereotypes.

❑ 3. You shouldn't attempt to convince people that you're right unless you are well informed on the subject.

❑ 4. Don't reject what other people say out of hand.

❑ 5. Don't use information about yourself to manipulate others.

❑ 6. Accept responsibility for the words that pass through your lips.

❑ 7. It's important to be careful when you talk about other people.

❑ 8. Avoid using private facts as a weapon.

❑ 9. Anticipate the effects of your speech.

❑ 10. Be aware of the limits of your knowledge.

Every answer you give to the "Are You a Responsible Communicator?" questionnaire is correct. If you got...

8–10 checks	We'll talk to you any day.
5–7 checks	You're on your way to becoming a responsible communicator.
1–4 checks	Dish that dirt, baby—but not about me!

The process of creating meaning is terribly complex. As a result, it is often easier to misunderstand people than it is to communicate with them. Even the most skilled communicators can benefit from training and practice.

The Least You Need to Know

➤ Good communication can correct misunderstandings, but communication alone cannot change deep-seated feelings and long-held values.

➤ Communication cannot directly improve problems such as war, poverty, and starvation.

➤ Silence can sometimes be the most effective form of communication.

Chapter 4

Types of Speeches

In This Chapter

➤ Meet the three kinds of public speaking

➤ Explore common speaking tasks

➤ Learn to walk the walk and talk the talk

When was the last time you were called on to "say a few words"? Perhaps you had to give a toast at a birthday party, wedding, retirement dinner, or installation ceremony. Or as part of your job, you might have been required to run a training session, sell a product, or interview a job applicant. Perhaps you were running for election or nominating the candidate who was running. Whatever the task, few of us have made it this far in life without giving a formal or informal speech.

Some people seem to be able to stand up in front of a group and talk about anything at any time. There are many reasons for their success. In large part, their social ease is due to a complete understanding of public speaking and the different speaking tasks. These speakers are familiar with each type of speech, inside and out! They know how every kind of speech is organized and delivered. They know how to be true to themselves and to their audience. Find out some of their secrets in this chapter.

In the previous chapter, you learned about the communication process and some widespread communication difficulties. In this chapter, you will explore the different kinds of public speaking tasks. I'm going to give you a "laundry list" arranged in alphabetical order for quick, easy reference. So let's plunge right into the overview of the three different kinds of public speaking.

Three Main Kinds of Public Speaking

All speeches fall into one of three categories: speeches that inform, persuade, or entertain.

Speeches that inform fulfill the following aims:

➤ Explain

➤ Report

➤ Describe

➤ Clarify

➤ Define

➤ Demonstrate

Whisper...

Tell Me About It
Because people absorb information much more readily when it is interesting, it is especially important to make informative speeches chock-full of delicious detail. Visual aids such as graphs, charts, and video clips are a great way to make heaps of information clear and palatable. See Chapter 21 for step-by-step instructions for using audio-visual aids to add zip and zing to informative speeches.

Even though sometimes these speeches may move your audience to action or belief, their primary purpose is to present facts, details, and examples. That's why they are classified as *informative* speeches. Speeches that inform are discussed in depth in Chapter 6, "Speaking to Inform" and Chapter 17, "Information, Please: Informational Speaking."

Speeches that persuade have as their primary purpose convincing their listeners about a specific topic. When your goal is to change your audience's beliefs or attitudes, you're speaking to *persuade*. You can use your own credibility to strengthen your argument. You can appeal to you audience's emotions, reasons, or sense of right and wrong. But whatever you do, your speech must include information that supports the logic of your position. *Persuasive* speeches are covered in depth in Chapters 7, "Speaking to Persuade," and 18, "See It My Way: Persuasive Speaking."

Speeches that entertain fulfill a social need by bringing people together. They do this by promoting a feeling of social unity that draws people together into a community. To accomplish this aim, you will most likely have to include elements of informative speeches: statistics, illustrations, and examples.

For instance, a speech honoring community member Bob Harris would likely discuss how he has taught a free writing program for ten years, led the Boy Scout troop for three years, and donated 55 pints of blood in the past decade.

Because these three different types of speeches often overlap, it is important for you to isolate and understand the primary purpose of your speech before you start writing. For example, if your supervisor asks you to deliver the opening speech at the annual sales convention and you read the sales report as your speech, you haven't fulfilled the primary purpose of your speech: to persuade. Check out Part 2, "Planning Your Speech" for guidelines.

> **Tell Me About It**
> Many people think that entertaining speeches must be funny, and indeed some of them are. But they don't have to be—nearly anything that is interesting can be the basis of an entertaining speech.
>
> *whisper...*

A-to-Z Speeches

OK, so I lied about that A-to-Z part, but just a little: it's not often that public speakers are called on to talk about zebras, zippers, or zeppelins. In this section, I'll cover some of the most common types of speeches that entertain. You *will* find that each type of speech is arranged in alphabetical order!

Addresses of Welcome

As the presiding officer or designee, your task is to give a brief speech that welcomes guests and members. Your role is to be gracious by extending a warm welcome that comes from the entire organization. See Chapter 8, "Speaking to Entertain" and Chapter 19, "Ever Hear the One About? . . . Entertaining Speeches."

Appreciation and Awards

It's an honor to present an award, but it's even more fun to receive it! When you're the recipient of an award, follow these four steps when accepting it:

➤ Offer your thanks to the giver and the organization he or she represents.

➤ Praise the donor.

➤ Say something appreciative about the gift or the honor. Recognize the assistance others gave you in this achievement.

➤ Explain what benefit or pleasure you expect to reap as a result of receiving the gift.

You can find more information about this type of speech in Chapter 8, "Speaking to Entertain" and Chapter 19, "Ever Hear the One About? . . . Entertaining Speeches."

Appeal for Funds

In you are active in community or public activities, you will likely have many occasions to "pass the hat" for funds or action. There are two steps to follow when you organize a speech appealing for financial support for a charity, service, or civic organization:

➤ Explain your reason for speaking. State the cause, purpose, or urgency of your appeal.

➤ Request the actual contribution to the cause.

Chapter 7, "Speaking to Persuade" and Chapter 18, "See It My Way: Persuasive Speaking" cover this speech task in depth.

Closing Remarks

As the head weenie at any roast, your job isn't over until you have adjourned the meeting. In so doing, your speech should express thanks for the audience's interest and cooperation and bid them a cordial good-bye. This is explained in detail in Chapter 8, "Speaking to Entertain" and Chapter 19, "Ever Hear the One About? . . . Entertaining Speeches."

Tell Me About It
It's especially important to keep your remarks brief when you close a meeting. People are ready to go, so you want your message short and sweet!

Dedicating Buildings, Ships, Vehicles, and So On

This type of speech cements a group, community, or organization by creating a feeling of goodwill. As such, this is a speech that entertains and builds social cohesion. Therefore, you want to go for emotional appeals and personal identification rather than appeals to reason, logic, or ethics. To craft and deliver a winning speech, you have to appeal to the interests and values you share with the audience. You learn how to do this by following the step-by-step directions in Chapter 8, "Speaking to Entertain" and Chapter 19, "Ever Hear the One About? . . . Entertaining Speeches."

Eulogies

A *eulogy* is a speech given in praise of a person. Most often, eulogies are given at funerals and memorial services, but they can also be delivered at retirement parties or any occasion when someone is being honored. The most effective eulogies focus on one or two of the subject's positive qualities. The speaker lists the quality and offers specific anecdotes from the person's life to illustrate the point. If the eulogy is offered at funerals and memorial services, it is appropriate to offer an expression of sorrow or shock at the person's passing and sympathy for the family of the deceased. Chapter 7, "Speaking to Persuade" and Chapter 18, "See It My Way: Persuasive Speaking" offer detailed instructions on writing and delivering eulogies.

Explaining a Process

Process analysis speeches tell "how to" do something: how to change a tire, prepare the perfect rice-and-beans casserole, assemble a widget, and that most difficult of all processes, program a VCR. These speeches often use transition words such as *first, second, next, finally,* and use numbered steps to make the process clearer.

To explain a process, start by telling why the procedure is important. Give an overview of the process by stating the steps you will be describing. Next, explain the steps, one at a time. If possible, demonstrate or illustrate each step. Look carefully at your audience to make sure that they understand what you're saying. Finish by summarizing the steps. This topic is covered in depth in Chapter 6, "Speaking to Inform" and Chapter 17, "Information, Please: Informational Speaking."

Giving Testimony

Giving testimony in court is a type of informative speaking. As a witness, your job is to give facts and evidence from which judges, juries, or committee members will draw conclusions. See Chapter 6, "Speaking to Inform" and Chapter 17, "Information, Please: Informational Speaking" for a list of rules that a witness should follow when giving testimony in court.

Installation Ceremonies

These speeches are used for the rites of installing officers such as the president, vice-president, secretary, and treasurer. They are also important for inducting people in union offices and other types of positions.

If you are the honoree, you must express your appreciation for the honor and pledge to faithfully perform the duties of the office.

If you are installing the officer, your speech should pay tribute to the person who is being honored. Such tributes are composed of two elements: praise for the person and good wishes for the task ahead. Call the person by name and offer specific reasons why he or she will be a fine officer.

Introductions

Follow these four steps when you introduce a speaker:

➤ First, present a brief statement about the speaker's background.

➤ Explain his or her qualifications to address the group.

➤ Praise the speaker.

➤ Give the speaker's name and the title of his or her speech.

Keep your introduction short: no more than two to three minutes long. Remember: This is the speaker's day to shine, not yours.

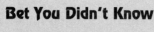

Bet You Didn't Know

OOOOH. It's crucial to introduce the speaker, honoree, or any other guest of honor by the correct title. Here's a list that should cover most of the introductions you'll be called on to make:

Speaker	Title
Governor	The Governor or The Governor of (state)
Mayor	Mayor (last name)
Senator	Senator (last name)

Speaker	Title
Member of Congress	Mr. or Ms. (last name), Senator or Representative from (name of state)
Cardinal	His Eminence, Cardinal (last name)
Archbishop	The Most Reverend, The Archbishop of (name of the state)
Bishop	Bishop (last name)
Priest	The Reverend Father (last name)
Monsignor	Monsignor (last name)
Protestant Clergy	Mr.(last name), Ms. (last name)
If D.D. or LL.D.	Dr. (last name)
Lutheran Clergy	Pastor (last name)
Rabbi	Rabbi (last name)

Job Interviews

Interviewing candidates for a job is one of the touchiest areas of informative speech because what an interviewer should—and should not say—at an employment interview is now subject to strict federal guidelines. In Chapter 17, "Information, Please: Informational Speaking," I explain the guidelines for this speaking situation.

Job Training Sessions

A type of informative speaking, job training sessions are unusual because they involve much more audience participation than most informative speech situations. As a result, you want to urge audience members to participate actively when you give a job training session. Often, the speaker functions more as a moderator. Here are some suggestions:

➤ Limit the information you will cover at the session.

➤ Organize the information in an easy-to-follow manner.

➤ Try to include ample visual aids, such as handouts, videos, charts, and graphs to clarify difficult concepts.

➤ Think about dividing the audience into small groups to discuss the presentation.

See Chapter 17, "Information, Please: Informational Speaking," for more detailed instructions on preparing to speak at job training sessions.

Nominations

A speech to nominate a candidate can be a simple statement: "I nominate Hector Ruiz for the office of president." Or it can be more elaborate: an explanation of your candidate's qualifications and an attempt to generate excitement about your candidate. The first type of nomination is an informative speech; the second type is a persuasive one. See Chapter 18, "See It My Way: Persuasive Speaking," for a detailed explanation of the second type of nomination.

Presentations

You've been selected to give the plaque, certificate, bond, or pat on the back to the deserving honoree. There are two main steps to these speeches: (1) praise the recipient; (2) give the gift. Your praise should be simple and sincere. Do your research to find a relevant but special aspect of the recipient's background to praise. Keep your speech factual and straightforward.

Presentation speeches can be thorny because they often pop up without much notice. Find out more about these speeches in Chapter 8, "Speaking to Entertain," and Chapter 19, "Ever Hear the One About? . . . Entertaining Speeches."

Reporting an Incident

Ever witness a traffic accident? A robbery? A natural disaster? If so, you know how important reliable eyewitnesses can be when it comes to settling the matter quickly and fairly. If you are an eyewitness to an incident that has to be reported to the authorities, your speech should present the facts as you saw them, without embellishment or commentary.

Another important aspect of reporting an incident is to understand cause-and-effect relationships.

➤ The *cause* is *why* something happens.

➤ The *effect* is *what* happens—the result.

When you are called upon to report an incident to the police, insurance investigators, or any other authorities, it's important to analyze the causes and effects. First, understand that causes come before effects. Second, realize that not all the events that came before the incident helped cause it. It's also important to remember that more than one cause can contribute to an effect, and if there are several causes, they may not contribute equally to an effect.

Retirement Speeches

A retiring officer, such as the chairman of a board, generally expresses his or her thanks to the organization and associates for the support they have given during the honoree's tenure in office. If you are ever in this position, begin your speech by expressing your appreciation for the honor of serving and thanking your associates and friends for the support you have received.

Speakers offering their good wishes to the retiree isolate specific examples of the person's tenure in office and end with heartfelt wishes for their happiness and continued success in the future.

Tell Me About It
Specific signal words identify cause-and-effect relationships. You can more clearly state a cause and effect relationship with the help of the following signal words:

As a result	Because
Consequently	Due to
For this (that) reason	For
If . . . then	Nevertheless
Since	So that
So	Therefore
This (that) is how	Thus

Running for Election

This is a classic persuasive speech—actually, a whole series of persuasive speeches, each tailored to the needs of your particular audience, time, and place. You can use a direct appeal: tell the audience what you want, give them the facts they need, and tell them again. Or you can appeal to their emotions as well as their reason. When combined with direct requests, emotional appeals make surprisingly strong election campaigns. Specific techniques to use for election speeches are described in Chapter 7, "Speaking to Persuade," and Chapter 18, "See It My Way: Persuasive Speaking."

Toasts and Roasts

When toasting or roasting a person, open with an overview of the purpose of the meeting. Follow this by introducing the members of the head table. Next, make a toast to the guest of honor and invite the guests to join in. Introduce the speakers. At the end of the roast, thank the guests and add one final sally. Hosting toasts and roasts is covered in Chapter 19, "Ever Hear the One About? . . . Entertaining Speeches."

Making a Sales Presentation

Sales presentations can be *direct* or *indirect*.

Direct sales presentations have three basic steps:

➤ A *hook* that grabs the audience's attention.

➤ A *list* that provides your audience with the facts.

➤ A *handle* that gives your audience a reason for supporting your idea.

Indirect sales presentations have eight basic steps:

➤ Analyze the audience.

➤ Establish common ground.

➤ Define the problem.

➤ Explain how your proposal will solve the problem.

➤ Show how the advantages outweigh the disadvantages.

➤ Acknowledge and deal with changing needs.

➤ Summarize benefits.

➤ Give audience directions for action.

See Chapter 18, "See It My Way: Persuasive Speaking," for a detailed description of direct and indirect sales presentation techniques.

The Least You Need to Know

➤ There are three main kinds of speeches: speeches that inform, speeches that persuade, and speeches that entertain.

➤ Different types of speeches demand different approaches.

➤ Successful speakers are familiar with the different types of public speaking tasks and what each one entails.

Part 2
Planning Your Speech

In a recent interview, John H. Johnson, the owner and publisher of Ebony *magazine said:*

"I developed my communication skills as a technique of survival. I was born in poverty and spent two years on the welfare rolls, and I learned early that I had to communicate or die. And so I talked my way out of poverty—I communicated my way to the top." (source: John H. Johnson, owner and publisher of Ebony *magazine, Qtd. in Gloria Gordon, "ECEL Award Winner John H. Johnson Communicates Success." IABC Communication World 6, no. 6 [May 1989]: 18–19.)*

As Johnson's experience shows, learning how to speak in public with confidence can have a tremendous positive impact on your life. So let's get down to the nitty-gritty and find out how you can plan speeches that will communicate your message effectively and powerfully.

Analyzing Your Audience

To be an effective public speaker, you must understand how your audience is likely to react to what you say and how you say it. Audience analysis also helps speakers decide how best to grab their audience from the very beginning and hold them throughout the entire speech. Successful speakers take into account the audience's interests, level of knowledge, and specific requirements. This chapter will guide you in analyzing an audience and matching your speech to their needs.

Why Me?

The obvious place to start an audience analysis is with the reason why you were asked to speak in the first place. In some cases, you received a letter asking you to speak at a specific occasion. The invitation should explain why you were invited. Consider what you have to offer to this group. Perhaps you have something to sell. Maybe they want the latest on industry or public policy ideas. The reason why you were selected will obviously affect the content of your speech.

People Who Need People

Next, figure out who will be in the audience. Members of the local Chamber of Commerce? Representatives from a manufacturing industry? Guests from financial companies? *Who* is in the audience makes a difference in *what* you say. Use this list to help you evaluate the composition of your audience and decide what to say:

➤ Retail workers: shopkeepers and salespeople

If you are called upon to speak before retail audiences, you'll find they are likely concerned about real estate costs, theft rates, and popular trends.

➤ Insurance brokers

Here, consider speaking about sales techniques, advertising methods, and the concerns of small-business owners, for example.

➤ Medical workers such as doctors and nurses

In this case, kicking off your speech with the same old medical jokes will likely fall flat. Odds are, the audience has heard every "classic" nugget about the doctor who left in the sponge or played golf with the rabbi, priest, and minister. And no jokes about cutting off the wrong leg, either.

➤ Lawyers

Unless you know your audience well, steer clear of lawyer jokes; they are often in questionable taste.

➤ Librarians

No quips about eagle-eyed matrons with buns, steel-rimmed glasses, and orthopedic shoes, please. Today's "information specialists" (as librarians are now called) are much more likely to be centered on computerized catalogues and retrieval methods.

➤ Educators, such as teachers and principals

Today's educational hot spots include homogeneous vs. heterogeneous class grouping, budgets, and tenure.

➤ Small-business owners

This audience is very different from its cousin, the large department-store owners. Small-business owners are often concerned about competition from malls and superstores.

➤ Industry regulators

An audience composed of industry regulators is likely to take offense at a speech about radical environmental ideas.

➤ Accountants

Don't assume that accountants are dull; that stereotype is as stale as yesterday's bagel. Consider how the latest software and recent changes in the tax code have transformed the industry.

➤ Computer specialists and Systems analysts

Be sure you know what you're talking about when you take on computer specialists and systems analysts. Don't throw around computer jargon without a real understanding of its meaning.

➤ Marketing personnel

Discuss what's in, what's out. Share ideas about vendors and trends.

➤ Engineers

Stick with the basics—solid information, professionally delivered. Engineers appreciate visual displays such as relevant, well-prepared charts and graphs.

➤ Stock and bond brokers

The market's volatile, so there's lots of room for discussion here.

➤ The self-employed, such as writers

Increasingly, self-employed professionals are concerned with issues such as medical coverage, retirement plans, child-care, computer hook-ups, and networking.

If the audience is the home team, they are apt to think they can anticipate the content of your speech. Suppose that you have the reputation for having a great sense of humor. If you decide to deliver a serious speech, the audience might be startled and unsure of your intent. Take this into consideration when you plan the content of your speech.

If people are from many different places, you can draw on your common experiences as visitors to the city. People will take your speech more seriously

45

if they feel you're trying to meet their specialized needs. But if you are speaking to a group of total strangers, you have to be that much more careful about making a good first impression. The way you come across in your speech is the way that people will remember you; there's no room for second tries.

Why Are They Here?

Is the audience present because they want to hear your speech, or did someone force them to attend? Compare the difference:

Captive Audience	Want to Attend
Less tolerant	More tolerant
"Prove it" attitude	"Accepting" attitude

Audience Size

The size of the audience is another key element to consider when you plan your speech. People in smaller groups tend to pay closer attention. They hesitate to show their restlessness or to zone off because it's much easier to be noticed in a small group—there's nowhere to hide.

The inverse is equally true. Individuals in larger groups tend to daydream more. They might shift in their seats or file their nails. After all, it's easier to be anonymous in a crowd.

Adjust your speech to the size of the audience. For example, if there are 15 or fewer people in attendance, you can make your points stronger with personal references to audience members. Here's how one speaker personalized her speech: "It's important to order at least ten extra books to account for late registration, as Dr. Malhotra discovered with his British Literature 101 course last semester."

Whisper...

Tell Me About It
To find out about the group, check the invitation you received, the corporate year-end report, members of the organization, friends who know about the group, and your public relations department. Don't be shy about getting as much information as you can about the group and the reason for the speech. Remember: more research = better speech.

Audience Age

Age is another consideration. Find out if you will be speaking to people younger than you are, your age, or older. Analyze your audience's age, and then select material that's right for the people in your particular audience. Consider what effect the age of your audience might have on these elements of your speech:

➤ Topic

➤ Purpose

➤ Main points

➤ Language

➤ Visual aids

Appearance Doesn't Matter . . . Or Does It?

It *is* important to consider appearance. How is your audience likely to be dressed? How do you think they expect *you* to look? These factors are important because if there is a great difference in appearance and style between you and your audience, you might feel either intimidated or superior. The same is true of your audience. For example, if your audience is dressed casually in shorts and T-shirts and you come dressed in a suit, they are apt to feel anxious and even hostile. This immediately makes it harder for you to win their trust.

What to do? Check with your host before the speech. Make sure that you are dressed appropriately for the occasion.

Tell Me About It
The most important tools in audience analysis are common sense and *empathy*, the ability to put yourself in someone else's place. Most likely, your audience is *not* just like you. Use what you already know about people and what you find out about the organization to predict likely responses to your message.

Whisper...

Gender and Male/Female Ratio

It's also helpful to find out what percentage of audience members will be female and what percentage will be male. Why? A number of researchers believe that the gender differences in conversational styles result in the miscommunication that often occurs in male-female conversations.

For example, researchers have learned that women are much more likely to indicate understanding by nodding and saying *yes* and *hmmm* than are men. Men, in contrast, interpret these signs as meaning "I agree," rather than "I understand." A male speaker who sees female audience members nodding may feel that they are inconsistent in action if they later question what he is saying. A female speaker who does not receive any feedback from male audience members may feel that they aren't listening to her.

Tell Me About It

Also consider whether male and female audience members might view your topic differently. Male and female audience members will very likely have different interests, experiences, and knowledge about the topic. This clearly affects your choice of topic and method of development.

Level of Knowledge

It's easy to overestimate the knowledge that your audience has. People outside your own area of expertise may not really know what it is you do. Even people who have once worked with you may have forgotten specific details now that their work is different. When you are presenting new information, try to open your speech with familiar facts, make a special effort to be clear, link new information to familiar information, and use visuals to illustrate difficult concepts.

Audience Knowledge and Opinions

How much do people know about my topic?

_____
_____
_____
_____
_____

How do people feel about it?

_____
_____
_____
_____
_____

Will my audience be against me, or will I be preaching to the converted?

_____
_____
_____
_____
_____

Does my organization have a history of conflict or cooperation with this group?

_____
_____
_____
_____
_____

Is my audience neutral?

_____
_____
_____
_____

Why was I asked to speak?

_____
_____
_____
_____

It's vital to know where you stand—before you step somewhere you don't want to be. Before each speech, analyze your audience's level of knowledge.

Spin Doctor

By all means, try to address the topic—but slant the topic to appeal most to your audience and meet your strengths. Next to elementary school orchestra concerts, there are few things as unendurable as listening to a series of speakers parroting the same weary platitudes. Speak to the audience's concerns.

If you think your audience is opposed to what you have to say, start your message on common ground. As you speak, try to be as clear as you can be. Never assume that your audience is getting your point: messages that might be clear to receptive audiences can easily be misread by negatives ones.

Stick with the topic. This is not the time to go out on a limb, because hostile audiences can have the verbal equivalent of a chain saw. Also, avoid flaming the fire; don't say anything that will rile up your audience. Spin doctor techniques are discussed in detail in Chapter 9, "Whose Speech Is It Anyway?—Speech Style," and Chapter 15, "Using Humor."

Your Place in the Sun

Your place on the agenda can determine the tone of your speech as well as its content. Sometimes, your speech may be the single most important speech at the gathering. Other times, you may be the opening speaker. Then, you set the tone for the event because you have a chance to affect how the audience receives the entire program. If you're the last speaker, you have to inspire and lead. You may be speaking in the middle of the program or at the end. In these instances, you are carrying the entire weight of the event.

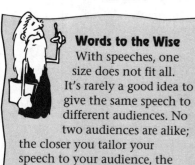

Words to the Wise
With speeches, one size does not fit all. It's rarely a good idea to give the same speech to different audiences. No two audiences are alike; the closer you tailor your speech to your audience, the better your speech will be.

If you're part of a panel, you want your speech to blend in with those of your peers. Listen to what they have to say. Match their time limit or speak for a little less time. At the same time, you also want your speech to stand out in a positive way.

Find out where your speech falls on the agenda. And don't be afraid to change your spot if you think it can lead to a better speech and better use of your time.

Location, Location, Location

Where you will be speaking can be as important as when and why. Researching the place where you will be speaking can help you tap topics of local interest, such as famous local people, inventions, and athletic teams. Put your hosts on the map of your speech, and you're already ahead of the game.

On the other side of the coin, there may be something going on in town that you would like not to mention in your speech. For example, jokes about California earthquakes fall flat if the place where you're speaking has just been hit with a series of tremors.

The room also has a great impact on your speech. Use the following guidelines.

In a small meeting room . . .

➤ There's no microphone, so project your voice.

➤ Make sure visuals are large enough.

In a large auditorium . . .

➤ Use a microphone.

➤ Use video or an overhead projector.

➤ Rope off the back to force people to sit up front.

On an outdoor platform . . .

➤ Bear in mind background noise.

➤ Take weather into account.

Bet You Didn't Know

OOOOH. Sophisticated audience analysis is commonplace in advertising. The Volvo campaign shows this. Its ads emphasize different benefits for different audiences: economy and durability in America, leisure and status in France, performance in Germany, and safety in Switzerland.

Special Circumstances

About 14 million Americans have some kind of hearing impairment. About 2 million of these people are deaf—unable to hear or understand speech. Deaf people use several methods to understand what others are saying. It's especially important to be aware of these methods when you are making public speeches so you don't ostracize anyone in your audience.

Some people who are deaf use lip reading to understand what others are saying. A great deal of your presentation will be lost, however, if you turn your head away from the listeners. It is also important to move your lips clearly when you are addressing lip readers.

People with hearing impairments also use two kinds of manual communication. One kind, *signing* or *sign language*, uses hand and arm gestures to represent words and ideas. Another kind of manual communication, the manual alphabet, uses the fingers to represent each letter of the alphabet. Many people with hearing impairments use manual language and lip reading.

There are many ways you can address these issues. For example, you can use title slides and overheads to communicate the outline of the speech.

Interpreters for people with hearing impairments will use signing to convey the outline of the presentation. Simultaneously, the interpreter will move his or her lips to reinforce the speaker's words. The interpreter will also use the manual alphabet to finger-spell unusual words or names.

Pull It Together

Before each speech, review and make notes about these questions to help you evaluate your audience:

➤ Who is going to be in the audience?

➤ How can I find out more about the people in the audience?

➤ How can I find out more about the organization?

➤ What is the political situation?

➤ How much do my listeners know about the topic?

➤ Are they on my side?

➤ How can I spin the topic to appeal to the audience?

➤ When on the agenda will my speech be given?

➤ How does the location of the speech affect its content?

➤ Are there any special circumstances I must take into account?

The Least You Need to Know

➤ Analyze your audience before you write a word of your speech.

➤ Find out as much as you can about the size of the audience, why they are there, and what they know about the topic.

➤ Try to meet the special needs and concerns of your audience.

Chapter 6

Speaking to Inform

In This Chapter

➤ Decide what to say in an informative speech

➤ Decide how to say it

➤ Fill in with great facts

➤ Learn what *not* to say in an informative speech

As you will recall from the discussion in Chapter 4, "Types of Speeches," the main purpose of a speech that informs is to convey information to the audience. That's because these speeches explain, teach, and clarify. To give the audience the information they've come for, it's especially important for this type of speech that you learn how to focus on a topic, decide on a clear method of organization, and get the facts.

In this chapter, you will first learn how to choose and narrow a topic. Next, I'll explain how to decide on an organizational pattern specifically suited to an informative speech. Finally, I'll provide step-by-step guidelines to researching the information that you need to make your informative speech fulfill its goal. You'll even learn what *not* to include in this type of speech.

Selecting a Theme

Said the after-dinner speaker: "I feel like Roseanne's fourth husband: I know what I'm supposed to do, but I'm at a loss as to how to make it different."

Word Power
Theme: The central idea in any speech; its one main idea.

I don't want you to feel like Roseanne's fourth husband—I wouldn't want *anyone* to feel like that. That's why you're going to start planning all your informative speeches by picking a central *theme,* the speech's one main idea. When planning your speech, ask yourself, "What is the one thing I want my audience to get from my speech?" That's your theme. A speech without a theme is like a swimming pool without water, a car without an engine, Roseanne's fourth husband without a clue—well, you get the idea.

Your theme must be general enough to fill the allotted time, but specific enough to respond to the topic, fit with any overall conference theme, and hold the audience's attention. Study this chart to see what I mean:

Topic Wide Enough to Tow a Battleship Through	Topic Narrow Enough to Fit in a Coach Seat
College	Paying for a college education in the 90s.
Work	Jobs for the 21st century.
Athletics	Should amateur athletes be paid?
Television	Should "infomercials" be banned?
Computers	Jump on the Information Superhighway.

Take the following quiz to see which topics have been sufficiently narrowed for a 20-minute speech. Circle the number for each topic that you think is specific enough for our mythical speaker. Ignore the ones that will have the poor sucker speaking until the cows come home.

1. Child care.

2. Ways to find caring, reliable, and inexpensive child care.

3. Divorce in the United States.

4. How counseling and mediation can help reduce the divorce rate.

5. Sexual harassment.

6. The problems of sexual harassment in the workplace.

7. Exercise classes/Aerobic exercise.

8. How to pick the exercise class that's right for *you*.

9. Stocks and bonds.

10. How to invest wisely in the bond market.

You're on to me, aren't you? In each case, the even-numbered choice is better because it has been narrowed enough to make a good base for a 20-minute speech. The odd-numbered topics are wide enough to make adequate suspension bridges.

Once you have your theme or *thesis*, you can find the second and third most important points to make—but everything in the speech must directly link to the theme. Make secondary points only if they do not detract from the impact of your primary theme. Keep your audience in mind as you develop your main ideas. Remember that your speech must be carefully tailored to meet your audience's needs and interests. Refer to Chapter 5, "Analyzing Your Audience," for guidelines.

Tell Me About It
Many people find that writing down their specific purpose—to convey information—helps them focus their thinking and stay on topic.

Be True to Yourself

There is an implied contract between audience and speaker. The audience must sit in their chairs and listen politely. The speaker must have something to say.

This only works if you believe in what you have to say; if *you* don't buy your message, the audience won't either. As Shakespeare said, "To thine own self be true." The advice may seem trite, but it's still true. Pick a theme that interests you as well as your audience. Settle on a theme that you are comfortable speaking about—a theme that suits your values, interests, and personality.

What If You Have Nothing to Say?

But what happens if you follow all this great advice and you find that the well is dry—you have absolutely nothing to say? Start by asking yourself some basic questions about yourself and your interests, such as your fraternal organizations, political affiliations and ambitions, hobbies, community work, company, business, or career. Here are some samples:

➤ Why did I join this civic group?

➤ What have we accomplished during my tenure?

➤ Why do I enjoy my hobbies?

➤ Have I been able to turn any hobbies into jobs?

➤ What community work gives me the greatest pleasure?

➤ What makes my company different or special?

➤ How has our organization helped the community?

➤ What was our company's most recent success?

Don't get too hung-up on setting aside time for thinking about themes. We're not pumping for procrastination as a lifestyle, but spending hours hunched over your desk pulling out your hair isn't a great solution, either. The best time for planning a speech can be while you're doing the dishes. Sometimes your best ideas will come when you least expect them. And the dishes get done, too.

Need more assistance priming the pump? Here's a list of useful sources. Which ones do you think would help you get ideas for important speeches?

➤ Academic journals

➤ Trade magazines

➤ Newspapers

➤ Training films

➤ Foreign publications

➤ Television

➤ Painting, sculpture

➤ Talking to coworkers

➤ Almanacs

➤ Encyclopedias

➤ Unfamiliar magazines

➤ Radio talk shows

Whisper...

Tell Me About It
Pick a theme you like. If you're interested in what you're talking about, your enthusiasm will rub off on your audience.

Deciding on an Organizational Pattern

The purpose of an informative speech is to make sure that the audience understands your ideas. It's not a race: the winner is not the person who covers the most information in the shortest length of time. Focus on helping others to grasp and remember the essential ideas you present.

To be sure that your informative speech is clearly organized, don't have too many main points—usually no more than three or four. Then, group the remaining facts under these main points. Be sure to link these main points logically and clearly. Don't jump back and forth among ideas.

The more clearly your speech is organized, the more easily your audience will grasp your ideas. The following sections review seven basic patterns for informational speeches.

Alphabetical—A-B-C Order

For this type of organization, simply arrange items in the order of the alphabet. But don't be misled by the ease with which this method of organization works—audiences find it a pleasure to follow a crisp, clear structure. It works best, of course, with discrete topics that lend themselves to easy division, such as the names of products, places, and companies.

Cause-Effect: What Happened and Why?

If you read a daily newspaper or watch the news, you are being exposed to cause and effect every day. Remember, the *cause* is *why* something happens; the *effect* is *what* happens—the result. Cause and effect is an especially suitable way to organize your speech because it is easy for an audience to follow. In most cases, start with the causes and lead into the results.

Chronological

Because with chronological order you present ideas in terms of time, it is an especially well-suited method of organization for an informative speech. For example, you might explain how to hook up a modem by taking the audience through the steps in order from first to last. See Chapter 10, "Decisions, Decisions: Finalizing the Organization" for more information on chronological order organization.

Numerical: 1-2-3 Order

As with alphabetical order, numerical order provides audiences with easy benchmarks to follow. Sometimes speechmakers include the numbers in their speech. Other times, they may use transitions that indicate order. Here are some of the most common signal words:

➤ First

➤ Second

➤ Third, and so on

➤ Then

➤ Next

➤ Following

➤ After

➤ Later

➤ Finally

➤ Subsequently

Problem-Solution: Dilemmas and Answers

This method of organization begins with the questions and moves to the answers. See Chapter 10, "Decisions, Decisions: Finalizing the Organization," for more information on the problem-solution method of development. This method can be used for persuasive and entertaining speeches as well as informative ones.

Spatial: The Order of Space

Here, information is arranged in the order of direction: up to down, down to up, north to south, east to west, inside to outside, right to left, and so on. A building can be discussed floor by floor, for example; the layout of a plaza can be described from the fountain in the center to parking fields in the outskirts.

Topical: The Order of Subjects

Some themes lend themselves to topical arrangements through long use: for example, financial reports are usually divided into assets and liabilities;

government is broken down into the federal, legislative, and judiciary branches. You don't want your method of organization to be shopworn, but remember: *audiences are listening, not reading.* Dividing your theme into familiar subtopics makes it easier for an audience to follow your logic. Because this method of organization can be used with all three kinds of speeches, it is covered in greater depth in Chapter 10.

Research Techniques

While their primary purpose is to tell, effective informative speeches are neither dull nor dry. Because people absorb information much more easily when it is interesting, make your speeches sizzle with juicy facts, tantalizing details, and delectable examples.

Someone once said to speak about what you know. That's good advice, but unfortunately we don't always have that luxury. Learning how to locate specific facts will give your speeches the backbone they need.

> **Tell Me About It**
> Recall that people learn new things by associating them with what they already know. Connect the new facts to the familiar ones to help your audience grasp your ideas.

Start by reading all about your topic. If you're plugged into the Information Superhighway, you can download piles of information from any of the on-line services to which you subscribe. If you know how to "surf the Net," you can get some of the latest and greatest reference material. I'm going to give you two more research techniques: five Ws and H, and interviewing.

Get the Scoop: Five Ws and H

One of the best ways to research is to ask yourself the reporter's questions: *who, what, when, where, why,* and *how.* As you prepare an informative speech, become a reporter: seek out the good stuff that you already know or can find out very easily. Start by brainstorming questions that answer each topic. Here's what I mean:

Who?

➤ Who should I ask for facts and advice?

➤ Who should my speech discuss?

➤ Who should I give thanks to in my speech?

What?

➤ What do I already know about this topic?

➤ What other information can I discover fast?

➤ What should I include? What should I cut?

When?

➤ When can I get this material?

➤ When will people be able to help me?

➤ When on the agenda do I have to speak?

Where?

➤ Where can I find information?

➤ Where can I find people to help me?

➤ Where am I going to deliver the speech?

Why?

➤ Why do I need this information?

➤ Why am I delivering this speech?

➤ Why will people help me?

How?

➤ How can I use what I already know?

➤ How will these facts help my speech?

➤ How can I make my informative speech better?

Interview People

If you want the right information, you have to ask the right people. What's the best way to conduct an interview? Here are some tried-and-true *Tell me about its*:

1. Always make an appointment for an interview. Because you are asking the favor, let the interviewee select the time for the interview.

2. Write out your questions before the interview. Keep them short and sweet.

3. Bring paper and a pen to the interview. Take detailed, legible notes.

4. Never tape-record an interview without getting the person's prior permission, preferably in writing.

5. Be sure to clarify confusing points. Double-check important information.

6. End the interview on time. Don't overstay your welcome. Be sure to thank the person for his or her time.

Types of Support

To be effective, informative speeches must be packed with *information*—the details that convey your theme. Effective support includes quotations, illustrations, analogies, and statistics. Each of these methods of support is covered in depth in Chapter 13, "Developing the Body."

Tell Me About It

To achieve their goals, informative speakers must:

➤ Structure the speech clearly.

➤ Present specific details, facts, and examples.

➤ Relate ideas to the listeners' existing knowledge.

➤ Use precise language.

What to Omit

As the speech writer and the speaker, you're in control. You get to decide what's in your speech, and what's out. What you don't decide to include can be just as important as what you do include. Use this checklist to decide what to include and what to leave out:

➤ Did I get rid of material that I can't verify?

➤ Have I cut out all extraneous details?

➤ Did I knock out anything I don't want to see in the newspaper tomorrow?

➤ Did I cut anything that might embarrass my friends or family?

➤ Did I cut anything that might embarrass me in the future?

➤ Have I cut information that is boring?

The Least You Need to Know

➤ Select an interesting theme (main idea) that appeals to you and your audience.

63

➤ Narrow your theme to fit into your allocated time slot.

➤ Select an organizational pattern that matches the theme and information in your speech.

➤ Include specific facts, details, and examples in your speech.

Speaking to Persuade

Getting right to the heart of persuasive speaking, a harried executive once said: "We're not paying you to make us look like a bunch of idiots. We're paying you so *others* won't find out we're a bunch of idiots." The guy had a point.

Effective persuasion is based on accurate logic, powerful appeals to emotion, and trust. All persuasive speeches have several purposes. They all:

➤ Provide information so the audience knows what to do.

➤ Overcome the listener's objections.

➤ Move the listener to belief or action.

In this chapter, you'll find out how to speak to persuade.

Researching Arguments Supporting and Opposing Each Side

There's one sure way to stop an argument. Drop one hard fact on it. The strength of your argument depends on three aspects of persuasion: logic, emotion, and credibility. Start with logic—the facts.

Willie Sutton once claimed that he robbed banks because "that's where the money is." Well, head off to the library because that's where the facts are.

There are over one hundred thousand libraries in the United States, with more than two billion books in them. There's a great deal of information you can easily find on your own at your local library. First, check basic reference sources such as dictionaries, encyclopedias, newspapers, magazines, almanacs, and *Facts on File*. Here are some reference sources chock-full of facts:

➤ Akey, Denise. *Encyclopedia of Associations.*

➤ American Society of Composers, Authors & Publishers. *Hit Songs.* (ASCAP).

➤ Asimov, Isaac. *Isaac Asimov's Book of Facts.*

➤ Hatch, Jane, ed. *The American Book of Days.*

➤ Levine, Michael. *The Address Book: How to Reach Anyone Who's Anyone.*

➤ Peter, Lawrence, ed. *Peter's Quotations: Ideas for Our Time.*

➤ *The World Almanac.*

> **Whisper...**
>
> **Tell Me About It**
>
> After you do your research, go for the heavy artillery—the reference librarian. A good reference librarian is a pearl beyond price. It pays to become friendly with these wonderful people; they can save you hours of toil. A cooperative reference librarian might even answer questions on the telephone, saving you a trip.

Deciding on Your Position and Creating a Thesis

Remember: There are two sides to every argument until you take one. Once you've gathered all the facts, decide how you stand on the issue. What do you want your audience to believe or do? Recall that the *topic* of your speech is called its *theme*. The specific *purpose* of your speech is called your *thesis*.

Then it's time to develop your case. Decide which of the following appeals will best serve your purpose and audience.

Appeal to Logic

Logical arguments rely on objective facts instead of personal opinions or preferences. In turn, each logical argument in your speech must be supported by evidence: facts, statistics, expert testimony, or details about the argument. The basic organization for a persuasive speech developed on logical arguments looks like this:

> *Introduction.* Catches the listener's attention. States your argument.

> *Body.* States each logical argument. Presents supporting evidence.

> *Conclusions.* Restates your argument. Summarizes your main points.

Logical arguments are developed in two basic ways: *inductive reasoning* and *deductive reasoning*.

Inductive Reasoning

Inductive reasoning is thinking from parts to the whole by drawing conclusions from specific facts. Scientists use inductive reasoning when they state a hypothesis and then conduct tests to see if it is valid. If repeated experiments produce the postulated result, the scientists are able to conclude that their hypothesis is likely valid.

For inductive reasoning to be solid, there cannot be any exceptions to the conclusions you draw. For example, if you saw three white cats and concluded that all cats are white, your conclusions would not be valid. To avoid this kind of faulty reasoning, be sure to use sufficient facts as the basis of your conclusion.

Deductive Reasoning

Deductive reasoning is thinking from the whole to the part. Start with a general statement and then proceed to specific facts that follow from the statement.

Sometimes, the deductive argument at the center of a persuasive speech can be stated in three sentences, like this:

> *Major premise:* All chocolate is fattening.

> *Minor premise:* This candy bar is chocolate.

> *Conclusion:* Therefore, this candy bar is fattening.

To use deductive reasoning correctly, first make sure that the major premise is true. If it is not valid, the rest of the argument will collapse. Then craft a minor premise that logically follows the first one. Finally, decide if the conclusion is sound. Make sure that any qualifications to the first statement are repeated in the conclusion. Rarely will a speaker lay out a deductive argument this neatly. In most cases, for example, the first statement will be implied rather than stated.

Use the following checklist when you write a persuasive speech using logical appeals:

- ✔ Is my topic appropriate to my audience?
- ✔ Have I sufficiently narrowed my topic?
- ✔ Did I research how other people feel about this topic?
- ✔ Did I select my side of the issue?
- ✔ Did I write my opinion as my thesis?
- ✔ Did I select the most effective facts?
- ✔ Did I weigh both inductive and deductive arguments?
- ✔ Did I check my inductive and deductive arguments to make sure they are valid?

Appeal to Emotion

An emotional appeal makes the audience want to do what you ask. A powerful speech can derive its strength from facts and logic, but if you rely on reason at the expense of emotion, you run the danger of ending up with a position paper instead of a speech. Listeners have a limited ability to relish a complicated argument or soak up reams of information. As a result, many effective public speakers make their case by emotional means as much as by intellectual ones.

Because speakers also have voice and nonverbal communication as part of their arsenal, a speaker can often use emotional appeals much more effectively than a writer. When speakers use emotional appeals, they are seducing by tapping the needs we all share. Here are some of these needs:

➤ **Physical Needs:** These are what you need to survive. They include the need for food, water, sleep, air, and protection from injury or harm.

➤ **Psychological Needs:** These are a person's inner life. They include the need for love, affection, security, and self-esteem.

➤ **Social Needs:** These are a person's relationship to a group. They include status, power, freedom, approval, belonging, and conformity.

Select a persuasive strategy based on your answers to the following four questions:

➤ What do you want people to do?

➤ What objections, if any, will people have?

➤ How strong a case can you make?

➤ What kind of persuasion does your organization value?

Good speeches are carefully crafted combinations of reason and emotion; strong messages and strong speakers are an uncommon luxury.

Credibility

Fact: Speakers need to have their audience identify with them if they are going to be persuasive. Want to make your speech powerful? Get your audience to trust you. Here's how.

Make the audience think that you, the speaker, are a person very like them—or like the way they see themselves on a very good hair day. Whatever the topic of your persuasive speech, work to get your audience to identify with you. To do so, you need to do the following:

Establish your own credibility by:

➤ Showing that you know what you're talking about.

➤ Explaining your credentials.

➤ Sharing information about your background.

➤ Being well-informed.

Evoke their goodwill by:

➤ Complimenting the audience on its good points.

➤ Identifying with a person the audience admires.

➤ Speaking with confidence.

➤ Using the appropriate tone.

➤ Showing powerful body language.

➤ Standing upright.

Be enthusiastic by:

➤ Avoiding false bravado.

➤ Saying it like you mean it.

What Not to Do—Logical Fallacies

Faulty logic can demolish the most carefully constructed speech. It's one of the surest ways to lose an audience. Following are the most common errors in reasoning, called "logical fallacies."

Oversimplifying the Issue

When speakers oversimplify the issue, they twist the truth by presenting too narrow a range of possibilities. For example:

> Here, we have a clear-cut choice between a plan that will result in international catastrophe or a plan that will result in a thriving economy both at home and abroad.

Are the two sides of the issue really that "clear-cut"? It seems unlikely. Unless the speaker can back up the assertion with convincing details, the audience is likely to shake its collective head in disbelief. The argument is not valid.

Begging the Question

This logical error is stating a position that needs to be proven as though it has already been proven. For instance:

> The question we must resolve is whether Dr. Wilson should be granted tenure with such an inadequate publication record.

The real issue is *not* whether Dr. Wilson should be granted tenure. The real issue *is* whether Dr. Wilson has an inadequate publication record. The speaker has avoided having to prove the real allegation by assuming that it is a fact. This leads the audience to make the same assumption.

Misleading Statistics

Someone once said that there are "liars, damned liars, and statistics." Misleading statistics are true but do not prove what the speaker claims. For example, you may have heard the advertisement that "four out of five dentists surveyed" endorse a certain brand of gum. All you know for sure is that five dentists were surveyed—not fifty, not five hundred, not five thousand. Because these dentists may not be typical of the entire population of dentists, their answers may not provide accurate information.

Post hoc ergo propter hoc

The phrase is Latin for "After this, therefore because of this." It is the mistake of confusing *after* with *because.* Here's what I mean:

> During the board of directors' term of office, the value of common stock has declined 25 percent; preferred stock by 15 percent. Should we reappoint people who cannot manage our money?

The fact that the value of the stock declined *after* the board of directors took office does not mean that it happened *because* they were in office. The speaker has to show that the events are indeed linked by a cause-and-effect relationship.

Reasoning Backward

This logical fallacy assumes that people belong to a group because they have characteristics in common with that group. Therefore, it assumes that anyone with that quality must be a member of that group. Study this example:

> Democrats are always proposing tax increases. Governor Harriman is proposing a tax increase. From this we can conclude that Governor Harriman is a Democrat.

Clearly, people other than Democrats have proposed tax increases; the ploy is likely known to any public official seeking re-election in a tough year.

False Analogies

False analogies are misleading comparisons. The correspondence does not hold up because the items or people being compared are not sufficiently alike. For instance:

71

A good marriage is like a game of baseball. In baseball, if a player follows the rules, the game will be a success. Likewise, in marriage, if the players stick to the rules the partners accept, the marriage will flourish.

No such luck. Marriage and baseball may have a few surface similarities, but marriage is much more complex than baseball. The relationship of the rules to "success" is infinitely more intricate in marriage than it is in baseball.

The Least You Need to Know

➤ Effective persuasive speeches rely on appeals to logic, emotion, and trust.

➤ Assertions are backed up with carefully researched facts, details, examples, and statistics.

➤ Errors in logic can destroy an argument.

Chapter 8

Speaking to Entertain

In This Chapter

➤ Discover what "entertaining" means—and how to craft a speech that really does entertain

➤ Explore organizational patterns and research techniques

➤ Learn how to make happy talk

➤ Why speeches that entertain are important to building social cohesion

Not all speeches deal with "big" issues. In fact, many speeches are ceremonial. These presentations include club meetings, dinners, parties, graduations, awards ceremonies, holidays, and ribbon cuttings—all our social rituals. These speeches are not the same as talks that inform or persuade. For one, speeches that entertain are usually much shorter than the other two types of speeches. In addition, they often take a personal approach.

Interestingly, speeches that entertain will often have a more immediate effect on your life than speeches with a more serious, lofty tone and purpose. That's because social occasions often present rich opportunities for you to score points with the audience. Those "points" are often cashed in for money for worthy causes and goodwill with business contacts and influential acquaintances.

In Chapter 4, "Types of Speeches," you learned that speeches that entertain do more than entertain: they also create social cohesion by creating good feelings. They do this by promoting a feeling of social unity that draws people together into a community.

On the surface, developing a good speech that entertains would seem to be easy, but this is far from the case. In this chapter, you will learn the skills you need if you are called on to speak at a ceremonial occasion.

Playing the Crowd

By this time, you're probably muttering in your soup, "Enough with the audience analysis already. Is this all that woman can talk about?" Well, as the length of this book shows, it's not *all* I discourse on, but it's so omnipresent here because it's so important.

Always start by assessing your audience. This is vitally important with regard to speeches that entertain because on these occasions, your listeners are not gathered to learn or be convinced: they're sitting at your feet to have a good time. Think about what topic and content will ensure that they get what they came for. Consider their likes and dislikes. Reflect on their level of sophistication. Here are your big three considerations:

➤ Audience

➤ Occasion

➤ Purpose

Make it your mantra for speeches that entertain. You may also want to review the information in Chapter 5, "Analyzing Your Audience" for super-specific ways to take the pulse of the people.

Developing a Clear, Central Theme

Next, select a theme that suits the occasion and audience. Go for a theme that's novel, provocative, and original. Not too novel, provocative, and original, though—you want to entertain, not shock. Remember: The easiest way to stay awake during an after-dinner speech is to deliver it.

Look back over the information in Chapter 5, "Analyzing Your Audience," for ways to slant your topic to suit your listeners.

Even when your main purpose in speaking is to entertain, you will often want to include at least one serious idea in your speech. Why? Like too much ice cream or chocolate (okay, bad examples), a speech that is all fluff can sometimes become tiresome and vacuous. Consider underlying your humor, therefore, with something of greater weight, such as a serious statement of loyalty for the group or organization that you are addressing.

Also remember that you want your audience to have a good time and that you cannot encourage other people to enjoy themselves unless you are a happy camper. It should be plain to your audience that you like what you're doing at that particular moment. Your topic should be genial and good-natured, suited to the audience and occasion. It should be a topic that you like speaking about. The overall theme should be:

> ➤ **Optimistic.** This is not the time to share your personal problems, paint a gloomy picture of the present, or offer dire predictions for the future. Keep it light, lite, or not heavy.

> ➤ **Uncomplicated.** Remember: People have come to be entertained. Don't make your audience strain to get your point. Develop your speech around one or two points that they can easily grasp.

> ➤ **Enlivened with anecdotes.** Avoid stale, familiar jokes. I recommend humorous anecdotes drawn from your own experience, about the guest of honor, or concerning the purpose of the speech. A colleague once gave a very funny speech about me by parodying my spring/summer/winter/fall allergies. Every other anecdote was accompanied by a blast of sneezes and a flurry of tissues.

Also, unless you are very skilled at wordplay, try to avoid commenting on your own jokes;

Words to the Wise

While the interjection of a serious note in an entertaining speech can serve as a much-needed anchor, the seriousness should never be allowed to predominate. Keep the purpose of your speech firmly in mind: to entertain.

Tell Me About It

If you're a gifted comedian or very comfortable with humor, go for it. Otherwise, consider taking a much simpler but equally effective course to win laughs: Play it straight. Sometimes, the best way to tell a joke is to tell it seriously. Hey, works for me. You, too, can use this approach to get a laugh while maintaining your cool.

instead, let one story flow naturally into the other. See Chapter 15, "Using Humor," for ways to work jokes into speeches that entertain.

Laying the Groundwork

A speech that entertains can be organized in a number of ways. Next, I describe two methods that have proven to be especially useful to beginning public speakers.

Method 1: Point and Proof

With the point and proof method, your speech is made up of a central idea or thesis supported by a series of examples, anecdotes, or amusing stories following on each other's heels. This method of development not only entertains your audience but also makes it easier for them to remember the main points in your speech. For a point and proof speech, follow these steps:

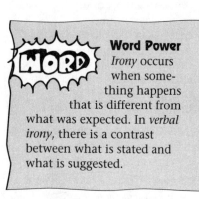

Word Power
Irony occurs when something happens that is different from what was expected. In *verbal irony*, there is a contrast between what is stated and what is suggested.

➤ Open with an anecdote, preferably amusing.

➤ Explain the point of the story. Describe how the entire speech will be organized around this point.

➤ Illustrate your point with additional anecdotes, each of which builds on the central point. Spread the stories out so the really good stuff isn't all bunched in the beginning, middle, or end.

➤ Close by restating your central point. Use a great story for a smashing ending.

Method 2: Poking Fun at Point and Proof

This method of organization lampoons the "point and proof" method:

➤ Start by relating an anecdote, referring to the occasion, alluding to a recent amusing event, or poking fun at the host.

➤ Present a serious problem exaggerated beyond all sense of proportion.

➤ Offer a ridiculous solution, described with a series of humorous anecdotes.

➤ Close the speech by lampooning an absurd call for action, telling a story to show the irony of your argument, or by summarizing the silly steps in your solution.

See Chapter 10, "Decisions, Decisions: Finalizing the Organization," for more guidelines on organizing entertaining speeches.

Researching the Topic

Now it's time to gather supporting material—examples, details, anecdotes, jokes—that help you make your point. Think of this step as trimming a Christmas tree. The supporting material adds glitter to a solid frame.

You should always gather more material than you think you will need. Vary the kinds of supporting material you select. Your speech writing task will be much less arduous if you have ample material from which to choose. It's not unlikely that what looked like a sure laugh-getter while you were researching turns out to be a dud when you're writing. If you have limited your research, you might find that you don't have enough material to fill out your speech.

Besides, speech writers are a thrifty lot; you'll find that any extra material, like left-over food, rarely goes to waste. Put it in your speech writing "freezer"—a folder that you'll keep for this purpose. That way, you'll have a stock of items to draw on for the next time you're asked to give an entertaining speech.

As you are researching, don't stop to panic about organization. Instead, jot down the following information:

➤ Facts about the sponsoring group.

➤ Anecdotes from news stories, TV, radio.

➤ Events from fact or fiction.

➤ Good, non-offensive jokes. Always err on the side of caution: Never insult anyone.

Tell Me About It
Irony is the most difficult form of humor to carry off; all too often audiences take it seriously. Before you use irony, be sure that your audience will understand that you're being ironic.

Words to the Wise
Satirizing the host, a guest, or any person in attendance can be a great way to open a speech—if it's done with taste and tact. It's *never* acceptable to be mean, vicious, embarrassing, or cruel. Judge everyone's "comfort zone" and stay well within it. If you have any doubt go with a personal anecdote, a reference to the occasion or news event, or a joke instead.

Then zero in on the specifics. Get statistics, quotations, names, dates, and places. If you can't get what you need, dig deeper into easy-to-get materials. Try this checklist:

✔ Did I look at high-interest newspapers? Don't shun those supermarket tabloids: they have some great stories for entertaining speeches. Even some of the headlines work. Here's my favorite: "Headless Body Found in Topless Bar."

✔ Did I look at family, club, or the organization's photo albums for ideas for anecdotes?

✔ Did I skim magazines on the topic? Look for magazines that match the interests of your audience.

✔ Can I call friends for information? How about the people who will be in the audience?

✔ Are there any other sources I can use?

I've given you so many "do's" in this lesson that it's time to have some "don'ts" for a change of pace:

➤ Don't start your research until you have your purpose and message firmed up.

➤ Don't ignore what you already know about a topic.

➤ Don't hesitate to ask for help from research librarians and experts.

➤ Don't consult sources that are very similar, such as only newspapers or only magazines.

➤ Don't use out-of-date materials, even if they are easier to get than more reliable and timely sources.

➤ Don't write down everything indiscriminately. Pick and choose: get the information that's relevant to your purpose and audience.

➤ Don't write down anything you don't understand.

➤ Don't record any key piece of information without making sure that it's true. Check all crucial facts in two reliable sources.

➤ Don't write down incomplete citations. Be sure to record the author, title, date, and page number with each source. You may need this later for any number of purposes.

Focusing on Shared Experiences

Speeches that entertain often focus on experiences that the speaker shares with the audience and guest of honor. These speeches are the most successful when the speaker relates anecdotes that help the audience tap into common events.

For example, imagine that you are speaking at a retirement dinner for a colleague. If you are already retired, you can relate some of the things that the guest of honor said about life at *your* retirement dinner. If you have yet to reach that blissful (or so I'm told) stage of life, you might recall shared work experiences, like the time the guest of honor got stuck in the snowbank trying to dig *your* car out of the drift.

If you are speaking at a wedding, you might want to recall your own wedding and marriage. Then again. . . If you are presenting an award, share some positive anecdotes about the recipient; if you are cutting the ribbon at the new library, remind the community how everyone pitched in to make the dream a reality. That's the idea. Remember this as you do your research.

Bet You Didn't Know

Speakers often memorize entertaining speeches to make sure that the show runs smoothly. See Chapter 19, "Ever Hear the One About?... Entertaining Speeches," for more on this.

Making Happy Talk: Building Goodwill

Whether your purpose is to entertain at a roast, toast the bride and groom, or honor a worthy award winner, speeches that entertain build good feelings. People who attend functions of this type do so because they affirm their commitment to their family, service group, country, religion, community, or nation. There are several ways that you can create a feel-good situation. And none of them calls for resorting to flowers, candy, or winning lottery tickets.

You-Attitude

Adopting the you-attitude is looking at events from the audience's perspective rather than from just your own viewpoint. Using the you-attitude helps

Words to the Wise
Keep it short and sweet. Nothing spoils an entertaining speech like too much of it. Make your point, illustrate your point, and summarize your point. For those of you who like things as specific as I do, figure about ten minutes of air time for an effective, entertaining speech.

you craft an entertaining speech that delivers what the audience expects and that respects their intelligence.

To use this method, imagine that you were sitting in the audience. What would you like to hear? What would you *not* want to hear? Rather than saying what you want to say, say what the audience wants to hear and what the occasion requires. After all, the purpose of your speech is to entertain, not to instruct or persuade. I tell myself that this is the time to leave my ol' soapbox home and make people feel good. This is especially important if you think the meal will be inedible rather than just merely indigestible.

Emotional Appeals

Another effective way to forge good feelings in speeches that entertain is through emotional appeals. This technique is very effective in helping reinforce values and unity.

With this method, you use an appeal to emotion to reinforce the audience's identification with you. You tap the values and interests that you share with the audience. Become one of them rather than the "sage on the stage."

The Least You Need to Know

➤ Speeches that entertain must be very closely linked to the audience's needs and wants.

➤ Develop a clear thesis and method of organization for these speeches.

➤ "Entertaining" doesn't necessarily mean humorous; avoid humor unless you're comfortable with it.

➤ Do thorough, careful research; there's no substitute for hard work.

➤ Build goodwill. You can use the you-attitude and emotional appeals to accomplish this.

Part 3
Writing the Speech

Once upon a time, when writing styles were more formal than they are now, some people were very careful never to end a sentence with a preposition. Even then, however, there were stylistic mavericks who let their prepositions fall with abandon. Winston Churchill was one these people. His secretary, appalled, always revised the drafts of Churchill's speeches to avoid ending sentences with a preposition. Exasperated, Churchill finally sent this message to his secretary: "This is the sort of English up with which I will not put!"

Let the writing begin!

Chapter 9

Whose Speech Is It, Anyway?— Speech Style

In This Chapter

➤ Learn how to write with grace, wit, and style

➤ Decide on a writing style that suits you and your audience

➤ Find out what *not* to do

As a speaker, you want to select the words that most accurately convey your meaning, suit your personal speaking style, and mesh with the audience and occasion. But how can you do this? That's what this chapter is all about.

Here, you'll discover that using words well depends on making good choices. You'll learn that no matter what the occasion for your speech, you'll go for the language that's simple, accurate, and appropriate. Sometimes the choices are clearly right or wrong; other times, however, the choices are more subtle. As you'll find out, your awareness of your purpose, audience, and situation will all influence your choice of words.

Words and More Words: Diction

Let's start with the building blocks of any speech—words. *Diction* is word choice. One of the most frequent questions I'm asked as I teach speech writing is, "Shouldn't I use long words to impress my audience? Won't they think I'm smart if I use a lot of hard words?" Those 25-cent words can sometimes make even the most stalwart stylist act like a kid in a candy shop. So many words—so little time!

Words to the Wise
The fastest way to discover whether you'll trip over a word or if a sentence is too long is to read what you read aloud. After all, if you can't say it smoothly, the audience won't understand it easily!

It *is* tempting to show off your vocabulary, but your point as a public speaker is to communicate a message. As a result, you will *always* want to pick the words that best convey your meaning. When people are reading, they have the time to study the words and think about them. Because listening is an oral skill, people can't go back to pick up something they didn't catch the first time. As a result, you should select the easier word, not the more difficult one. If your listeners have to try too hard to figure out what you're saying, chances are they will lose entire chunks of your speech. By the time they decipher one sentence, you'll be three ahead. Strive for clarity, not complexity. Here are some examples of what I mean:

Hard to Understand	Easier to Understand
Precipitous	Steep
Mellifluous	Golden, mellow

For informal speeches, use an *everyday level of diction*, with standard vocabulary, conventional sentence structure, and contractions. Eulogies, commencement addresses, and other formal speeches call for *formal language:* long, complex words; complex figures of speech; few contractions.

Instead of puffing up your words, give specific details, facts, and examples that prove your point. Set out the statistics that people can use as benchmarks. If you want to prove that speed skater Bonnie Blair is an extraordinary athlete, dazzle your audience with the facts:

> Bonnie Blair blasted the competition off the ice in the 1994 Winter Olympics at Lillehammer, Norway. Blair won gold in both the 500-meter and the 1,000-meter speed skating races, giving her a career total

of five gold medals. That's one more medal than any American woman has ever won in an Olympics—winter or summer. Only speed skater Eric Heiden, the hero of the Lake Placid Winter Games in 1980, has brought home as much winter gold for the United States.

Hone the Tone

Your choice of words affects the *tone* of your speech. Tone in writing is your attitude toward your subject and audience. The tone can be highly formal, informal, or somewhere in between. Different tones are appropriate for different occasions, audiences, and purposes. An informal tone, for example, can be well suited to a brief speech at a birthday party; a highly formal tone, in contrast, would be more appropriate for a commencement address or a speech at a stockholders' meeting.

No matter what tone you adopt for your speech, it's not a bad idea to downplay your own importance in the Great Chain of Being. You can almost always score a few points with a little humility. Arrogance and smugness rarely play well. Try to avoid absolutes, which convey a black-and-white rigidity. Study Table 9.1 for more guidelines.

Words to the Wise

In most cases, avoid slang and regional expressions. Slang—words like *rad, dead-head, groovy, neat*—passes out of usage quickly and can make your speech not only confusing but also dated. Regional expressions are words particular to a specific region, such as *grinder, poorboy, hero,* or *sub* for a cold cut sandwich. Like slang, regional expressions can backfire and confuse your listeners.

Table 9.1 Alternatives for Words That Could Make You Seem Rigid or Smug

Words to Avoid	Words to Use
Always	Sometimes
Invariably	Occasionally
Constantly	From time to time
Forever	Now and then
Never	Occasionally
Never again	Once in a while
At no time	Seldom

continues **85**

Table 9.1 Continued

Words to Avoid	Words to Use
In no way	Rarely
Certainly	Likely
Assuredly	Reasonableness
Without fail	Potential
Positively	At times
Unconditionally	At intervals
Absolutely	Not infrequently

Avoid Clichés Like the Plague

While we're on words, strive to craft fresh, new phrases. As a general rule, try to stay away from *clichés*—phrases are so shopworn that they have lost their capacity to communicate with impact. If you have heard these phrases over and over again, so has your audience. Here are some clichés to avoid "like the plague." (That's our first one!)

➤ Dead as a doornail

➤ Gentle as a lamb

➤ Sweet as sugar

➤ Tough as nails

➤ Straight as an arrow

➤ Ripe old age

➤ Raining cats and dogs

➤ Face the music

➤ Happily ever after

➤ Hard as rocks

Occasionally, clichés *can* work for you. When people listen to speeches, they like to hear familiar ideas and sentiments sprinkled among the new ideas, like sugar on berries.

But for a cliché to work, it can't be used in its tired, old way. Instead, stand the cliché on its head to make it work for you in a fresh, new way. Take the cliché "The business of America is business," for instance. This was probably a cliché when Calvin Coolidge first used it! To give the cliché new life, try this:

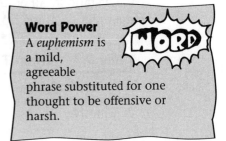

Word Power
A *euphemism* is a mild, agreeable phrase substituted for one thought to be offensive or harsh.

> Calvin Coolidge once said that the business of America is business. That was in the past. Today, the business of America is minding everyone else's business.

What does this prove? Clichés can be an asset, if you use them cleverly.

Tell It Like It Is: Avoid Euphemisms

Euphemisms are sometimes necessary for tact in social situations. For example, most people find it more comfortable to offer condolences by saying "I'm sorry that your dog *passed away*," rather than "I'm sorry that your dog *died*." The euphemism "passed away" cushions the uneasy situation.

But in speech writing, euphemisms drain away your meaning. For instance, using the phrase, "He is between assignments" rather than "He lost his job" fools no one and is unlikely to spare feelings. Table 9.2 provides some examples of what I mean.

Word Power
Jargon is the specialized language of a particular organization, occupation, or group.

Table 9.2   Out with the Euphemisms—In with Plain English

Euphemisms	Clear English
He came within the venue of the law enforcement establishment.	He was arrested.
Her occupation is domestic engineering.	She is a homemaker.
She announced herself to be in favor of terminating the employment of the computer engineer.	She wanted to fire the computer engineer.

What Language Is That? Avoiding Jargon

Jargon is a bad idea because people outside the organization are not likely to understand it. All occupations have their own jargon. Table 9.3 gives some examples of jargon from different professions or hobbies.

Table 9.3 Jargon Terms from Different Areas of Expertise

Stamp Collecting	Computer	Speech
Adhesives	Address	Articulation
Sidebar	Bit	Phonation
Glassine	Chip	Resonance
Commens	Hacker	Dysphonias
Definitives	Hard copy	Aphasia
Mint	Floppy	Phoneme
Hinged	Program	Aphesis
Reprints	Windows	Apheresis
Covers	Virus	Phonic

As you draft your speech, consider your purpose and audience to decide whether a word or phrase is indeed jargon. For example, an audience of baseball fans will easily understand a speaker who refers to *RBIs, ERA,* and *homer,* but those words are jargon to an audience not familiar with baseball. They may even have a different meaning in the jargon of another group. For example, *ERA* would refer to the Equal Rights Amendment in the jargon of the National Organization of Women. The computer jargon *virus, program, chip, bit,* and *floppy* also have other meanings. It's important to avoid jargon unsuited to the audience because it shuts out your listeners.

Hey, Babe, Avoid Sexist Language

Sexist language assigns roles or characteristics to people on the basis of gender. The term was originally used to refer to practices that discriminated against women. Now, the term *sexist language* also includes any usage that unfairly limits the aspirations or capabilities of either sex. Here are some guidelines to follow:

➤ Avoid outdated stereotypes such as "Men are terrible housekeepers" or "Women are bad drivers."

➤ Do not describe women by their looks, age, or clothing—unless you do the same for men.

➤ Do not use a wife's first name when you use the husband's last name.

No: Mr. Green and his wife Amanda.

Yes: Chet Green and his wife Amanda, or Chet and Amanda Green.

➤ Do not use the word *girls* to refer to adult women. Use the word *women* instead.

➤ Avoid using the masculine pronoun to refer to males and females together. Use a pair of pronouns or recast the sentence into the plural form.

No: An electrician cannot afford to make mistakes in *his* job.

Yes: An electrician cannot afford to make mistakes in *his or her* job.

Yes: *Electricians* cannot afford to make mistakes in *their* jobs.

➤ Avoid the use of *man* when women and men are both included. Try to use gender-neutral words like *people, humanity,* and *humankind.*

No: *Man* does not live by bread alone.

Yes: *People* do not live by bread alone.

➤ Avoid expressions that demean one gender.

No: career girl, gal Friday, male nurse, lady doctor (lawyer).

Yes: professional woman, assistant, nurse, doctor, lawyer.

➤ Avoid expressions that exclude one sex.

No: a man-sized meal, old wives' tale, the common man, mankind.

Yes: a huge meal, superstition, the average person, humanity.

➤ Avoid stereotyping occupations by gender when men and women are included.

No: businessman, mailman, policeman, chairman, stewardess.

Yes: business executive, postal carrier, police officer, chair or chairperson, flight attendant.

➤ Avoid racist language or language based on ethnicity. For example, the term "gypped" comes from "gypsies." As a result, "gypped" is highly offensive to gypsies, since it implies that they are thieves.

They Get the Picture with Figures of Speech

Figures of speech (also called *figurative language*) are words and expressions not meant to be taken literally. Figurative language uses words in fresh, new ways to appeal to the imagination. Figures of speech create comparisons and connections that use one idea or image to enhance or explain another. This can make your speech especially memorable—even quotable! Figures of speech include *images*, *similes*, *metaphors*, *hyperbole*, and *personification*.

Illustrate with Images

An *image* is a word that appeals to one or more of our five senses. Imagery can be found in all sorts of writing, but it is most common in poetry. Imagery is important in speech because it can make your address memorable by telegraphing meaning. A memorable image can stay in your mind long after you have forgotten the rest of the speech. Good ideas can be expressed in visual terms. If you can get pictures rather than words floating through people's minds, your speech will be the one they remember.

A striking image transforms a ho-hum address into an unforgettable experience. A case in point is former President George Bush's image of "a thousand points of light" for the spirit of volunteerism. The image produced an emotional response, fulfilling the role of the politician to inspire. Here's a longer example from Martin Luther King, Jr.'s famous "I Have a Dream" speech:

> I have a dream today that one day in the state of Alabama, whose governor's lips are presently dripping with the words of interposition and nullification, will be transformed into a situation where little black boys and black girls will be able to join hands with little white boys and white girls and walk together as sisters and brothers.

> I have a dream today that one day every valley shall be exalted, every hill and mountain shall be made low, the rough places will be made plains, and the crooked places will be made straight. . . .

In 1963, when this speech was delivered, it presented a waterfall of images that were somehow within our grasp. Many people have told me that this is the most powerful speech in their memory.

Speechmakers in any realm—business, politics, and private life, to name just a few—can apply the same techniques to their speeches. To find images that you can use, look at the usefulness of your topic or commodity. Trace the subject—such as agribusiness, pharmaceutical, chemical companies, machinery, or publishing—from the producer to the consumer.

Dare to Compare with Similes and Metaphors

A *simile* is a figure of speech that compares two unlike things. Similes use the words "like" or "as" to make the comparison. "A dream put off dries up like a raisin in the sun" is an example of a simile.

A *metaphor* is also a figure of speech that compares two unlike things. However, metaphors do not use the words "like" or "as" to make the comparison. "The rush-hour traffic bled out of all the city's major arteries" is a metaphor.

Hyperbole (or Overstatement) and Personification

Hyperbole is exaggeration used for a literary effect such as emphasis, drama, or humor. Here is an example: "If I don't get this report in on time, my boss will kill me."

Personification is giving human traits to nonhuman things. For example: "This speech begged to be given." Hyperbole and personification are like spice: a little goes a long way to make a speech especially delicious.

Throw Out the Rule Book: A Look at Grammar

Ever have your knuckles smartly rapped because you had broken one of the cardinal Rules of Writing such as "Never Use Contractions in Formal Essays"? Fortunately, for those of us who are still massaging our knuckles, a lot of these rules don't apply to speech writing. Feel free to cut out all the contractions in your speech—but be ready to have it collapse under the weight of its own pomposity.

When you write a speech, you try to capture the rhythms of spoken English. This means that you can throw out these old Formal Writing Rules:

➤ Never use contractions in formal writing.

➤ Never end a sentence with a preposition.

➤ Never use clipped words (such as "till" for "until").

➤ Never interchange *which* and *that*.

➤ Never split an infinitive. For example, "To boldly go where no one has gone before." If it were "To go boldly . . . ," it would sound silly.

You're always better off if your speech accommodates your natural speech patterns. (Notice that I snuck in the contraction "you're" for "you are.") This is because we're most at ease when we are speaking in our normal voice, with our normal speech patterns. Words and grammatical constructions that are unfamiliar are hard for speakers to deal with, even with a lot of rehearsal time.

Short and Sweet Sentence Length

Give yourself and your audience a break: keep the sentences short. Long, complex sentences are hard to read. There's more chance that you'll trip over the sentences, lose their rhythm and pacing, and make a hash out of the whole speech. Long sentences are also more difficult for the audience to follow.

A Final Word: Be True to Yourself

Writing and delivering a speech is especially difficult if the subject has nothing to do with your business, hobbies, or interests. For example, you may have to give a speech at a commencement, the opening of a supermarket, or the groundbreaking for the new dog-racing track.

> **Whisper...**
>
> **Tell Me About It**
> Many speakers select an important phrase from their speech and use it as a refrain, a technique called *repetition*. If you have an important point to make, don't try to be subtle or clever. This is the time to apply the polo mallet to the side of the audience's head with a tremendous whack. Repetition makes a speech resonate, which makes it easier to remember and thus more significant.

Why are you on the top of everyone's dance card? Maybe you look good in a suit, have a great voice, or come cheap. Whatever the reason, don't sell yourself short. You don't have to resort to greeting-card sentiments to fill the air time. Avoid such shopworn clichés as "Do the right thing" and "Tomorrow is the first day of the rest of your life."

You don't have to pretend to be Oprah, Phil, or even Father Flanagan. Think about what makes you important. It's your wisdom, common sense, and experience. You don't have to cross-stitch your accomplishments on a sampler. They asked you and not someone else to speak because you earned it.

Generally speaking, your speech will be better if it deals with concrete stories, examples, and illustrations that make sense coming from your mouth. Your speech will be better if you use natural language, brief sentences, and vivid figures of speech.

The Least You Need to Know

➤ Select the words and level of diction that suit the audience, purpose, and occasion.

➤ Avoid sexist language, clichés, and jargon.

➤ Include colorful figures of speech and repetition.

➤ Match your words to your personality. To thine own self be true.

Chapter 10

Decisions, Decisions: Finalizing the Organization

Every time you make a speech, you want your audience to think about what you're saying as you say it. You want them to process the message by considering your main idea and its supporting points. You want your speech to be memorable, too. In order to help your audience understand your points and recall them with clarity and pleasure, you need to organize your speech into a recognizable and easy-to-follow pattern. (Strong organization has another key benefit: it helps you remember what you planned to say!)

In this chapter, you will first learn about time limits. How long is long enough for an effective speech? Then I'll show you how to analyze different organizational patterns. Next, I'll discuss how to select the organizational pattern that suits your purpose, audience, and occasion. I'll take you through the process of organizing a topic, step-by-step.

Setting a Time Limit

William Henry Harrison's inaugural address in 1841 was 9,000 words long. It took two full hours to deliver, and it was a freezing day. Harrison came down with pneumonia and died a month later. The moral of the story? A speaker who is going to go on for hours better have a good speech, deliver it well, and stay out of the cold.

Abraham Lincoln was once asked how long a man's legs should be. "Long enough to reach the ground," he answered. How long should a speech be? Long enough to "reach the ground"—to accomplish what it intends. Lincoln's Gettysburg Address, recognized as one of the finest speeches of all time, is 265 words long—and it accomplished what it intended.

Once during a meeting, I was on my way back from the restroom when I ran into another member of the audience. Wondering whether it was safe to go back into the room where the speaker was talking, I asked, "Has the speaker finished what he had to say yet?" "Yes," my colleague replied, "but he's still talking."

When deciding how long to speak, your first consideration should be how much time you are allocated. You don't have much control over this. Whatever length of time you're given, you're always better off going under the time limit rather than over. Cheat on the short side. Do your audience a favor: the only thing worse than listening to a bad speech is listening to a long bad speech.

Few people resent a good, brief speech, but almost everyone resents a waste of time. With speech, long does not equal better. If you have successfully communicated up to—but no more than—three points, you have done well. If you try to get too many points across, it's possible (in fact, probable) that your audience will remember none of them clearly. In fact, a great way to undo the effects of a barn-storming speech is to exceed your allotted time or to keep talking when you've said your piece.

Remember: No matter how good your speech is—and no matter how good a speaker you are—people get cranky sitting in those hard wooden chairs and listening, listening, listening. Many attempts to communicate are nullified by saying too much. Don't be one of those orators who makes up in length what they lack in depth.

The "20-Minute" Rule

Twenty minutes is a good benchmark for the average speech for the average occasion. Obviously, a wedding speech will be much, much shorter; you're going to want to save the bride and groom some time to dance and eat their cake. By the same token, the keynote address at the Democratic National Convention will likely run a tad longer (especially if you're using it as a career builder, as Bill Clinton tried in 1988). Twenty minutes is fair to you, the speaker, and the audience, the listeners. If you need more time to make your point, don't be afraid to take it. But give everyone in the room a break. Say what you have to say and be done.

> **Tell Me About It**
> You can't go wrong if you think of the first two minutes of your speech as an audition. It's a 120-second sample that has to convince your listeners that the remaining 20 minutes are worth their time and attention.

Listening to a speech is very different from reading one. Because your audience can't go back to your speech and review confusing parts, it's important for you to provide an especially clear organization and to repeat your central points. Every speech needs a beginning, middle, and end. The following three-part structure is simple—and it works. If you use this organization, your speech will be clear, organized, and powerful.

Here's the way that I recommend that you break down a 20-minute speech:

Tell 'em what you're going to tell 'em: In the first part of your speech, tell your audience your themes and major points. This should take one to three minutes. See Chapter 12, "Begin at the Beginning," for specific guidelines for writing effective speech openings.

Tell 'em: In the middle part of the speech, illustrate all the points that support your theme. This should take about twenty minutes. Guidelines are provided in Chapter 13, "Developing the Body."

Tell 'em what you told 'em: At the end of the speech, recap. Be sincere, be brief, be seated. Allow one or two minutes. See Chapter 14, "Finishing Touches: Conclusions, Revisions, and Titles."

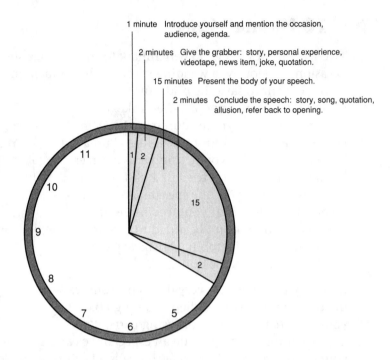

1 minute   Introduce yourself and mention the occasion, audience, agenda.

2 minutes   Give the grabber: story, personal experience, videotape, news item, joke, quotation.

15 minutes   Present the body of your speech.

2 minutes   Conclude the speech: story, song, quotation, allusion, refer back to opening.

Here's how to allocate the time during a 20-minute speech on any topic.

Another Look at Methods of Organization

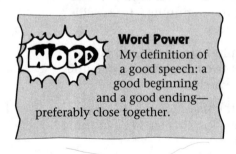

Word Power
My definition of a good speech: a good beginning and a good ending—preferably close together.

Now it's time to turn to the body of the speech. As I explained in Chapters 6, 7, and 8, there are different ways to organize your speech. In Chapter 6, "Speaking to Inform," I explained the organizational patterns most often used in informational speeches: alphabetical, cause-effect, chronological, numerical, problem-solution, spatial, and topical. At that time, I promised you I would discuss chronological order, problem-solution, and topical order in greater depth in this chapter, so here they are.

Chronological Order: The Order of Time

Begin at a certain time or date and move forward or backward. For example, in your speech you can discuss the development of the computer from 1970 to the present or trace the methods of making plastic from start to finish.

Here's one way the career of a colorful president can be arranged chronologically, for example:

The Political Career of Lyndon Baines Johnson

1. 1937, elected to Congress as a supporter of FDR.

2. 1948, elected to the Senate by a margin of 87 votes.

3. 1953, elected Senate Democratic leader.

4. 1960, lost Presidential nomination to Kennedy.

5. 1963, sworn in as President after Kennedy's assassination.

6. 1964, elected President, defeating Barry Goldwater.

Problem-Solution Order: Presenting Dilemmas and Answers

Sometimes, you'll want to first explain the problems with a specific situation and then offer the solutions. For example, you might describe the problems with launching a new stock fund and then explain how your division can resolve these problems. Or you might want to discuss declining blood reserves and then convince your listeners that they should roll up their sleeves and participate in the company's blood drive. Here's a sample outline:

Declining University Enrollment

Problems:

1. Fewer students in the region

2. Declining enrollment

3. Decreased revenue

Solutions:

1. Invite prospective students to visit campus

2. Increase advertising on television and radio

3. Place posters in high schools

4. Set up billboards on main roads

5. Establish chat rooms, web site, and on-line admissions hot-line

6. Increase scholarships

Topical Order: The Order of Subjects

Some themes lend themselves to topical arrangements through long use: for example, financial reports are usually divided into assets and liabilities; government is broken down into the federal, legislative, and judiciary branches. You don't want your method of organization to be shopworn, but remember: audiences are listening, not reading. Dividing your theme into familiar subtopics makes it easier for an audience to follow your logic. Here's how a topical speech on storms could be arranged:

Whisper...

Tell Me About It
Consider these three methods of organizing a speech in terms of your own specific theme, thesis, main points, and audience. For example, does your topic lend itself to the order of time, or would it be better served arranged by subjects? Keep this in mind: select the method that best helps you accomplish your purpose.

Storms

1. Thunderstorms

2. Hurricanes

3. Tornadoes

4. Tsunamis

5. Dust Devils

Don't forget your audience! You want to make it easy for them to follow your logic. Your organizational pattern must be very apparent so they can clearly identify it. They should not have to struggle to figure out what you're saying and where your speech is going. But at the same time, your speech doesn't have to follow a tried-and-true, boring old pattern. Instead, analyze your audience and topic to discover which pattern will best help you make your point in a fresh, new way. No one will snooze while *you're* speaking!

Arranging Supporting Points

After you have decided on the appropriate organizational pattern, the next step is deciding how to arrange the supporting information to maintain internal logic.

Subordinating Information

Never make a point without supporting it with an example, detail, illustration, or some other form of proof. It's not enough just to include several subpoints under your main ideas. Instead, the way you *use* the supporting material helps create the strength of your argument, provide the information your audience needs, or give the humor or detail that makes your speech entertaining.

But you can't just set down a heap of facts. If every point in your discussion is given equal emphasis, nothing stands out as significant. Stringing ideas together like beads is tiresome at best, confusing at worst. No matter how vivid your examples, your point will be lost unless your subpoints are correctly subordinated. To make your speech strong and logical, subordinate the following information:

➤ **Causes and effects.** As discussed in Chapter 6, "Speaking to Inform," causes and effects rarely occur individually. To clarify this relationship, list each cause and effect singly in order of importance. The most important causes of smoking, for example, might be listed as peer pressure, advertising campaigns, and an oral fixation: the most important effects might be listed as cancer, emphysema, loss of appetite, nervousness, and premature wrinkling.

➤ **Examples.** What can you do if you have a series of examples that back up your main idea? You can arrange them from most to least important or least to most important. Or you can put the best examples in the opening and close of the speech.

➤ **Qualities or functions.** If you are writing an informative speech that describes an object or process, the supporting details describe how the object works or they trace the steps in the process. For example, the purpose of a food processor can be described by explaining its slicing, shredding, and mixing blades; the production department of a major corporation can be illuminated by describing its functions.

➤ **Parts of a whole.** For example, you can discuss the modem, hard drive, floppy drives, and monitor as part of a computer; the fabric, stitching, and finishing as part of a well-made suit.

Imagine that a mythical figure named Bob has been invited to speak before a rabid group of comic fans because he is a noted comic book collector with an enviable comic art and comic book collection. He read the first part of this chapter carefully, so he has already limited his speech to a brisk 20 minutes. His topic is Comics.

After he does some research, he discovers that there's pretty close to a ton of books on the subject. He realizes that there's no way that he can explain everything there is to know about comics in 20 minutes, even if he speaks at super-speed like The Flash. Therefore, recalling what he already learned in this chapter about limiting his topic and remembering what he learned in Chapter 5 about analyzing his audience, he asks himself, "What will my audience most want to hear about comics?" He decides to limit his talk to the *history* of comics. His narrowed topic is:

Comics: A brief review of their history from the 1930s to the 1990s.

101

Now he lists his points on paper to see how they can be organized. His list looks like this:

➤ Horror Comics (1950s)

➤ The Golden Age of Comics (1938–1950)

➤ The Marvel Age (1962–1980s)

➤ The Silver Age of Comics (1952–1972)

➤ Direct market (1970s–present)

➤ Comics in the Mainstream (*Batman, Richie Rich, Casper*)

The ideas are good, but there are too many of them for a 20-minute speech. Also, there are some overlaps, especially with the Silver Age and the Marvel Age. Bob decides to combine The Silver Age with the Marvel Age to get rid of the overlap. Then he decides to delete Horror Comics and the Direct Market to limit the topic.

Further, the ideas are not in any specific order that an audience could follow. Which method of organization is best suited to the topic? After looking over the list, he decides to arrange his information in chronological order. Here's what his revised list looks like:

➤ The Golden Age of Comics (1938–1950)

➤ The Silver Age of Comics (1952–1972) and the Marvel Age (1962–1980s)

➤ Comics in the Mainstream (*Batman, Richie Rich, Casper*)

Bob's next task will be to arrange his ideas into an outline. This will be covered in Chapter 11, "Sketching It Out on Paper: Outlining."

The Least You Need to Know

➤ Everyday garden-variety effective speeches usually run about 20 minutes.

➤ Speeches should have a clear beginning, middle, and end.

➤ Speeches should also have a clear method of organization. Three of the most common methods are chronological order, problem-solution, and topical order.

➤ Details, examples, and other back-up proofs must be subordinated to help the audience follow your main idea.

Chapter 11

Sketching It Out on Paper: Outlining

In This Chapter

➤ Discover why it's important to outline your speeches

➤ Learn how to build an outline

➤ Trace the steps on sample outline templates

In earlier chapters, you learned how to develop and organize the ideas in your speech. In this chapter, I'm going to explain how to take those ideas and arrange them in an outline to form the framework for a written speech. First, I'm going to explain the importance of outlining for any kind of speech. Then, I'll cover the different kinds of outlines. Finally, I'll share some of the tricks of the trade to help you prepare outlines quickly and easily.

What, Me Outline?

Why bother with an outline—why not skip right to the speech writing itself? There are *a lot* of good reasons to take the time to make an outline. First of all, an outline sets out before you the entire structure of your speech. This enables you to see whether you have arranged the main ideas and supporting details in the best possible way. It also helps you make sure that you have given each part of your speech enough emphasis. Outlines let you see at a glance if you have forgotten anything important.

An outline also helps you make sure that you have supported your main points with sufficient detail—before you begin to write. Outlines, like tight spandex bike shorts, have a startling ability to reveal deficiencies. Looking back over your outline might reveal that you have used only one kind of detail, for example. Finally, an outline helps you see clearly what it is that you want to communicate to your audience. It's all neatly laid out for you to review.

In addition, reading your outline over helps you memorize the way your speech is organized. When you stand before your audience, you'll have a visual image of your speech's "bones." As a result, you will a have the confidence that comes with being well prepared.

How to Know a Good Outline When You Meet One

Of course, the amount of detail and arrangement of subtopics on your outline will depend on your topic, audience, and previous experience in public speaking. Often, novice speakers tend to feel more comfortable with fuller outlines; more experienced speakers go with pared-down versions. But even accomplished speakers will prepare a detailed outline when the audience and occasion demand it. There are two types of outlines used for public speaking: the *full-text outline* and the *key-word outline*.

Full-Text Outline

As its name suggests, the full-text outline is the complete speech in outline form. Each major idea and all supporting ideas are written out in complete sentences. This provides you with the full meaning of all ideas as well as their relationship to other ideas. In addition, the sources for all research are included, either in the outline itself or in a Works Cited section in the back of the outline. This outline offers speakers a complete scaffolding for their speech.

Key-Word Outline

The key-word outline, in contrast, provides trigger words rather than complete sentences. Every main idea and supporting detail is reduced to a key word or phrase that the speaker can remember more easily. Preparing and then skimming this type of outline can help you fix the structure and content of your speech firmly in your mind. While it does not offer as much detail as the full-content outline, it can be prepared in much less time.

Note-Card Outline

You can also create an outline on your note cards. As you speak, you use your note cards as the outline. This type of outline works best in informal speaking situations that don't require a fully written speech.

Outline Rules

Whether you prepare a full-content or key-word outline, all outlines must obey the following Official Outline Rules covered in the next five sections.

Use Uniform Letters and Numbers

Traditionally, the body of the speech is shown by roman numerals (I, II, III, and so on). Subheads are indicated by capital letters (A, B, C, and so on). Subdivisions under the subheads are shown by cardinal numbers (1, 2, 3, and so on).

Conventional outlines call for at least two entries at each outline level. For example, if you have roman numeral I, you must have roman numeral II; if you have an A under I, you must have a B. Follow this rule if you're going to turn in your outline for school credit. Otherwise, list only those heading, subheadings, and details that you need for your speech. Don't pad the outline just to satisfy a need for order.

As you study these sample outlines, notice that items of the same logical importance have the same letters and numbers throughout. I've followed the conventions of pairing entries—but you don't have to.

Tell Me About It
For those rugged individualists who like to do things their own way, the outline police won't get you if you don't use roman numerals, capital letters, and cardinal numbers—but you do have to adopt a consistent set of numbers, letters, or symbols.

I. Main Head	I. Main Head
A. Subhead	A. Subhead
B. Subhead	1. Subdivision
C. Subhead	2. Subdivision
1. Subdivision	B. Subhead
2. Subdivision	1. Subdivision
3. Subdivision	2. Subdivision
II. Main Head	C. Subhead
A. Subhead	1. Subdivision
B. Subhead	2. Subdivision
C. Subhead	II. Main Head
1. Subdivision	A. Subhead
2. Subdivision	1. Subdivision
3. Subdivision	2. Subdivision
III. Main Head	3. Subdivision
A. Subhead	B. Subhead
1. Subdivision	III. Main Head
2. Subdivision	A. Subhead
B. Subhead	B. Subhead
1. Subdivision	C. Subhead
2. Subdivision	
C. Subhead	

Include Only One Idea Per Line

Include only one idea under each roman numeral, capital letter, or number. Running multiple ideas together defeats the very purpose of the outline: to separate and differentiate ideas. Here's what I mean:

No-No

    I. Circumstances sometimes force people to live alone. Grown children leave the nest. They go to college. They move to other cities to get jobs. They marry and move away to start families of their own.

Yes

    I. Circumstances sometimes force people to live alone.

        A. Grown children leave the nest.

           1. They go to college.

           2. They move to other cities to get jobs.

           3. They marry and move away to start families of their own.

Study this template:

Thesis statement:

    I. First main idea

        A. First subordinating idea

           1. Reason or example

           2. Reason or example

        B. Second subordinating idea

           1. Reason or example

           2. Reason or example

Subordinate Ideas Properly

It's not enough just to place each idea on its own line; the items listed as subordinate must actually *be* subordinate. This means that they must be less important in meaning, not of equal or even greater importance.

Further, ideas must be related logically. Outlines cannot include subpoints unless they are directly linked to the main point under which they are placed. Each subpoint must directly support the point under which it appears.

No-No

    I. Noise pollution comes from many sources.

        A. Music blasts into headphones.

        B. Music in clubs assaults the senses.

        C. Lawn movers and leaf blowers roar.

II. Jackhammers and other construction tools blast.

III. Noise pollution occurs in many large cities.

A. Noise pollution occurs during leisure time.

B. Radios blare.

C. Cars and buses honk their horns.

Yes

I. Noise pollution comes from many sources.

A. Noise pollution occurs in many large cities.

1. Jackhammers and other construction tools blast.

2. Radios blare.

3. Cars and buses honk their horns.

B. Noise pollution occurs during leisure time.

1. Music blasts into headphones.

2. Music in clubs assaults the senses.

3. Lawn movers and leaf blowers roar.

Indent Lines to Show the Relationship of Items

Each succeeding level of the outline shows more specific detail than the one before it. The more important an idea is, the closer it will be to the left margin. Traditionally, main ideas are flush left. Indent subheads five spaces and subdivisions ten spaces. If an outline entry is longer than one line, the second line is indented as far as the first word of the preceding line. Study this template:

Thesis statement:

II. Main idea

A. First subordinate idea

1. Supporting evidence

2. Supporting evidence

B. Second subordinate idea

   1. Supporting evidence

   2. Supporting evidence

Bet You Didn't Know

You can use computers to help you organize your research into a speech outline. All the major software companies have programs available that you can use to write outlines. They're nifty because they enable you to move around ideas quickly, resulting in better-organized speeches and a greater willingness on your part to experiment with patterns of organization.

Use Parallel Structure

Make all ideas grammatically parallel. This means that they are in the same form, such as all phrases or all sentences. All of the phrases are in the same form, such as all adjectives, all adverbs, all gerunds (*-ing* forms). Here's what I mean:

No-No

   A. *Use* earplugs.

   B. *To avoid* excessive noise.

Yes

   A. *Using* earplugs.

   B. *Avoiding* excessive noise.

Recipe for a Great Outline

Unlike grandma's cooking, outlining is not a little bit of this and a pinch of that. Rather, outlining is an explicit process. Follow my recipe for a speech outline, and I guarantee great results every time!

➤ First write down your topic, purpose, audience, and audience attitude. For example:

Topic	Community's need for a new library
Purpose	Persuasive
Audience	Civic association
Audience attitude	Antagonistic, unfriendly

➤ Then build the framework for your outline. The skeleton of your ideas begins with your topic and purpose. Keep these firmly in mind to guide you as you develop your outline.

Remember that the body of your speech will contain three main ideas, designated by roman numerals. The main ideas will support the topic and purpose. Under each main head will be subheads, which relate to the main heads. Any subdivisions (1, 2, 3) under the subheads provide support. Here's a sample general structure:

I. First main idea

   A. First subordinating idea

      1. Reason or example

      2. Reason or example

   B. Second subordinating idea

      1. Reason or example

      2. Reason or example

➤ Third, write each of the specific points you intend to cover. Study this model:

I. Tennis is one of the best sports to play.

   A. Provides all-around exercise.

      1. Improve cardiovascular system.

      2. Build agility and stamina.

   B. Is enjoyable.

      1. Make new friends.

      2. Feel invigorated and refreshed.

➤ Finally, revise, reword, and rearrange your ideas. Go back over your out-line to make sure that items are parallel and logical. See if every item is in the correct place and subordinated properly. Make sure that you have sufficient support for each of the statements you have included.

All-Purpose Speech Outline

One size doesn't fit all—but in many instances it can come close. Below is a sample outline form. Adapt it to suit the special needs of your audience, purpose, and thesis.

    I. Introduction

       A. Grab your audience's attention. (See Chapter 12)

       B. State your topic and purpose. (See Chapters 4, 6, 7, 8)

       C. Preview your speech. (See Chapter 10)

   II. Body (See Chapter 13)

       A. State first main idea.

          1. Support

          2. Support

       B. State second main idea.

          1. Support

          2. Support

       C. State third main idea.

          1. Support

          2. Support

 III. Conclusion (See Chapter 14)

       A. Restate your main idea.

       B. Add a memorable conclusion.

See the Appendix for additional sample outlines.

The Least You Need to Know

➤ Outlining is an equal-opportunity skill: Any type of speech can—and should—be outlined.

➤ Outlining your speech is a crucial step in clarifying ideas.

➤ Full-text outlines describe the speech in complete sentences; key word outlines use important words and phrases to sketch the speech's contents.

➤ Outlines must use a consistent system of letters and numbers, subordinate ideas, and be in parallel grammatical form.

➤ Once you get the hang of it, outlines are not difficult to construct—and are well worth the time.

Chapter 12

Begin at the Beginning

In This Chapter

➤ Discover what purpose speech openings serve

➤ Experiment with different openings

➤ Find the opening that suits your purpose, topic, audience, and style

Are you like the mosquito at a nudist camp—you know what you ought to do, but you don't know where to begin? One of the questions I'm asked most often is, "How do I begin my speech?" In this chapter, you will explore many different ways to get your speeches off to a great start. You will also discover how to choose the method of introduction that best suits your audience, topic, purpose, and personal speaking style.

You can begin your speech in a number of ways. Whatever method you select, your opening should accomplish the following five tasks:

➤ Forge a bond with the audience.

➤ Establish credibility and goodwill.

➤ Create interest.

➤ Preview the speech by introducing your main points.

➤ "Hook" the audience by grabbing their attention.

Think about all the movies, television shows, and plays you've seen—they all open with a hook. The same is true of novels, short stories, and essays. And the same will be true of all your speeches.

Before you write the introduction, put yourself on the other side of the lectern and think about what kind of opening would really grab your attention. Would a brief anecdote do it? How about a question? A quotation? A joke?

Hand-in-Glove: Intro and Speech

Everyone has one really good anecdote, question, quotation, or joke. It's been stored up for just this occasion. So you take your great opening out and slap it down right in the beginning of your speech. There's only one problem: it doesn't fit. It's just not right. What to do? Some speakers try to cram that sucker in, twisting it to fit. Don't.

Be merciless when it comes to using a favorite story or a beloved quotation. Include it only if it precisely fits the audience, occasion, and purpose. If not, put it back in the folder for another day.

Telling a Story

Here's how a speaker at an insurance convention used a story to open a speech:

So this patient makes an appointment to see a specialist. After a week of expensive tests, the patient gets the bill.

She rushes back to the specialist's office and screams, "Are you nuts? This bill is outrageous. There's no way I can pay this!"

The doctor replies, "Okay, so pay me half."

"Half? Half? I can't pay half!"

"Well," the doctor replies, "what amount can you pay?"

"Not a cent. I'm a poor, old woman."

The doctor let out a long sigh. "Why did you come to me—one of the most famous specialists in the country?"

"Listen, doc," the patient replies, "when it comes to my health, money is no object."

We Americans want the best health care that money can buy, but we are appalled when we get the bills. Unfortunately, these bills will only increase as the American population ages and medical tests become more complex.

Speakers in demand are constantly on the look-out for good anecdotes to use to catch the audience's attention. The obsessive-compulsive crowd (of which I'm a charter member) keeps files of newspaper and magazine clippings, piles of photocopies, and notes from their reading. This is a good thing. Who said all neuroses are bad? Join the club! Start a story folder today. Cram it with clippings, and you'll have a good start for some of your speeches.

An off-shoot of the anecdote is the fact-ette, commonly called the "factoid." It's that small bit of trivia that can make an audience snap to attention. *USA Today* is a great source of these tasty tidbits. Here are a few that caught my eye this week—but remember, factoids have to suit the audience, purpose, tone, and your individual style.

> **Words to the Wise**
> For generations, speakers have opened their presentations with "Good evening, ladies and gentlemen." Openings like this are usually fluff. Unless you feel compelled to include one or you feel that your audience will be appalled by its absence, skip it and get right to the *real* opening of your speech.

➤ Lightning strikes the U.S. 40 million times each year.

➤ A lightning bolt has enough power—30 million volts—to light up all of New York City.

➤ The average thunderstorm is more powerful than an atomic bomb.

➤ Boris Karloff modeled his mummy face and costume in the film *The Mummy* after Rameses III.

Asking a Question

One of the easiest and most effective ways to open a speech is with a question. People immediately begin to frame an answer, and then listen closely to your speech to see if their answer matches yours. It's a common opening technique because it works. The next few sections review three different forms that your question can take.

Personal Touch

Prodding a person's ego immediately gets every member of the audience roped in because now they're thinking, "Hey, this speaker is talking about *me*!" Here's a personal opening tailored for a charity fund-raising event for a new hospital wing: "Can I trust you? Are you someone I can rely on to do the right thing? I know I can. Let me tell you why I need your trust now more than ever. It's a matter of life and death."

Mini-Mystery

Open with a question that leaves the audience wondering. Here's one that a motivational speaker used at a marketing seminar: "There's a buzz in this room, an electric charge in the air. I've spoken at a lot of meetings, and I'm never wrong about this. Can you feel the power? The high voltage excitement? What is it?" The answer the speaker provided was "Conviction." In addition to pumping up the audience members, this opening also flattered them.

Tailored to the Occasion

An expert on dieting opened her after-dinner speech with these questions: "How many calories do you think you've just eaten? How much fat? How much protein? Well, I'm going to tell you. The facts will amaze you." These questions grabbed the audience because they were suited to the occasion.

Greetings from the Home Team

Everyone likes to have a moment in the sun. It's easy to make this part of your opening if you're speaking at an out-of-town event. I'm not talking about a rehash of the Chamber of Commerce pamphlet handed out at the drive-through hospitality window. The opening has to be *personal* about the town.

Isolate a handful of specific, representative, flattering things you have learned about the city, town, or community. Do your research. Follow these guidelines:

➤ Read up on the town, especially in the local newspaper.

➤ Speak to some people who live there. Stop for a chat at the Blue Moose Diner.

➤ Take a drive through the community and see what it's like.

Using an Appropriate Quotation

Quotations inspire nearly as much controversy as Long Island lothario wanna-be Joey Buttafuoco. Most speakers love quotations, but there is a vocal minority that won't open a speech with anything less than an original utterance. Ironically, the oft-quoted famous 19th century American philosopher and minister Ralph Waldo Emerson was a member of the later crowd. "I hate quotations," he said. "Just tell me what you know." Actress Marlene Dietrich, in contrast, was a standard-bearer for the quote crowd: "I love quotations because it is a joy to find thoughts one might have, beautifully expressed with much authority by someone recognizably wiser than oneself."

Controversy aside, it can be surprisingly comforting to let other people's words carry the opening of your message. Using an appropriate quote in a speech is like using a good illustration in a book: it illustrates your point and grabs the audience's attention. Good quotations should be a standard part of your speechmaking bag of tricks.

When you select a quotation, remember your own personality and the impression you want to convey. When you look for quotations, think about your audience, the subject, and the person you're quoting. To give the impression that you are the master of your material, draw quotations from material that it seems likely you would have read. This also lessens the chance that you'll sound like a pompous fool.

By now you know that I'm an enthusiastic supporter of using quotations in the opening of a speech. But too many quotations are like too much of anything (except good quality chocolate—you can never have too much of *that*). You don't want your audience to spend most of your speech wondering if you actually read all the books, saw all the movies, and spoke

Tell Me About It
Never read greetings to the home team. To preserve the spontaneity and sincerity of this opening, the tribute should be recited from memory. If you're concerned about remembering the opening, jot down notes on separate index cards. Make it appear that this is not part of your regular speech—although of course it is.

Words to the Wise
Don't feel compelled to quote the quotation verbatim. The quote police won't come after you, I promise. Put the quote in different words—your own words. Change words. Have a good time with the quote. You have to be careful, of course. Not attributing a quote can be called "plagiarism"—theft— under certain-situations. To avoid this, state that you're paraphrasing the quote before you attribute it to its author. For example, you can say: "To paraphrase Kurt Vonnegut . . ."

to all the people you quote from. Savvy people will be checking out your back pocket to see if that's where you hid your copy of *Bartlett's Familiar Quotations*. What you really want is your audience to concentrate on you and your message. Think of quotes like garlic: a little goes a l-o-n-g way.

So where do you find the good quotes? Obviously, the better read you are, the more material you have to draw on.

Here are some suggestions for finding pithy quotations:

➤ Books of quotations and trivia, such as *The Guinness Book of World Records*, *The Trivia Encyclopedia*, and *199 Things Every American Should Know*.

➤ Newspapers and magazines.

➤ Television, especially "classic" 50s shows.

➤ Literature: short stories, essays, novels.

➤ Witty friends with good memories.

➤ Comic books and other popular literature.

➤ TV and radio commercials.

➤ Public personalities, living or not.

You should know the first law of using quotations in speech introductions: If you're quoting someone who is dead, make it clear in the speech that they are dead; that is, "In the words of the *late* Herbert Hoover . . ."

Here are some pointers to follow when using quotations:

1. Use the quotation to reinforce your message.

2. Don't use quotations to show off what you know.

3. If you don't know how to pronounce the author's name, don't fake it. Cop out instead. Try these lines: "A famous person once said . . ." or "An author once wrote . . ." or "It's been said that . . ."

4. Include context or background to make the quote more meaningful. Quotes are illuminated when the writer, date, or situation is included.

5. Quote it right. Misquoting a direct quotation in the beginning of a speech shoots your credibility to the moon. Even if you abbreviate your notes rather than writing out the full text, be sure to write out completely any quotation that you are directly quoting. Obviously, paraphrasing lets you off this hook.

6. Be sure the quotation is relevant to what you're saying, appropriate to your audience, and fresh.

Bet You Didn't Know

OOOOH. If you are a recognized authority in your field, your reputation will automatically convey credibility. As long as your speech stays within the boundaries of your area of expertise, you're going to be trusted. If you're not recognized as an expert, the host should read off your credentials to confer on you an aura of credibility.

If the host fails to share your credentials with the audience and they are important to the success of your speech, don't shy away from introducing yourself as part of your opening. Meet the situation face on by saying, "Let me tell you a little bit about myself"—and then do. This is going to mean a little adjusting to your prepared speech opening, but under certain circumstances, it's a must.

Using Statistics

"Statistics" mean numbers, but numbers are meaningless unless they are taken as part of a whole. This means you have to place the numbers in the context of something understandable to your audience. Your task is to cut and stitch them to fit the fabric of your speech. Never, never distort the numbers; instead, make them work to suit your audience and purpose.

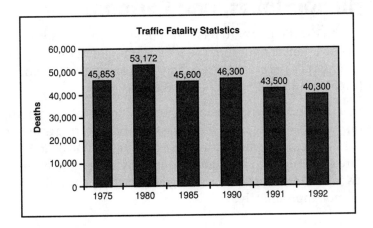

Here are some example statistics from the 1995 Information Please Almanac *about traffic fatalities.*

Depressing and dull. Can you imagine the reaction you would get if you started a speech that way? You would have to go from table to table picking the heads off the plates. It's more interesting to re-phrase the statistics this way: "Motor vehicle colli-sions cause one death every 13 minutes and one injury every 14 seconds." But I'm still not jumping off my seat to hear more, are you?

Here's how then-President Harry Truman used statis-tics successfully in 1947 to open a speech before a highway conference:

> When I was in the Senate . . . I found at that time more people had been killed in automobile accidents than had been killed in all the wars we had ever fought beginning with the French and Indian War. This is a startling statement. More people have been permanently injured than were injured in both the world wars from the United States.

Tell Me About It
Whatever type of introduction you use, remember to keep it short. After all, you're dealing with your introduc-tion, not the body of your speech. As I discussed in Chapter 10, the introduction (the opening hook) should be no more than one to two minutes long. That's allowing one minute for a formal "Ladies and Gentlemen" introduction (if you must have one) and two minutes for the "grabber."

Truman put the numbers into a meaningful context. He used them to shock his audience into an aware-ness of the seriousness of the problem.

Using Humor, Jokes, and Cartoons

Humor is an excellent way to relax the audience and the speaker. It serves to plunge your listeners right into the topic while simultaneously establishing instant rapport. You can also use humor to instruct the audience because it's a nonthreatening way to get to a moral or lesson.

But if you decide to open with a joke, be very sure that it is appropriate to the occasion. Few things are more embarrassing than hearing a speaker start off with "A rabbi, a priest, and a minister were out in a rowboat . . ." And few things are as painful as a joke poorly told. Stay away from ethnic, racist, and religious jokes. See Chapter 15, "Using Humor," for a detailed discussion of using humor appropriately.

Using Dates

Try opening your speech by linking the date with the subject of your speech. For example, here's how one speaker used dates for this slight tongue-in-cheek opening for a review course for standardized college admissions tests:

"Did you know that today is the 50th anniversary of the first standardized test? Yes, on this very day the Army administered a standardized test to sort its recruits. That was the only wide-spread standardized test that existed. Think how far we've come in only 50 years. Now we give these tests all the time. Now, don't you feel lucky?"

How can you find these great dates? Look through reference books about great discoveries, publications, performances, wars, sports events, films, personalities, and culture. One of my all-time favorite sources is *Timetables of History*.

Using Videotapes

If you have the resources, videotapes and other equally sophisticated audio-visual materials can make great openings. Some speakers are uneasy about relying on visual aids because of possible technical problems, a problem I cover in Chapter 21, "Preparing Visual Aids, Audio-Visual Aids, and Props." Nonetheless, in this age of visual images, the old saw "A picture is worth a thousand words" is more valid than ever before. Clips from old movies make especially good openings.

Using News Items

News items make great openings, especially because they're topical. Keep an eye out for offbeat news stories, headlines, and other topical stories. Cull these from the media. But remember, like fish and house guests, topical news stories get stale very fast.

Using References

A brief personal reference or reference to the occasion is another great way to begin a speech. But be sure that the references really fit the occasion.

Sharing a personal experience, giving some biographical information, praising the audience, and using definitions are some other effective ways to open your speeches. Remember: Pick the method that suits you, your audience, and your purpose.

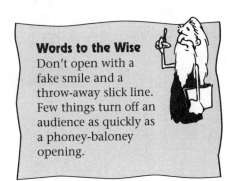

Words to the Wise
Don't open with a fake smile and a throw-away slick line. Few things turn off an audience as quickly as a phoney-baloney opening.

The Least You Need to Know

➤ Open your speech with a bang by a method suitable to your audience, topic, and purpose.

➤ Possible openings include quotations, humor, news stories, videos, dates, and statistics.

➤ Use an opening gimmick only if it fits your natural style. If the shoe doesn't fit, don't wear it. There are plenty of shoes that *do* fit.

Chapter 13

Developing the Body

In This Chapter

➤ Learn how to allocate your "writing" time

➤ Focus on organization

➤ Add supporting information

➤ Liberally apply the "glue" that holds it all together

Someone once said that speeches are like steer horns: a point here, a point there, and a lot of bull in between.

Not mine—or yours! In this chapter, you'll learn all about making the body of your speech clear, powerful, and enjoyable. You will learn how to craft a forceful statement of your beliefs and personality.

The body of your speech is the heart of your message. It's the burger in your bun, the cream in your cupcake.

If you're writing an informational speech, the body is where you provide the facts the audience needs and wants. If you're writing a persuasive speech, the body is where you move your audience to action or belief. If you're writing an entertaining speech, the body is where you beguile, delight, and divert your listeners.

I start off this chapter with a description of the writing process. Then I'll explain how to select an organizational pattern that you think will best appeal to your audience, most clearly convey your ideas, and most successfully accomplish your purpose. Next, I'll show you how to flesh out this framework with effective details, examples, and support. Last—but not least!—you'll discover how to unify your ideas with transitions and other rhetorical devices.

The Writing Process

Graceful, logical speeches seem artless. In reality—as any good speech writer will tell you—they are the result of great practice, hard work, attention to detail, and intense concentration.

The body of your speech is the longest part of your talk. As a result, you will most likely spend the most time writing it. Since it is the heart of your talk, I recommend that you write it first, before you write your introduction.

To get the best result from your writing time, spend only about a third of your "writing" time actually writing. Spend the first third of your time analyzing your audience and purpose and researching back-up information. Spend the last third evaluating what you've written. Study this diagram for a more detailed description of time allocation.

If you have three hours to write your speech, divide your "speech writing" time this way to maximize your efforts.

Take a closer look at the steps you should follow as you write your speech:

➤ **Preparing.** In this stage, formulate your topic, analyze your audience, define your purpose (to inform, persuade, entertain), and think of ideas.

➤ **Getting it all together.** Here's where you physically gather all the material that you need. Do your research by hitting the books or CD-ROMs; talk to your sources. Select a method of organization and prepare your outline.

➤ **Writing.** Now, do the actual drafting, the putting pen to paper or fingers to computer keys. Hammer out a formal draft of your speech.

➤ **Evaluating.** Read the speech over and think about what you wrote. Measure it against your audience and purpose. Is your speech informative? Convincing? Entertaining? Is your support adequate and convincing?

➤ **Getting Comments.** It's try-out time! Draft a willing participant or two and see what they say about your speech. Don't be shy about asking for help; turnabout is fair play. No doubt you'll soon be in a position to offer constructive criticism about the draft of a speech to the friend who read yours!

➤ **Revising.** Make the changes you noticed in your evaluation or those suggested by your readers. Here's where you will add, subtract, rearrange, and revise. Reshape the speech to suit your needs.

➤ **Editing.** Check the speech to make sure that you used standard written English. Fix all your spelling and writing errors. This is important even if no one else is going to read your speech. Why should your speech be letter-perfect? It will help you make sure that you read and pronounce each word correctly.

➤ **Proofreading.** Check the final copy to make sure that there are no typing or writing errors.

Tailored to Fit

One serious mistake that beginning speech writers make is clinging to an unshakable determination to include everything in every single speech. "But my topic is so important," you're probably protesting at this very minute. "How can I not say it all?" Or, "I've waited years for the chance to speak about this topic. How can I cut myself short now?" You're probably quite correct. I have no doubt that your topic *is* important and that you are very knowledgeable about it. It's very likely an interesting topic, too. After all, you've done a great deal of serious research about your topic, so I know that you know your stuff.

But it's important for you to recognize right from the start that you cannot fit everything you want to say into the body of your speech: you have neither the time nor the room. And if you try, you'll end up getting very little of anything across to your listeners.

Instead, zero in on the audience, purpose, material, and the key point you want to make. If you focus on one central idea, your audience will be much more likely to get your point. No matter what your topic, you must limit, focus, and organize your material. Fortunately, there are many different ways to do this. Select the method that best suits your topic, purpose, audience, and personal speaking style. Follow these guidelines:

➤ Select the major point or points.

➤ Keep the points of equal importance.

➤ Arrange them in a logical manner.

➤ State your thesis in a simple sentence.

➤ Make your point clear with explanations, details, facts, and examples.

➤ Restate the idea you have explained.

Take a closer look at some of the most common organizational patterns.

It's as Simple as A, B, C

Don't dismiss this method because it's simple and clear. Simple and clear are very good in speeches. This method works especially well with individual points, such as the names of people, places, and things. Besides, there are times that alphabetical order is the only logical and effective way to arrange your information.

Cause-Effect

Use this organizational style when you are tracing why something happened and what happened as a result. For instance, did you start a community program that produced clear results?

Suppose that you secured a federal grant to establish a summer Youth Council program. The program offers free athletic, educational, and enrichment programs to the kids in your area. As a result of your efforts, there are 100 kids involved in a six-week theater program; 300 kids in summer sports; and 75 kids taking computer, writing, and science classes. Explain the effects: helping children by reducing the number of "latch-key" kids, having fewer kids involved in accidents, and reducing levels of teen drinking.

Time Marches On

Here, you take the audience from the beginning to the end. This method is effective because it unifies and connects ideas. Explaining a process, tracing an historical event, and giving directions are all well suited for this organizational plan.

1, 2, 3

Use numbers or transitions to walk the audience through your speech. You can go from the highest numbers to the lowest, or the lowest numbers to the highest. Whichever way you order your numbers, stick to just a few numbers, such as 1, 2, 3, or 1–5.

As I said in Chapter 10, "Decisions, Decisions: Finalizing the Organization": "Tell 'em what you're going to tell 'em; Tell 'em, and then Tell 'em what you told 'em." This means that you will likely announce something like: "There are three stages to my plan. Let me present them one at a time. First . . ."

If you say *first,* you have to say *second;* otherwise, you're leaving your audience dangling. If you announce that there will be three steps, be sure to say *one, two*, and *three.* Otherwise, people will be sitting and waiting for the other shoes to drop, and there goes your point.

> **Tell Me About It**
>
> If at all possible, show how the method of organization you have selected directly relates to your audience's life. For example, if you're using chronological order, you might show how the historical changes you describe directly affect the quality of life for your audience. Or if you're using numerical order, link the numbers to human events. That will make the events important to your listeners.

Whisper...

Problem-Solution

Here, start with the questions and move to the answers. For instance, is there a problem with the shipping procedure used in your company? First explain the problem and then offer one or more solutions. If you have multiple solutions, offer them from least to most effective. Always try to finish with your best shot. It will be what your audience remembers.

Also, don't hide the problems. Speak with honesty. Odds are, your audience already knows about the problems. Hiding them won't make them go away, but it will very likely damage your credibility. For example, what would you do if your company faced a serious problem, and you had to be the one to speak about it? Here's how to structure a problem-solution that addresses this situation:

➤ Start by presenting some facts that show how serious the problem is. Let the facts speak for themselves: don't underplay or overplay them.

➤ Discuss possible ways to solve the crisis. For example, you might propose limited layoffs, benefit givebacks, or increased hours.

➤ Invite everyone to suggest other solutions. Make it clear to the audience that everyone must pull together for any solution to work.

Psychological Needs

Another way to organize your speech is according to the psychological needs of your audience. What issue concerns them the most? Place that issue first. What issue concerns them least? Cover that issue last.

Tell Me About It
Be very careful judging what situations really are crisis material. If you treat every problem as an emergency, you'll be the manager who cried "wolf." Even in a high-pressure career, no more than one zero-hour a year, please.

You can also start with the issue they find the most acceptable and work to the issues they find least acceptable. This will help you establish credibility and win over your audience early on—before you have to deal with the thorny topics that are apt to spark resentment. For example, assume you are a labor leader addressing management. There's apt to be more than a little resistance to your point of view. As a result, you should open your speech with the point that's apt to cause the least resentment.

The psychological method of organization requires the most thorough audience analysis. Consider where your audience stands on the issues. Start with common ground and move to differences of opinion.

Map It Out

Spatial order is geographical order: east to west, north to south, right to left, up to down. Here, information is arranged in the order of direction. For example, say that you have to give a speech to evaluate the success of your hospital's outpatient program. You can arrange the facts region by region and area by area. Or survey the district from the most northern point to the most southern point. Discussing a shipping plan? Arrange the speech according to the route that a delivery truck might take.

Topics

Break down a major topic into its components or subtopics. For instance, health care can be subdivided into types or costs. Discuss each topic in turn.

Supporting Information

To be most effective as a speaker, you must use information that backs up your point. You read, discuss, and observe as you gather material for your speech. The supporting material in your speech proves the accuracy of your statements, illustrates points of interest, or entertains the audience. You will use these verbal supports to reinforce and clarify your statements. This is how you build understanding and audience support. This is how you make your points more vivid and clear, as well.

Never make a statement of a major point in a speech without presenting at least one of the forms of support to clarify, illustrate, or support it. The substance of what you say rests in the examples, details, facts, and testimony you include. The most powerful speeches use a combination of sources. These include:

➤ Anecdotes

➤ Comparisons and contrast

➤ Examples

➤ Facts

➤ Statistics

➤ Testimony by authorities

Often, one or more of these forms of support are combined, as when anecdotes are used to provide examples or facts are added to personal experience. Now, take a look at these methods of support one at a time.

Once Upon a Time . . .

Anecdotes are brief narratives, stories, or verbal illustrations that provide vivid support for your point. These stories can be drawn from personal experience, the experience of others, and your reading and research. Be sure to distribute your anecdotes throughout the body of the speech so the really good stuff isn't all bunched in the beginning, middle, or end.

Comparison/Contrast

A *comparison* points out the similarities between something that is already known and something that is not. A *contrast* shows the differences between the two situations. Comparisons and contrasts illuminate the unknown. For example, I can explain the unfamiliar game of cricket to Americans by comparing it to a familiar American game, baseball.

Because a comparison tries to draw a judgment based on a single instance, it must be a valid analogy to be believable. The two objects being compared must be closely alike in all essential respects. The question you must ask yourself is, "Do the similarities between the items outweigh any differences that might be important to the conclusion I am trying to draw?"

Examples

An *example* is a type of support where you state several specific, brief instances or facts. It recounts an incident that brings out the point you are making. Sometimes an example describes a typical instance; other times, the actual situation. Your general statement becomes specific by using examples.

There are two main types of examples: *factual* and *hypothetical*. The former tells what actually happened; the latter, what could happen. To be convincing, a hypothetical example must make sense and match the facts. Hypothetical examples make abstract explanations more vivid and specific. They are especially useful in explaining a complicated plan. Instead of just outlining the details, you can create a hypothetical situation and trace the process. Factual examples are discussed in the following paragraph.

Facts

Facts are statements that can be proven. Factual examples describe situations that have actually happened. Facts are a particularly effective means of support because they cannot be easily refuted. The incident becomes vivid to the audience; because it is true, it has great persuasive power.

Facts create credibility. They help convince your audience that you know what you're saying and that you deserve to be taken seriously.

Consider these points when selecting facts:

➤ Is the fact clearly related to the main point of the speech?

➤ Is the fact a fair example? Select representative facts and examples; details drawn from left field have little power because they are anomalies.

➤ Is the fact vivid and impressive?

Stats It!

Not all figures are statistics; some are just numbers. That's because *statistics* are numbers that show comparison, the relationship between ideas and things. They point out how something gets larger or smaller, how one circumstance affects another. Statistics impress an audience because they help convince the audience of your claims. Here are some examples:

➤ Today, about 60 percent of first marriages are likely to end in divorce.

➤ According to the most recent statistics, in 1991, the median age at a first marriage for women was 24.1; for men, 26.3.

➤ In 1970, the Federal government collected $195,722,096 in taxes; by 1993, the number had jumped to $1,176,685,625 collected.

To maintain your credibility, be sure that the statistics you cite are accurate. Consult only reputable, up-to-date, recognized sources, such as the latest almanacs, government document, or statistical abstract. I also recommend that you cite the source of your statistics. This helps build even stronger credibility. The statistics I quoted in the previous paragraph are from the 1995 *Information Please, Almanac,* a respected reference source known for its accuracy and impartiality.

But like pepper, a little statistic goes a long way. Masses of figures are difficult for an audience to understand. Follow these guidelines when using statistics as support:

➤ Round figures off to make them easier to understand. For example, make 5,879,932 into 6 million.

➤ Slow down when you present statistics. Emphasize the importance of the numbers by your voice and gestures.

Words to the Wise

Be sure to present the statistic in terms that your audience can grasp. For example, say that you include this figure: "At 525 feet tall, the new Union Hall will be the largest building in the area." This is virtually meaningless. To give the statistic meaning, compare it to something the audience can grasp: "The building is as tall as the Washington Monument."

➤ Copy the statistics onto handouts or present them on overhead projectors.

➤ Don't saturate your speech with too many statistics. If you do, your audience will likely tune out all those confusing numbers.

Testimony by Authorities

You may wish to cite another person's opinions to reinforce your point of view. When a speaker cites the opinions of others word-for-word or nearly verbatim, the speaker is using *testimony*. The testimony can clarify an idea or supply proof.

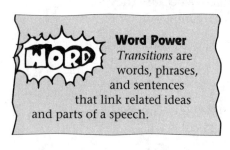

Word Power
Transitions are words, phrases, and sentences that link related ideas and parts of a speech.

To be most effective, this testimony should come from a recognized expert or authority in the field. It's not enough that you know the authority—the audience must recognize the person, as well. Also, the testimony must not be overly influenced by personal interests. This makes the testimony appear prejudiced and weakens your credibility. As you present the testimony, state the person's name and qualifications so your audience can be sure of the authority's specific expertise in the subject area.

Tell Me About It
You can also link ideas by using (1) deliberate repetition, (2) parallel structure, and, (3) pronouns. With the first method, select a key word related to the main idea and repeat it at important points to help your listeners follow your ideas. Parallel structure is matching grammatical forms. Using pronouns that clearly refer to nouns helps your listeners follow the bridges you build between sentences.

Get with the Flow: Transitions

No matter which method you use, make sure that your ideas are arranged logically and smoothly. As you move from one point to the next, give your listeners some clear toe-holds. Make it easy for them to follow your points. Information that may seem evident to you may be muddy to your audience; leaps of logic that appear perfectly reasonable when you wrote them may leave your audience stranded in midair.

Never assume that your audience will necessarily see the connections that you see between arguments, facts, and anecdotes. Lead your audience from point to point, example to example, and issue to issue. Your goal: To create your conclusions for your audience.

A speech is logical and coherent when its sentences and ideas are related to each other. Decisions about coherence are often made after you write the first draft of your speech, and you can begin to see how the ideas fit together. One of the best ways to make it easy for your audience to follow your points is to include *transitions*. These are words and phrases that signal how ideas are connected. Each transition serves to show a specific relationship between ideas. Table 13.1 lists different kinds of transitions you can use to convey different kinds of relationships between ideas.

Table 13.1   Consult This List to Select the Transitions That Best Link Your Ideas

Relationship	Transitions
Place	at the side, adjacent, nearby, in the distance, here, there, in the front, in the foreground, in the back, in the background
Summary	in brief, in conclusion, finally, on the whole, as a result, hence, in short
Result	therefore, thus, consequently, so, accordingly, due to this
Time	meanwhile, subsequently, immediately, at length, eventually, in the future, currently, before, soon, later, during, first, second, third, next, then, finally, afterwards
Concession	of course, to be sure, certainly, naturally, granted
Contrast	on the other hand, but, yet, however, nevertheless, nonetheless, conversely, in contrast, on the contrary, still, at the same time
Comparison	similarly, likewise, in like manner, in the same way, in comparison
Example	for example, for instance, thus, as an illustration, namely, specifically
Addition	also, in addition to, moreover, and, besides, further, furthermore, equally important, next, then, finally

Getting It On Paper

Let's focus for a second on the mechanics of getting your words on paper. I recommend that you always keyboard your speeches to reduce the chances that you will misread your handwriting.

As you type, follow the accepted rules of capitalization: capitalize the first word in a sentence and direct quotation, proper nouns, and proper adjectives. Avoid typing your speech in all capital letters: capital letters can make your speech confusing to read by giving you the impression that you're delivering a life-or-death message, something about UFOs, the emergency broadcast system, or Elvis' reappearance. All those capital letters look so imposing that you're apt to adopt a doom-and-gloom urgency in your delivery.

Use at least a 12-point font to make the letters easy to read. Select a clear, standard font, such as Courier or Times New Roman. Avoid elaborate fonts with lots of flourishes.

Leave at least three inches blank on the bottom of the paper. That way, you won't be forced to lean your head all the way down to your chest to read the paper and thus muffle your voice. Also leave generous margins—at least 2 inches—on the top and sides. This helps keep your head focused straight ahead at your audience. Be sure to number the pages to keep the order clear.

The Least You Need to Know

➤ Savvy speech writers make effective use of their time by dividing their task into three parts: planning, writing, and revising.

➤ Like a good undergarment, a method of organization supports the whole shebang. Pick the method of organization that suits your purpose, audience, and material.

➤ Don't stint on the details, examples, statistics, facts, and other back-up information. That's what makes your point or entertains your audience.

➤ Use transitions and other rhetorical devices to create unity and coherence.

➤ Be complete, but exhaust neither the topic nor the audience.

Chapter 14

Finishing Touches: Conclusions, Revisions, and Titles

In This Chapter

➤ Learn different techniques for drawing your ideas to a satisfactory close

➤ Explore ways to polish your speech until it shines

➤ Discover how to write a memorable title

If the body of the speech is the cream in your cupcake, the conclusion is the icing on the top. Your conclusion may be the only part of your speech that people remember, so it's crucial that you make it memorable. It's reassuring to think that no good speech ever came to a bad end, but it's just not so. As with every other part of your speech, writing a good conclusion requires a lot of effort.

In this chapter, you will learn some tried-and-true ways to end a speech with power and assurance. I will also explain how you can add that "finishing touch" to all your hard work. You'll learn why it's important to complete the revising and editing now and how it can help you avoid making mistakes when it really counts—during show time!

Finally, I'll guide you to select a title that says what you want it to say and stays in people's minds.

Writing the Conclusion

An effective conclusion has three main goals:

➤ To restate the main points you made in your speech.

➤ To focus on your desired response.

➤ To leave the audience with a sense of completion.

Take a look at each purpose in detail.

To be effective, the ending of your speech should make your point clearly and forcefully. To do so, it often sums up the individual subpoints you have made in your speech. The summary can hammer home your point like the rat-a-tat-tat of a wood-pecker, or it can be more subtle—but it must reinforce the purpose of your speech.

Tell Me About It
One way to make sure that you focus your conclusion is to read your thesis statement aloud. Then think of your conclusion as a variation on it—the same ideas in more emphatic words. To give your conclusion the proper emphasis, consider using parallel structure, repetition, and brief, forceful words.

At the same time, your conclusion should leave your audience with the feelings you want them to have. For example, if you are giving a persuasive speech and you want your audience enthusiastically fired up, your speech should bring them to their feet cheering. If you want your audience to think deeply about what you said, your conclusion should leave them in a calm, reflective mood.

Finally, the conclusion should convey a feeling of finality. Your words must give the sense that your speech is over. Few things annoy an audience as much as a false ending. Sensing that the speech is coming to a close, the audience begins to gather up its psychological and physical belongings only to find that the speaker has taken a deep breath and started anew. False endings cheat the audience and destroy much of the effect of a speech. An effective conclusion ties together all the strands of your speech while telegraphing to the audience that the end is indeed in sight.

Some of the most practical methods you can use to end your speeches involve the use of:

➤ Appeal

➤ Illustration

➤ Inducement

➤ Quotation

➤ Summary

It's rare that these methods are used in isolation: adept speech writers often combine two or more methods. For example, quotation works extremely well with summary and appeal; an inducement is sometimes prefaced with a summary. Nonetheless, I'm going to present these methods to you one at a time. That will make it easier for you to pick out the specific elements of each conclusion. But you'll notice that some of the examples do indeed combine methods—just as you will, if they serve your purpose and audience.

Appeal

Here, the speaker directly reminds the audience of its responsibilities to take action or follow a specific belief. To be successful, the appeal must be powerful and commanding. Folded within the appeal should be the main ideas that support the reason the appeal is valid.

Here's how the famous abolitionist William Lloyd Garrison ended his 1831 appeal to abolish slavery. Notice that he gives his listeners a specific direction to follow. He describes exactly what he wants them to think—and do. He uses strong, biblical diction to marshal the forces of right on his side.

> What then is to be done? Friends of the slave, the question is not whether by our efforts we can abolish slavery, speedily or remotely—for duty is ours, the result is with God; but whether we will go with the multitude to do evil, sell our birthright for a mess of pottage, cease to cry aloud and spare not, and remain in Babylon when the command of God is "Come out of her, my people, that ye may not be partakers of her sins, and that ye receive not her plagues." Let us stand in our lot, "and have done all, to stand." At least, a remnant shall be saved. Living or dying, defeated or victorious, be it ours to exclaim, "No compromise with slavery! Liberty for each, for all, forever! Man above all institutions!"

Illustration

An *illustration* is a detailed example of the idea or statement you are supporting in your speech. When you give an illustration, you are recounting an incident to make a point. To be effective, the illustration must be vivid and memorable. Recall that illustrations can be true or hypothetical. True illustrations are called *facts*.

Just as you can open your speech with an illustration, you can close it the same way. The following surrender speech by the leader of the Nez Perce Indians, Chief Joseph, is a quietly eloquent illustration of the need for peace. In 1877, a dispute between the tribe and federal government erupted into a war. Hoping to join forces with the Sioux, Chief Joseph led his people on a long march from Oregon to Canada. The tribe was heavily outnumbered by government troops; on October 5, Chief Joseph was forced to surrender.

The core of the speech is the factual illustration of his tribe's situation. Notice the powerful effect of the repetition, parallel structure, and simple words. The speech is reprinted below in its entirety.

> Tell General Howard I know his heart. What he has told me before, I have in my heart. I am tired of fighting. Our chiefs are killed. Looking Glass is dead. Toohoolhoolzote is dead. The old men are dead. It is the young men who say yes or no. He who led on the young men is dead. It is cold, and we have no blankets. The little children are freezing to death. My people, some of them, have run away to the hills and have no blankets, no food; no one knows where they are—perhaps freezing to death. I want to have time to look for my children and see how many I can find. Maybe I shall find them among the dead. Hear me, my chiefs. I am tired; my heart is sick and sad. From where the sun now stands, I will fight no more forever.

Inducement

You can also conclude a speech by revisiting the key ideas and then supplying one or two additional examples for accepting the belief or taking the action you proposed.

See how the writer of the following speech combines summary and added inducement to urge the use of mandatory air bags in all cars.

> In conclusion, there is no doubt that air bags save lives and prevent serious injuries. The Johnson/Juarez study I cited earlier demonstrates the effectiveness of airbags in sharply reducing vehicular casualties and injuries. In addition, the cost of including them in all cars is minimal. Further, having airbags in your car may reduce your insurance costs. The only argument that can be raised against air bags is their cost, which shows how casual many people are about their safety and survival. Even if you are willing to take chances with your own life, you owe this additional safety to your family. Only buy cars that come with airbags. Insist that car manufacturers install them in *all* cars.

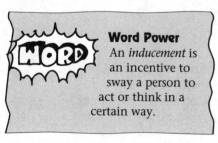

Word Power
An *inducement* is an incentive to sway a person to act or think in a certain way.

Quotation

Quotations can be another good way to end a speech—but they only work if the quotation directly relates to the main points that you made in your speech. The quotation can be directly quoted or slightly paraphrased.

This method is notably effective if you opened your speech with a quotation. Matching the opening and closing format gives your speech unity and cohesion. It also subtly serves to remind your audience of your opening points.

Following is the entire text of the speech Justice Oliver Wendell Holmes wrote for his 90th birthday tribute. Holmes delivered the speech over the radio on March 7, 1931. Notice the effectiveness of the quotations.

> In this symposium my part is only to sit in silence. To express one's feelings as the end draws near is too intimate a task.
>
> But I may mention one thought that comes to me as a listener in. The riders in a race do not stop short when they reach the goal. There is time to hear the kind voices of friends and say to oneself, "The work is done." But just as one says that, the answer comes: "The race is over, but the work never is done while the power to work remains. The canter that brings you to a standstill need not be only coming to rest. It cannot be, while you still live. For to live is to function. That is all there is to living."
>
> And so I end with a line from a Latin poet who uttered the message more than fifteen hundred years ago, "Death plucks my ear and says, Live—I am coming."

Bet You Didn't Know

OOOOH. Even if you are only going to use a small part of a quotation, always check the entire quotation—and double-check it. I once heard this story about a speaker who finished his address to a prominent public figure with two lines from John Dryden:

A man so various he seemed to be

No one but all mankind's epitome.

The honoree liked the conclusion so much that he went back to check the rest of the quote. Here's how it goes:

Stiff in opinions, always in the wrong

Was everything but starts and nothing long;

But in the course of revolving moon

Was chemist, fiddler, statesman and buffoon.

139

Summary

In this method of ending a speech, the speaker reviews the main points of the speech and draws conclusions from them. This type of ending is especially well suited to the informative speech because it helps remind your listeners of the main points of your argument. It also works very well with a persuasive speech because it allows you one last chance to go back over the main arguments you presented.

Following is an excerpt from the speech that playwright-dissident Vaclav Havel delivered when he became president of Czechoslovakia. He gave the speech when he assumed office on New Year's Day, 1990. Notice how he reiterates the most important elements of his speech in his conclusion. See if you can tell from this conclusion whether he is speaking more to inform or persuade.

> In conclusion, I would like to say that I want to be a president who will speak less and work more. To be a president who will not only look out the windows of his airplane, but who will always be among his fellow citizens and listen to them attentively.

> You may ask what kind of republic I dream of. Let me reply: I dream of a republic that is independent, free, and democratic; a republic with economic prosperity yet social justice; a humane republic that serves the individual and therefore hopes that the individual will serve it in turn; a republic of well-rounded people, because without such people, it is impossible to solve any of our problems, whether they be human, economic, ecological, social, or political.

Whisper...

Tell Me About It
Craft your conclusion with words that convey strength. Consider using memorable *imagery,* words and phrases that appeal to the senses. Also use *alliteration,* the repetition of initial consonant sounds. Abraham Lincoln used alliteration in the opening line of the Gettysburg Address. Notice how he repeated the initial *f* three times: "Four score and seven years ago our fathers brought forth on this continent. . . ."

Body Shop: Matching the Conclusion to the Speech

If you write your opening and closing first, chances are they won't be an integral part of your speech. On the other hand, by writing the introduction and conclusion *after* you write the body, your speech will be much more cohesive and logical.

For a brief speech, start with a catchy opening that refers to your topic. In the body, present all the supporting information. Close with a challenge, summary, or appeal. With a longer speech, you may wish to start with a less direct opening, such as a quotation. After you develop your main idea, close with the same method you used in the opening. The structure of the body remains the same, but the introduction and conclusion have been dovetailed to your audience, purpose, and subject.

Reading and Revising

As you learned in Chapter 13, "Developing the Body," the three final stages in writing your speech are *revising, editing,* and *proofreading.*

Revising entails adding, subtracting, and changing material in response to self- or outside evaluation. *Editing* involves checking for mechanical errors: spelling, punctuation, grammar, and usage. These are the errors that might make you slip up as you deliver the speech or cause you embarrassment if the speech is later reprinted.

Write for the ear, not the eye. Remember that your speech is being written to be heard, not to be read. The spoken word (oral writing) is straightforward and conversational. It calls for short, familiar words, active verbs, personal pronouns, contractions, and subject-verb-object order. You can even use incomplete sentences if they convey your meaning well. I recommend that you read your speech aloud as you revise and edit to hear as well as see any rough spots that need polishing.

Proofreading is the last step. Here's where you make sure that your speech is typed, printed, or written correctly. Type the speech with upper- and lower-case letters and triple-space the manuscript for ease of reading.

Bet You Didn't Know

OOOOH.

There's no magic bullet that works for all speech writers all the time. Nonetheless, effective speech writers are most likely to:

➤ Accept that their first draft will have to be revised.

➤ Break their writing into manageable tasks.

➤ Focus clearly on audience and purpose.

➤ Seek feedback and weigh it carefully.

➤ Be flexible in their approach to writing.

Crafting a Title

Speech titles have two purposes: They suggest the general contents of the speech while simultaneously grabbing the audience's attention. Think of the title as an advertisement. If successful, the title should make the listener want to hear more about your product. A good title is:

➤ Relevant

➤ Intriguing

➤ Brief

Relevant means timely or up-to-date. As a general rule, avoid recycling titles. Unless the fit is perfect, your speech is going to seem dated. Avoid last year's slang and local expressions that are apt to be misunderstood.

Words to the Wise
Be careful that the title doesn't tip your hand. An effective title makes the audience sit up in anticipation. It doesn't give away the entire contents of the speech or provide too much advance information.

Intriguing does not mean undiplomatic. If you're addressing a community group that's opposed to sidewalks being installed in the neighborhood, it's not politically wise to title your speech "Why This Neighborhood Must Have Sidewalks." Better to suggest the topic of your speech more subtly. Here are some possibilities: "A Walk on the Wild Side," "An Important Community Issue," or "The Issue of Sidewalks."

Brief means the title must be punchy. The title should be as short and to the point as possible. Senator Margaret Chase Smith realized this when she called her speech against Senator Joseph McCarthy a "Declaration of Conscience." The only exception is scientific talks, for tradition demands that those speeches are prefaced by long, descriptive titles.

Write the title last, after you have finished the entire speech. Creating a title that is both intriguing and suitable will be easier after you have written the rest of the speech.

The Least You Need to Know

➤ Powerful conclusions restate the main points you made in your speech, focus on your desired response, and leave the audience with a sense of completion.

➤ You can end a speech in several different ways. Select the method that best suits your audience and purpose.

➤ Time spent revising and editing is time well spent.

➤ Most speakers don't need an introduction—just a conclusion.

Using Humor

The most popular way of beginning a speech is with humor. That's because a good story entertains the audience. It convinces them that you're an everyday person, a person just like them, and with a good sense of humor. Experienced speakers and speechwriters know that the perfect comedic line can immediately get the audience on your side. The audience feels safe and relaxed; you've got 'em right where you want 'em. With one suitable joke, you've taken command.

But the key word here is *suitable*. Few things are as dismal as a bad, tasteless, or otherwise unsuitable joke. Humor has to be handled correctly if it is to succeed. Some jokes are right for some occasions and dead wrong for others. I'm not asking you to become a comedian—the field's too crowded as it is. In this chapter, you will learn how, when, and why you should use humor. I'll discuss jokes that work and those that don't. I'll also cover how to match your natural speaking style to the demands of humor.

All About Humor

Humor is a key element in all but the most gloomy speeches and occasions. But you must consider your own natural style before you decide how much humor—and what kind—to use. Some people like Alan King, David Letterman, and Henny Youngman are naturally funny and can deliver even the lamest comic lines with a timing that makes them funny. Other people are not blessed with this gift.

Further, the standards for humor are rising. With comics like Jay Leno, Robin Williams, and Jim Carrey plying their trade, audiences have gotten used to great topical jokes, perfectly delivered. Few of us are that talented. But not to despair: the audience is almost always on your side. People gathered to hear a speech are often already primed to enjoy themselves.

So let's explore the basic rules for using humor in speeches.

➤ **Social conventions.** To be effective, jokes depend on a shared frame of reference. You and your listeners must understand the social conventions underpinning the joke, or your efforts will fall flat.

➤ **Audience analysis.** Further, the humor must fit the audience. Jokes that work with the Parent-Teacher Association likely won't match the needs of the annual shareholders' meeting.

➤ **Appropriate to the occasion.** Use humor only when it is appropriate. For example, if you use too much humor when delivering a funeral eulogy or delivering the news about poor corporate performance, the humor will likely be viewed as inappropriate.

➤ **Personal style.** The joke also has to suit your specific style. Sweet young things can look foolish acting like tough Rosie O'Donnell and Roseanne; button-downed stockbrokers usually shouldn't try to impersonate coarse Rodney Dangerfield. Some comedians can work against type, but this requires years of practice and carefully honed techniques.

➤ **Make a point.** When used effectively in a speech, humor does more than just entertain the audience, it makes a point. It supports your thesis. Audiences might forget the actual joke, but they remember the point it was meant to reinforce.

Ask yourself the following questions before you decide to use a joke in a speech:

1. Is the joke genuinely funny?

2. Can I comfortably say this joke?

3. Does this joke match the mood of my speech?

4. Does this joke fit with the purpose of my speech?

5. Will my audience understand the joke?

6. Will my audience appreciate and like the joke?

7. Is the joke tasteful?

8. Is the joke fresh?

If you can answer "no" to any these questions, play it safe—deep-six the joke. Follow this iron-clad rule: When in doubt, cut it out. If you can answer "yes" to all these questions, here are some detailed ways to make humor a part of your public speaking style.

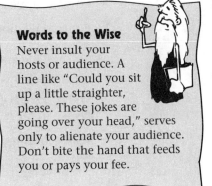

Words to the Wise
Never insult your hosts or audience. A line like "Could you sit up a little straighter, please. These jokes are going over your head," serves only to alienate your audience. Don't bite the hand that feeds you or pays your fee.

Jokes That Never Work

So, there you are at the podium rattling away from your prepared speech when you notice that a number of people seem to be nodding off. You think, "Perhaps I should come up with a great joke to make them laugh."

Think again.

All too often, humor in speeches backfires because most speakers don't use humor correctly. They tell jokes that are insulting, stupid, or just not germane to the speech. They come up with jokes at the last minute without carefully considering the ramifications of their remarks. Sarcasm and irony can also backfire, creating sympathy for the opposite point of view. This can lead to bad press for you and the group you represent.

The most dangerous kind of humor is the kind that makes fun of other people. Avoid these topics:

➤ Religion

➤ Race

➤ Sexuality

➤ Intelligence

➤ Birthplaces

➤ Handicaps

➤ Ethnicity

➤ Sexual orientation

145

➤ Religious leaders

➤ Childlessness

➤ Physical appearance

➤ Political leanings

These jokes have a way of blowing up in your face, even if they are genuinely funny. Here's an example of what I mean:

> The first speaker asks: "John, why do people take such an immediate dislike to me?"
>
> The second speaker answers: "Because it saves time."

This is funny, but it's also nasty. Being nasty usually doesn't make it, either. What is acceptable at a roast, for example, won't cut it at a commencement speech.

Unfortunately, the rules of good taste don't stop some professional performers from offending people. The fact that insulting material has been written, rehearsed, and performed to a laughing audience would seem to give it some legitimacy. You might be tempted to use one of these jokes. "After all," our beginning speaker might think, "it worked on television, so it should work in my speech."

Tell Me About It

Speakers almost never have the chance to try their material out on the road. Giving a speech is a one-shot deal—do or die. Is it worth the gamble that you might upset your audience with an offensive joke? Nope.

What you don't see is the stack of irate letters from viewers, the scores of enraged telephone calls, the list of canceled advertisements. So my beginning speaker makes a joke about a quadriplegic, a childless woman, a lesbian. Sure enough, someone in the audience starts to cry; someone else walks out in a huff; a group complains to the conference sponsor. These exact situations really happened. I present them as a warning to you. Look carefully at the jokes you select. Play it safe, not sorry.

The Mechanics of a Good Joke

You can't tell a joke successfully without knowing how it works. What makes a joke funny? In part, it's the way the joke is constructed. Try this one:

> In my neighborhood, we have a word for sushi: bait.

The humor comes from the contrast between the expectations that "sushi" sparks: delicious little expensive morsels of fish and the flat, stinky, reality of "bait." By placing the word "sushi" right next to "bait," the contrast is underscored. The colon (:) allows the speaker to take a breath and pause for effect. This pause sets up the punch line; or in this case, the punch word.

Rewrite the same words in a different way, and the joke falls flat. Here are some examples:

> In my neighborhood, we call sushi something else. We call it bait.

Nope.

> In my neighborhood, we call sushi bait.

No dice.

> Some people in my neighborhood call sushi bait instead of calling it sushi, but it's really the same thing.

Get real.

This is not to say that there's only one way to word a joke. It *is* to say that you must arrange the words to achieve the greatest punch and laughter. Play around with the words until the joke works for you. Then try it out on people whose judgment you respect, preferably people with a sense of humor. If they laugh, you'll know that you're on to something.

Methods to Achieve Humor

So what *can* you say that will be funny to most people most of the time? Toastmasters International recommends a number of different ways to develop humor in speeches. I've adapted some of these below and added some of my own. Here they are, as recommended by proven joke meisters.

"Borrow" Good Jokes

Take a little bit of well-tested material from people you know are funny. But make sure that the jokes suit your audience, purpose, and individual style. Tried-and-true humorists include Will Rogers, Mark Twain, Robert Benchley, Woody Allen, and Dave Barry. The first three are better suited for an older audience; the last two, for younger audiences.

Be judicious in your borrowing. Don't take a joke from the previous speaker on the agenda—unless you have a topper and want to one-up the previous speaker. In my experience, an audience will only find a joke funny once per occasion. And one-upping can be dangerous.

What about wading through stacks of joke books to find a nugget of humor? I don't recommend it. Reading through scores of joke books to find one good joke is like reading the telephone book for fun. By the time you find something that you think may be funny, you'll probably be so numb that you won't know what's funny any more. It's like eating cookies. A few are delicious, but by the bottom of the bag, you're feeling slightly green.

Tell a Joke About Yourself

The safest kind of humor are jokes that use the safest target—yourself. For example, a child once asked John F. Kennedy how he became a war hero. "It was absolutely involuntary," he answered. "They sank my boat." The linguist S. I. Hayakawa once opened a speech by saying, "I'm going to speak my mind because I have nothing to lose."

Take a page from the masters. Poke fun at yourself before you poke fun at someone else.

Draw from Real Life

Many events that happen to you, people you know, and people in the news are funnier than anything you could make up or find in a joke book. These events also have the advantage of being fresh, original material. As a result, you won't have to worry that everyone in the audience heard the joke last week on Leno or Letterman.

But avoid drawing from stories that are too prominent in the news because they are apt to be overworked. It's likely that most clever speakers have thought of using them, too. In addition, they get stale fast.

Tell Me About It
What should you do if a joke falls flat? Nothing. Never explain a joke. In any audience you're apt to see that some people got the joke and some people didn't. Even if the entire audience seems baffled, don't retreat. Let it go and move on with your speech.

Original stories from your own life are especially effective. They bring people in the audience closer to you because they help your listeners understand that you can poke fun at yourself.

When you're brainstorming, think about your last encounter in the food store, parking lot, or water cooler.

Think about things that set you off from the audience. I sometimes make jokes about being a Long Islander. For added humor, I use a little "Lawn Guyland" pronunciation. Here's a true story I used in a speech about the need for patience and tolerance in marriage.

One night, my husband and I were sitting in the local diner talking about the week's events and eating huge slabs of cake. As a member of a large and voracious family, I quickly polished off a slice of cheesecake the size of an ocean liner. My husband, raised in a smaller, more restrained bunch, was taking human bites out of his apple pie. Batting my lashes at my long-suffering husband, I poised my fork over his pie. When he protested, I said, "I bore your children." He replied, "You bore a lot of people. Take your fork out of my pie."

If necessary, embellish your stories with a little stretching of the facts. Stay within the confines of reality and reasonableness, however.

Include Clever Wording

For entertaining speeches, my method is to go to the utmost trouble to find the right thing to say, and then to say it with the utmost humor. I find Yogi Berra a great inspiration. Here are two of my favorite Yogiisms:

➤ "I don't mind being surprised, as long as I know about it beforehand."

➤ "It's *deja vu* all over again."

Take the time to craft and polish the joke. A well-phrased witticism can go a long way toward building audience good will, even if your delivery is a little stiff.

Bet You Didn't Know

Yiddish is a language suited to indigestible food, serious complaining, and great curses. No one curses like Yiddish speakers. Okay, maybe the Greeks. Here are some of my favorite Yiddish curses:

➤ Corns should grow on your nose.

➤ May a band of gypsies camp in your belly and train bears to dance on your liver.

➤ May all your enemies move in with you.

➤ May your sex life be as good as your credit.

➤ May all your teeth fall out—but one should remain for a toothache.

Making Humor Work for You

An effective storyteller has many ways to reinforce humor, such as facial expressions, exaggerated lines and gestures, and pauses. But even if you're not a natural comedian, you can tell a joke successfully. Follow my tricks of the trade:

1. **Don't apologize for your inexperience.** Never use lines like "I'm not much of a comedian" or "I don't tell jokes too well, but I'll do my best." This destroys your humor even before you start.

2. **Stick to the basics.** If you clutter up your joke with unnecessary details, your audience will lose interest. Include only the names, dates, and things that you need in order to make your joke work.

3. **Don't overplay your hand.** If you promise the audience the moon, they are going to expect the moon. Avoid lines like "This is the best joke you ever heard," or "Wait until you hear *this* one." Don't promise humor; just deliver it.

4. **Enjoy yourself.** Smile and look happy. Your mood will be contagious, making it that much easier for you to get a laugh.

5. **As you tell the joke, look the audience members in the eye.** Shift your gaze around the room, pausing to focus on individuals.

6. **Keep your jokes short.** Dragging a joke out can often spoil the humor.

7. **Leave the audience enough time to enjoy the joke.** If you rush the laughter, you're undercutting the effect you worked so hard to achieve.

8. **Speak slowly and clearly.** Make sure the audience can understand every word of your joke—especially the punch line.

The Least You Need to Know

➤ Successful jokes are built on a common frame of reference.

➤ The humor must fit your audience, purpose, topic, and personal style.

➤ Avoid any joke that demeans, insults, or might make anyone in the audience uncomfortable.

➤ If you're still uneasy about taking a walk on the comic side, you're better off using relatively little humor in your speeches.

Chapter 16

Writing International Speeches

In This Chapter

➤ Analyze cultural values, beliefs, and practices

➤ Say it right in any language

➤ Meet the demands of a foreign audience

➤ Work with a translator

Experts agree: To succeed in international business, you need international experience and an understanding of other cultures, beliefs, and patterns of acceptable behavior. Communicating with people in other countries and from other cultures is crucial if you want to sell your products abroad or manage a multicultural workforce.

In the past, America used the metaphor of the "melting pot" to describe the assimilation of different cultures into the whole. Today, the metaphor has become a "mosaic" or "quilt" to more accurately reflect our cultural diversity.

In this chapter, you will learn how to make speeches that meet the needs of international audiences—at home and abroad.

Culture Quiz

❏ **1.** Are you aware that your values are influenced by your culture?

❏ **2.** Do you think your values are not necessarily "right"?

❏ **3.** Are you flexible and open to change?

❏ **4.** Are you sensitive to nonverbal clues?

❏ **5.** Are you knowledgeable about the values, beliefs, and practices of other cultures?

❏ **6.** Can you perceive differences among individuals within a culture?

Are you attuned to successful intercultural communication? Take this test to find out. Check each of the items that applies to you. Then score your test by giving yourself one point for each question you checked.

5–6 Checks	You're ready to address the U.N.
3–4 Checks	Maybe you could serve cookies at the U.N.
1–2 Checks	Think about visiting the U.N.

Even if you never leave the United States—and maybe not even your own hometown—you will deal with people whose culture and background differ from yours. America is becoming an increasingly multicultural society.

Words to the Wise

Don't assume that colors convey the same meaning in other cultures. In the America, for example, brides wear white, and mourners wear black. In Mexico, purple flowers are left on coffins. In Korea, red ink is used to record deaths, but never to write about the living.

For example, in the 1990 census, about one-quarter of the people living in America chose to identify themselves as minorities. There are 2,000 Hmongs from Laos living in Wisconsin. Nearly half of all Californians are African-American, Latino, or Asian. According to one estimate, today there may be twice as many Muslims as Episcopalians in America. This would place Episcopalians in the minority when compared to Muslims. The 350 employees at the Digital Equipment Corporation plant in Boston come from nearly 50 countries and speak 19 different languages; the plant's announcements are printed in English, Portuguese, Haitian Creole, Vietnamese, Spanish, and Chinese.

Unfortunately, few speakers have much experience dealing with international audiences or have much knowledge about the special needs that come with these speeches. As a result, they approach the podium with great trepidation. How many of these concerns worry you? Read the following list to find out:

➤ Will I make a cross-cultural blunder?

➤ Can I use humor effectively?

➤ How can I show respect for my host's culture?

➤ How can I show respect for my foreign hosts?

➤ How can I show pride in my own heritage?

➤ How can I be sure that my message is understood?

➤ How can I meet the special demands of a foreign audience?

➤ How can I use translators effectively?

Because all these worries are valid, you need to be familiar with some specific ways that you can deal with the special problems that international speeches bring.

Bet You Didn't Know

Learning another language involves more than words. Even laughing is different. In Japan, for example, polite laughter requires holding your arms at your sides, shoulders forward, head bowed, with a hand covering your mouth. Laughing in America, in contrast, requires a more open body position. Usually the head is back and the mouth open. In America, loud laughter is acceptable, even expected, when something is genuinely funny.

Ways to Get Your Message Across in Any Language

Cultural awareness has a tremendous impact on speaking situations. Diplomats, for example, carefully and thoroughly prepare to meet with diplomats from other cultures. The following suggestions can teach *you* how to communicate with people from other cultures.

153

1. **Declare your pleasure at speaking to this foreign audience.** Acknowledge the honor of addressing a cross-cultural audience. At the opening of the speech, state your positive feelings about being invited to speak to people from another country or of another culture. The acknowledgment should be direct and sincere, not obsequious or hollow. For example, you might say, "I am most grateful for the honor of being the first representative from the XYZ Company to address a Japanese audience."

2. **Cite an expert from you guest's country or culture.** Select an authority from the host's country or culture whose views match the theme of your speech. Possibilities include educators, respected public officials, writers, artists, or famous historical figures from the host country, for example. As with any authority you cite, be sure that the reference is appropriate to the speech and that the figure is indeed admired by the members of your audience.

3. **Include a quotation from your guest's country or culture.** Select an apt quotation from a well-known, well-respected source that reinforces your message and flatters your audience. Consider quoting a well-known person or work of literature from your host's culture, for example. Be sure to include context or background to make the quote more meaningful. See Chapter 13 for more information about using quotations.

4. **Make references to your own culture.** Focus on your culture's values. Emotional appeals help bridge gaps between customs and traditions by showing that people share common feelings—no matter how diverse their backgrounds.

5. **Deliver your most powerful line in the audience's language.** Learning a line or two of another language makes an impression greater than the effort required. This illustrates in an especially dramatic way the importance of intercultural understanding. The line can be as simple as "My country extends its thanks to everyone here." Your guests will appreciate the effort you expended to learn a few words of their language. It is also an effective way to build instant rapport with your audience.

6. **Use the country's measurement terms.** America is one of the few places in the world (maybe even the universe!) that does not use metric measurements. If you are delivering a speech in a country that uses metric terms, translate your figures into metric. It's a small touch that goes a long way toward impressing an audience.

7. **Check your timing.** If you are delivering a major speech in another country, try to adjust the time of your presentation to accommodate everyone's internal clock. Try to avoid speaking when you—or members of your audience—are jet lagged. Also, if the speech is going to be carried on the media, try to time it so it can be broadcast at home as well as locally.

8. **Reinforce the need for intercultural communication.** Address the issue of cultural diversity head-on to reassure your audience that everyone is singing from the same hymnal. You can cite statistics, specific examples, and vivid anecdotes that stress the need for international understanding. This data is easily available in an up-to-date reference text such as an almanac. Here are some examples to illustrate this point:

> **Words to the Wise**
> Be completely, totally sure that the phrase you have selected accurately expresses your sentiments. Study with a competent foreign speaker to make sure that you are pronouncing every word correctly. Few things are as embarrassing as making a fool of yourself in a language you don't even understand.

> ➤ The U.S. has more than $500 million invested abroad.

> ➤ The bulk of America's foreign investments are in the European countries, including Belgium, Denmark, France, Germany, and Italy.

> ➤ Foreign countries have nearly $500 billion invested in the U.S.

> ➤ Five countries account for over 75 percent of the direct foreign investment in the U.S. In order from most to least direct foreign investment, these countries are the United Kingdom, Japan, the Netherlands, Canada, and Germany.

International Speech Bloopers and Ways to Avoid Them

The great increase in international communication has resulted in scores of linguistic blunders. Many of these concerned potentially lucrative business deals. For example, when Pepsi entered the Chinese market, its slogan, "Come alive with the Pepsi generation" was translated into Chinese as "Pepsi brings back your dead ancestors." It's tempting to lay all the blame on people, but a technological approach doesn't always get out all the bugs, either: A United Nations translating computer translated the cliché "Out of sight, out of mind" as "invisible insane."

Hotel signs seem to be especially susceptible to becoming gibberish when translated. For example, a Tokyo hotel posted this sign in something resembling English: "It is forbidden to steal hotel towels please. If you are not a person to do such a thing, please not to read notis." The same hotel tried to explain the mechanics of bathing this way: "Please to bathe inside the tub." This sign was seen on the door of a Moscow hotel room: "If this is your first visit to the USSR, you are welcome to it." We assume that with the breakup for the USSR has come better translation.

You might want to have your laundry done in this Yugoslavia hotel: "The flattening of underwear with pleasure is the job of the chambermaids." This Vienna hotel is prepared for fire: "In case of fire, do your utmost to alarm the hotel porter." The following Athens hotel has a clear policy on criticism: "Visitors are expected to complain at the office between the hours or 9 and 11 a.m. daily."

Elevators are also at special risk for garbled translation, such as the following:

➤ This sign was seen in a Bucharest hotel lobby: "This lift is being fixed for the next day. During that time, we regret that you will be unbearable."

➤ In a Leipzig elevator: "Do not enter the lift backwards and only when lit up."

➤ In a Belgrade elevator: "To move the cabin, push button for wishing floor. If the cabin should enter more persons, each one should press number of wishing floor. Driving is then going alphabetically by national order."

➤ A Paris elevator: "Please leave your values at the front desk."

Bet You Didn't Know

OOOOH.

Even British and American English can involve translation bloopers because the two languages often use different terms to mean the same thing. Many of the people in Europe, Asia, Africa, and the Caribbean have learned British English, not American English. Study this chart to avoid embarrassment in a language closer to home:

American English	British English
legal holiday	bank holiday
white-collar job	black coat job
attorney in non-court work	solicitor
attorney who goes to court	barrister
ground floor	first floor
elevator	lift
hood	bonnet

Shopping signs overseas can make it tricky for even the most intrepid mall crawler:

➤ In a Hong Kong supermarket: "For your convenience, we recommend courteous, efficient self-service."

➤ A Tokyo shop advises: "Our nylons cost more than common but you'll find they are best in the long run."

➤ A tourist found this sign in the shop of a Swedish furrier: "Fur coats made from ladies with their own skins."

➤ Seen in a Hong Kong tailor shop window: "Ladies may have a fit upstairs."

➤ An Athens tailor had this sign posted in the shop: "Order your summer suit. Because is a big rush will execute customers in strict rotation."

➤ Even trendy Paris boutiques are not exempt from the terrors of Bad Translation: "Dresses for street walking," the sign in a chic shop window read.

➤ And to add insult to injury, a sign in a Moroccan shop window bragged: "Here speaching English."

And what about keeping your purchases clean?

➤ A Bangkok dry cleaner gets right to the heart of the matter: "Drop your trousers here for best results."

➤ A Roman laundry likely didn't mean what they wrote on this English sign: "Ladies, leave your clothes here and spend the afternoon having a good time."

The size of the transaction doesn't seem to affect the skill of the translator, as the following sign spotted in a car rental firm in Japan shows: "When passenger of foot heave in sight, tootle the horn. Trumpet him melodiously at first but if he still obstacles your passage, then tootle him with vigor."

Tourist attractions are equally apt to attack by the language-impaired:

➤ An ad for donkey rides in Thailand reads: "Would you like to ride your own ass?"

➤ A Budapest zoo cautions: "Please do not feed the animals. If you have any suitable food, give it to the guard on duty."

➤ A sign in Germany's Black Forest states: "It is strictly forbidden on our camping site that people of different sex, for instance men and women, live together in one tent unless they are married with each other for that purpose."

➤ A Czech tourist agency suggests: "Take one of our horse-driven carriage tours. We guarantee no miscarriages."

Woe be to those who dare to drive, fly, or otherwise try to get around in a foreign land by reading translated signs:

➤ A Japanese detour warns: "Stop. Drive Sideways."

➤ A sign in a Copenhagen airline ticket office: "We take your bags and send them in all directions."

➤ This sign was spotted in a Chinese railroad station: "Please keep cleanness. Sanitary important."

Eating abroad can be imperiled by bad English:

➤ A Swiss restaurant menu reads: "Our wines leave you nothing to hope for."

➤ A Swiss inn's sign reads: "Special today—no ice cream."

➤ An Acapulco hotel assures its diners: "The manager has personally passed all the water served here."

But it goes both ways. Armed with a German-English dictionary, one tourist ordered a "heisser hund," a literal translation of the American "hot dog." Unfortunately, the literal translation just didn't cut the mustard. What did it mean? "A dog in heat." Dinner was a real dog.

You don't want to get sick, either, as the following two signs show. A sign in the window of a Roman doctor says, "Specialist in women and other diseases." A Hong Kong dentist posted this notice: "Teeth extracted by latest Methodists."

Bet You Didn't Know

In North America, clothing conveys nonverbal messages about competence, success, and influence. In Japan, clothing denotes occupational group as well as status. Company badges include rank; workers wear different colors when they are on strike.

How to Use a Translator

These mistranslations serve to illustrate one of the toughest aspects of translating from one language to another: keeping idioms intact. Many times, idioms cannot be translated from one language to another. Skilled translators can help you avoid these blunders. Let's take a look at using translators.

As the number of people speaking languages other than English has grown in America, so has the need for translators. Recently, for example, translators have been called upon to translate courtroom testimony, operating manuals, and business contracts.

Unfortunately, there is a huge difference between someone who happens to speak a foreign language and someone who has the ability to translate between speakers and writers of different languages. The first is an amateur; the second, a professional. Competent, effective public speaking demands the professional.

If at all possible, take your own translator when you travel to another country on business. Discuss with the translator the nature of your work abroad, the speech or speeches you will be giving, and any technical terms you will be including. A good translator can also help you interpret nonverbal behavior and negotiating strategies.

If you are giving a speech in English to an audience that speaks another language, how can you find a translator who can do the best possible job for you? Start by word-of-mouth. Ask people in your field for recommendations. Unfortunately, people tend to guard good translators with the same zeal they use to safeguard trusted child-care workers, cleaning help, hairdressers, and the last of the super-premium ice-cream. If no one steps forward with a recommendation or two, consider advertising for a translator. In any event, carefully interview all candidates.

During the interview, see if you feel comfortable with the candidate. If you feel uneasy, this is not the right translator for you—no matter how good the individual's reputation and skills may be. Remember: You are essentially trusting this person with your reputation. You want to select a person you can work with easily. See if the person projects the image you want. Is the candidate professional, well-groomed, and competent? A translator is literally a stand-in for you. The candidate must be someone you want to represent you. Use this checklist when you are interviewing candidates for a position as a translator:

Words to the Wise

If you are writing a speech that will be translated, leave about one-third more white space than you would on an English document. When text is translated from English into most other languages, it usually takes up more space.

➤ How did you learn the language?

➤ Where did you study?

➤ What was the nature of your training?

➤ Did you ever live in this foreign country?

➤ What are your teachers' credentials?

➤ How long have you been a translator?

➤ How often do you work?

➤ What types of materials do you feel most comfortable translating?

➤ What were your last three translating jobs? Request specific details: length of assignments, types of materials, clients, fees, and so on.

➤ Have you ever translated speeches within my particular industry or field?

➤ Why do you want this job?

➤ What do you see as your role in it?

➤ What references can you offer?

The Least You Need to Know

➤ It's crucial that you learn the traditions, attitudes, and beliefs of the people you deal with at home and abroad.

➤ Don't be a martyr: use a competent translator to help you deal with speeches in other languages.

➤ It's a small world after all.

Part 4
Tackling Specific Types of Speeches

Ever see a Marx Brothers movie? How about A Night at the Opera? *Or* A Day at the Races? *If you've ever seen one of these classic flicks, you know that Groucho was the brother with the big mustache and bigger cigar, Chico was the brother with the outrageous Italian accent, and Harpo was the curly haired brother who played the harp and spoke by honking a horn. No one ever heard his voice on film. As a result, people assumed that he couldn't speak.*

Years after the Marx Brothers stopped making movies, Harpo would occasionally host charity functions. His standard opening line was to step onto the stage, sidle to the microphone, and say, "Unaccustomed as I am to speaking in public . . ."

This section of the book shows you how to craft speeches that work—so you won't shock people with your eloquence!

Chapter 17

Information, Please: Informational Speaking

In This Chapter

➤ Tell how things work

➤ Train and teach

➤ Interview and be interviewed

➤ Testify in court

➤ Give (and get!) criticism

There can be little doubt that the reaction sought by the after-dinner speaker at a banquet differs quite a bit from that sought by the Production Director explaining the offset printing process to her staff. The first wants the audience to *enjoy* themselves; the second wants them to *understand*.

Ours has become an information society. More than ever before, we are compelled to inform and be informed. When you try to clarify a concept or process for your audience, define terms and relationships, or in any way expand their knowledge, the object of your speech is to *inform*. Common understandings and solutions to problems are based on accurate exchanges of information. The success of governments, businesses, community organizations, and even social groups depends on this type of communication.

As a result, much of the time we spend communicating is spent in trading information. Whether the audience is an intimate group of personal friends or a huge gathering of strangers, the speaker of an informative speech attempts to give the audience more information than they already had. Take a closer look at each of these public speaking tasks.

Explaining a Process

At a public meeting, can you describe your plan to revitalize the town park? On the job, can you describe the steps your colleagues must take to install new software applications, order materials, or complete an accident report? Use these guidelines to help you remember how to explain a process.

You will often have to explain a process to another person. The process may be as simple as ordering flowers or as complex as installing a fax modem. Whatever the process is, your explanation should have three parts: *introduction, body,* and *conclusion.*

Tell Me About It

I recommend that you join Toastmasters International if you have to do a lot of informational or persuasive speaking. Toastmasters provides an ideal forum to hone and improve the skills you need to make these kinds of speeches. Look in the telephone book to find the chapter of Toastmasters closest to your home or office.

In the *introduction*, explain to the other person or people why the process is important and what steps you will be describing.

In the *body*, explain the steps one at a time. Demonstrate or illustrate each step as you discuss it. As you speak, look at your audience to be sure they understand what you are saying. If not, repeat the step and explanation. Try to use different words in your restatement to help your listeners grasp the ideas in another way.

In the *conclusion*, briefly go over the steps again. Remind your listener about any important rules, safety regulations, or cautions. To make sure that your listeners understood the process, ask them to restate the rules in their own words. You can do this at the end of the process or after each step.

Follow these steps when you explain a process:

➤ Tell why the process is important. State the steps in the process.

➤ Explain the steps, one at a time. Have listeners restate the steps.

➤ Quickly restate the steps. Repeat important safety rules. Have listeners restate the steps.

Remember what you learned in Chapter 6, "Speaking to Inform," about using numbers and transitions in a speech to help you make the order of events easier for your audience to follow. See Chapter 13, "Developing the Body," for a list of the most common transitions to use in informational speeches.

Running Job Training and Teaching Sessions

Job training sessions are unique, informative speech situations because here, audience members learn by doing, not just by viewing and listening. As a result, when you run job training sessions, you should encourage people to become actively involved. The more people are involved—the more questions they ask, the more give-and-take there is—the more effective the session will be. At many job training meetings, the speaker functions more as a moderator. Don't be afraid to let go of the reins.

But that does not mean that these sessions are Speaker's Day Off. On the contrary: it's important to really prepare for these meetings in advance. You will need to make the sessions long enough so that people will really get involved. Be sure to save some time for audience members to go over what they learned.

Tell Me About It
When you are explaining a process, keep your sentences short. Use vivid, concrete language and precise terminology.

Strong speaking skills are especially important in teaching sessions because these presentations too easily become boring and tend to be filled with too much information. Follow these guidelines to make your teaching sessions clear and effective:

1. Decide what knowledge is most important. You can't cover everything—nor do you want to.

2. If a number of people are speaking, review all the presentations beforehand to see if they can be pared down.

3. Arrange the information in a logical fashion. The order of time (first to last) or importance (most to least important) work best.

Tell Me About It
Remember to always keep your audience firmly in mind. Consider their needs and goals. It helps to recall that *public speaking* is an audience participation event; if it weren't, it would be *private speaking*.

4. Be precise in presenting measurements, sizes, numbers, colors, time, and other technical facts.

5. Present complex or crucial technical information by using visual aids. This is explained in Chapter 21, "Visual Aids, Audio-Visual Aids, and Props."

6. Consider using small discussion groups to cut down on information overload and allow people time to digest crucial facts.

7. Be lavish in your use of visual aids. Don't skimp on slides, displays, and video.

Interviewing and Being Interviewed for a Job

Before you even get to the interview, you have to inquire about the job. It is likely that most of the job inquiries you make will be oral rather than written. For example, you may telephone about a job you have seen advertised or speak in person to a personnel manager or job recruiter. Whether you find out more about a job by phone or in person, use the Interview Preparation checklist to help you say it right.

Interview Preparation Checklist

❏   Prepare a list of questions about the job.

❏   Know the name and title of the person you must contact.

❏   Have a pencil or pen and paper ready to take notes on your conversation.

❏   Identify yourself at the start of the conversation.

❏   Explain why you are calling.

❏   Give the person any helpful information about prior meetings or contacts, such as "We talked last week at Andy Helfer's party."

❏   Be prepared to answer questions about relevant work experience and interests.

❏   Follow up the conversation with a phone call or letter.

Check off each item on this list as you complete it.

So you've made your inquiries, sent a follow-up letter and perhaps a résumé and cover letter, and are given an interview for a job. In the mid-90s, many employers expect you to be more aggressive during the interview than was common in the past. The key is to present yourself as qualified, assured, and personable. Follow these guidelines:

1. Do your homework: find out as much as you can about the job, company, and industry. Read stock reports, newspaper articles, and magazine pieces. If possible, speak to people you know in the company and industry to get additional information.

2. Leave yourself plenty of time to get to the interview. This will help prevent you from rushing in all frazzled.

3. Dress neatly and appropriately for the interview.

4. Bring an extra copy of your résumé, a list of references, and a pen. It's also a good idea to have identification, such as a social security card or a driver's license.

5. Be ready to answer questions about your education, experience, job qualifications, and interests.

6. Be confident and polite, but convey your enthusiasm about the job.

7. Ask intelligent, thoughtful, well-researched questions about the job.

8. Stash the gum, elaborate jewelry, overpowering perfume, and other distracters someplace far from the interview.

9. Watch for cues that the interview is over. To signal the end of a meeting, many interviewers look at the clock or their watch, push back their chairs, or shuffle papers.

10. Thank the interviewer for his or her time.

Interviewing candidates for a job is one of the touchiest areas of informative speech because what an interviewer should and should not say at an employment interview is now subject to strict federal guidelines. For example, in the United States it is illegal to ask job applicants about their race, religion, or marital status. Some topics may be illegal or legal depending on how they are asked. It is illegal to ask, "How old are you?" but it is legal to ask, "Can you prove that you are over 18?" All questions must be relevant to the job and asked of all applicants.

In court cases, companies have been at fault when women have been discouraged from applying for jobs, when African-Americans have been judged solely by a group of whites, when interviewers have not been trained, and when companies have not kept adequate records.

If you are employed by a major corporation, speak to your human resources department to obtain a copy of these guidelines and the company's interview policy. In many companies, it is mandatory that a representative of the human resources department sit in on any job interviews.

If you belong to a small company or run your own shop, be sure to obtain a copy of these guidelines and study them carefully before you conduct a job interview.

Giving Testimony

More than 14 million people are arrested every year. With this number of malefactors, it's likely that at some point in your life you'll be required to testify under oath in the course of a trial. You may be called to testify before an investigative committee or commission.

The purpose of testimony is to present facts and evidence from which other people will draw conclusions. The "other people" include judges, juries, or committee members. A witness should follow these rules:

1. First, listen carefully to the entire question before you answer.

2. Do not interrupt the person asking the question or anticipate what the questioner has to say.

3. If an objection is raised, the person testifying should also wait to hear the court's response to the objection before answering.

4. Be sure that you understand the question before you answer.

5. If you do not understand the question, ask for an explanation.

6. Give precise, factual answers. Cite dates, times, and other specific details, when possible.

7. Answer only what was asked in the question.

8. Do not offer your own opinion unless specifically asked to do so. In these instances, back up your opinion with specific details.

9. Answer carefully. Take the time you need to make sure that your answer is correct and concise.

10. Keep cool. Don't lose your temper, even if you are baited.

11. Tell the complete truth. Do not withhold facts that should be part of the response. Recall that you promised to tell the "whole truth."

Let's Get Critical

Criticism, like the common cold, knows no bounds. But unlike the cold, criticism does serve a useful purpose. Constructive criticism points out the weaknesses in people's work and suggests ways they can improve their performance.

Criticism Checklist

❑ Did I limit my criticism to one specific aspect of the job or assignment?

❑ Did I focus on the behavior, not the personality?

❑ Did I make my criticism helpful, saying things like, "Please proofread your typing," rather than "You're a poor administrative assistant"?

❑ Did I listen closely to the person's defense? Did I understand the other person's point of view?

❑ Did I give positive as well as negative criticism?

❑ Did I include praise by telling the person what parts of the job he or she does well?

Use this checklist to help you keep your criticism helpful, not hurtful.

Can you take it as well as dish it out? Constructive criticism can come from a superior, colleague, or subordinate. When you accept criticism, listen carefully. Be sure you understand what specific criticisms the person is making. Think about whether the criticism is valid. Do not rush to defend yourself. Instead, ask the other person for specific suggestions for improvement. Jot down these ideas.

If you do not understand all the criticism, calmly ask the other person to clarify any confusing points. Try to correct your performance according to the other person's suggestions. Evaluate your progress by asking the other person how you are doing. For example, you might say, "Is this closer to what you had in mind?" rather than "Is this good enough for you now?" Remember: more trouble is caused in the world by indiscreet answers than by indiscreet questions.

Describe an Object, Person, or Place

The key to describing a person, place, or thing is *organization*. Select and arrange your points systematically. With these speeches, you must exercise the most care to make your organization of ideas clear, for the audience must be able to follow your description without any problems.

169

The most common method of organizing these speeches is space sequence, using location or position as the basis for arrangement. For instance, you might arrange your details from top to bottom, bottom to top, inside out, and so on.

Define a Concept

One of the most common informative speaking tasks is defining a concept. Why? Because it is often necessary to define an obscure term or establish the special meaning you wish to attach to a particular word or phrase before you can go any further. Otherwise, you will fail to communicate your meaning adequately, no matter what else you may say. There are five main ways to clarify a concept. Let's look at each one in turn:

➤ **Dictionary definition.** To use this method, place the concept or term you are defining into a category or general class. Then, carefully distinguish the concept from other members of this class. For example, "*Democracy* is a system of government by the people, of the people, and for the people."

➤ **Etymology.** What's the history of the concept? How was the word created? What is its background? With this technique, you clarify the meaning of a concept by providing the history of the word or phrase. For instance, a *pandemic* disease is one that is very widespread. An example of a serious disease of this sort was the viral influenza that caused thousands of deaths in 1918. A less serious example is the common cold, which seems to always be with us. *Pandemic* means "general, universal, affecting most of the people." The concept comes from two Greek roots—*pan*, which means "all," and *demos*, which means "people."

➤ **Negation.** Clarify the meaning of a concept by telling what it is not. For example, "By *socialism* I do not mean communism, which supports the common ownership of the means of production. Instead, socialism means . . ."

➤ **Example.** Try explaining the meaning of a concept by giving an actual example or illustration of its meaning. For instance: "You have all seen the new Skydome on the parkway. This is what I mean by modern architecture."

➤ **Use in a sentence.** Sometimes, the best way to clarify the meaning of a concept is to use it in a sentence. This can help make the meaning concrete to the audience. Here's a sample: "*Rad* is a slang term for 'exceedingly fashionable' or 'trendy.' It has a positive connotation. For instance, if I say, 'What a rad hairstyle,' I mean, 'What a stylish hairstyle.'"

The Least You Need to Know

➤ Informative speeches explain concepts, define terms, and explain processes.

➤ Use vivid, concrete language and precise terminology.

➤ Be careful what you say while you are interviewing a candidate. Certain questions and topics are legally off-limits.

➤ Anyone can learn to give informative speeches—and good ones, too!

Chapter 18

See It My Way: Persuasive Speaking

In This Chapter

➤ Explore different types of persuasive speeches

➤ Discover how to sell your ideas

➤ Learn how to use persuasive speeches to solve problems on your own and in groups

Political candidates wooing voter support and TV commercials pitching the latest toothpaste. Salespeople urging you to buy their widget and a charity trying to convince people to donate money. A committee trying to iron out a difficult problem and two people working together to solve a dilemma. What do all these situations have in common?

All are forms of persuasive speech. When your purpose is to influence or alter the beliefs or attitudes of your audience, you're speaking to persuade.

Whether you're selling houses or ideas, effective persuasion is based on accurate logic, powerful appeals to emotion, and trust. Persuasive speeches include making sales presentations, selling budgets and ideas, solving problems, running for election, and delivering a eulogy.

In this chapter, you will learn how to construct the most important and useful types of persuasive speeches. I'll teach you specific techniques for making these persuasive appeals convince a wide variety of audiences and situations.

Types of Persuasive Speeches

There are three types of persuasive speeches:

➤ Speeches of fact, where you try to prove that someting is or is not so, or did or did not happen. "Our candidate has always supported the family farmer." "Our company has never missed a shipment."

➤ Speeches of value, where you try to prove better or worse, good or bad. "Our car is better than their car." "This movie is superior to that one."

➤ Speeches of policy, where you try to prove that something should or should not be done. The key word is *should*. "You should elect our candidate." "You should pass this bill."

All persuasive speeches have several purposes:

➤ To provide enough information so the listener knows what to do.

➤ To overcome the listener's objections.

➤ To move the listener to belief or action.

Select a persuasive strategy based on your answers to the following four questions:

➤ What do I want people to do?

➤ What objections, if any, will people have?

➤ How strong a case can I make?

➤ What kind of persuasion does my organization value?

Now, it's time to apply these techniques to specific types of persuasive appeals.

Making Sales Presentations

Sales presentations demand special persuasive techniques. Your appeal can be *direct* or *indirect*. Your choice of technique depends largely on your audience and the amount of resistance you can expect to encounter.

In the next two sections, I apply these techniques to two very common sales tasks: selling an idea and selling a budget. You'll find the direct approach explained with regard to selling an idea and the indirect approach explained with regard to selling a budget. However, you should apply each technique to the specific situation, depending on your specific needs in each individual case.

The Direct Approach

Use a *direct approach* when your audience is receptive to your ideas. This persuasive technique allows you to present your ideas at once. Here's how.

Open with a *hook* to catch the audience's attention. In the body, provide a *list* of reasons people should act on your idea. Finish by giving the audience a *handle*—tell them what to do and why they should act fast. Take a look at each part in detail:

➤ *Hook:* Provide a one-minute motivation to grab your audience.

➤ *List:* Give the audience the information they need to support your idea. Include specific reasons why your idea is worth their support. Don't stint on details. Remember: "The more you tell, the more you sell."

➤ *Handle:* Make the action sound easy. Give the audience a positive reason for supporting your idea. Avoid *if* and *why not* closes. They lack positive emphasis and encourage your reader to say *no*.

Bet You Didn't Know

OOOOH.

In other cultures, making a direct sales pitch might backfire. Brazilians, for example, are often offended by a direct solicitation. Even supervisors are expected to suggest, not request. In India, people often assume that a direct request really conceals a more subtle message. Often, people ignore the direct statement and focus on the supposed "subtext."

The Indirect Approach

Use an *indirect approach* when you expect resistance from your audience. This pattern allows you to demobilize your opposition by showing all the reasons in favor of your position before you give your audience a chance to say *no*.

Follow these steps:

1. *Start by establishing common ground.* For example, show that the budget is beneficial. Or you may wish to grab your audience's attention with a negative, which you then proceed to show can become a positive or can be solved.

2. *Define the problem you share, which your budget will solve.* Your task is to convince your audience that something has to be done before you can convince them that your budget is the solution.

3. *Explain how your budget will solve the problem.* Keep personalities out of the discussion; don't use the words *I* or *my*.

4. *Show how the advantages outweigh the disadvantages.* Depending on your budget, possible disadvantages might include a decrease in personnel, supplies, office space, or vacation time. Possible advantages might include greater profits, market share, promotions, office space, or vacation time. This is the equivalent to asking for the order.

5. *Summarize any additional benefits to the audience's supporting your budget.*

6. *Tell the audience members what you want them to do: support your budget.* Get your audience to act quickly, perhaps by offering an additional incentive. For example, "By passing the budget now, we can avoid laying off additional people this quarter," or "We can move into the new office space this year instead of next."

Tell Me About It
A strategy that works in one situation may not work in another. Some organizations expect direct requests; others, a more indirect approach. Study role models and solicit advice when selecting a persuasive approach for selling a budget or an idea.

Using a Sales Presentation Checklist

"Would you buy a used car from that person?" To make sure that no one says that about *your* sales presentation, use the Sales Presentation Checklist to help you prepare for your sales speeches.

Sales Presentation Checklist

❑   Did I analyze my audience?

❑   Did I meet my audience's needs?

❑   Did I adjust my speech to deal with changing needs?

❑   Have I used specific facts and figures?

❑   Did I effectively answer questions about the product?

❑   Did I remember that "the customer is always right"?

❑   Did I speak with enthusiasm and confidence?

❑   Did I know when to stop talking?

As you edit and revise your sales speech, check off the important elements you completed or considered.

Delivering a Eulogy

A *eulogy* is a speech given in praise of a person. Speakers often deliver eulogies at funerals and memorial services, but they can also be given at retirement parties or any occasion when someone is being honored.

For the most powerful eulogies, concentrate on a few specific qualities of the person being honored. For example, a eulogy for a retiring volunteer fire-fighter might concentrate on the effect of the person's bravery by giving instances when the person helped others. This approach would simultaneously honor the person while persuading the audience to become involved in the volunteer fire department. A eulogy for a deceased teacher might explain the teacher's high standards in order to honor the individual and to persuade people to set similar high standards for themselves. Remember: Words are what hold society together.

Solving a Problem

Whether you're a student, an employee, an employer, or a community volunteer, you need to be able to work with others to solve problems. It's not unusual that the problem-solving process sparks tempers, making it more difficult to reach an equitable resolution. Follow these problem-solving guidelines to keep the waters calm and to help ensure smooth sailing:

1. In your speech, describe and understand the problem. Define the scope and causes of the problem.

2. Be sure to isolate criteria to use in order to judge possible solutions. Establish standards for evaluating solutions.

3. Identify all possible solutions. Keep an open mind. Don't discard any possibilities as you speak.

4. Evaluate each possible solution according to the standards that were set earlier.

5. Select the best possible solution and present it in your speech.

6. Address people from every involved group. To solve a work-related problem, for example, be sure to address the needs of union workers, sales associates, and management in your speech.

7. To make sure that no one is left out in the cold, don't withhold any relevant information as you speak.

8. Don't let personality conflicts infringe on your address. Work to maintain the group's cohesiveness and ability to work together after you finish speaking.

Running for Election

Ever hear this well-known campaign maxim: "You campaign in poetry, you govern in prose"? Even though people have individual differences in temperament and ability, their responses to persuasive appeals are surprisingly similar—so similar, in fact, that politicians have been able to develop a fairly standard pattern for campaign speeches. Remember: These are speeches of policy. As a result, they always try to prove that something should or should not be done. The password is *should*.

Nearly all candidates attempt to create dissatisfaction with existing conditions in order to convince the audience that these conditions need to be changed—and they are the one to do it. Candidates craft speeches that point out flaws and failure. Follow these steps:

Direct Appeal	Election Campaign
1. Tell the audience what you want.	"Elect me."
2. Give them the information they need to act on your request.	"We're paying too much in taxes. I can lower taxes."
3. Tell the audience what you want.	"Vote for me."

But people don't make decisions based on logic alone. Emotional appeals make the audience want to do what you ask. When combined with direct requests, emotional appeals make surprisingly strong election campaigns. See Chapter 7, "Speaking to Persuade," for more information about making an emotional appeal.

Nominating a Candidate

A speech to nominate a candidate has two aims: to explain why your candidate is qualified for a specific office and to whip up support for your candidate. The excitement of your speech should carry over to the voting. Try these guidelines when you prepare a nominating speech:

➤ First, list the requirements for the office.

➤ Then, explain how well your candidate's training and knowledge fulfill each requirement.

➤ Don't provide the candidate's entire life history.

➤ Instead, provide examples of your candidate's positive qualities, such as judgment, loyalty, energy, and intelligence.

➤ Link each character trait to one aspect of the office.

➤ Reinforce the positive character traits you listed by using the candidate's name often.

➤ Speak with conviction and vigor.

➤ Don't attack the other candidate.

➤ Keep your speech short.

➤ End the speech with your candidate's name and a flourish to create excitement.

Tell Me About It

Savvy candidates follow these three caveats:

Be factual. Don't stretch the truth—not even a little.

Be specific. Give details to support your claims.

Be reliable. Don't promise what you can't deliver.

Whisper...

The Least You Need to Know

> ➤ Persuasive speeches include speeches of fact, speeches of value, and speeches of policy.

> ➤ Use a *direct approach* when your audience is receptive to your ideas; use an *indirect approach* when they are not.

> ➤ Powerful speakers are factual, specific, and reliable.

Chapter 19

Ever Hear the One About? . . . Entertaining Speeches

In This Chapter

➤ Learn how to prepare and deliver entertaining speeches as part of a ceremony

➤ Discover how to make 'em laugh and make 'em cry

➤ Become a regular on the rubber-chicken circuit

For centuries, speakers have addressed audiences at a number of different occasions. Sometimes these speeches help create greater unity within an organization. Other times, they honor individuals or fulfill part of a social ritual or special ceremony. What makes these speeches different from the other forms I have described so far is their purpose: they don't inform or persuade. Instead, their primary purpose is to entertain and thus bring people together. They create social unity.

In this chapter, I will show you how to write speeches that build goodwill, create social cohesion, and delight audiences. First, you will learn how to introduce a speaker, give a graduation speech, and present and receive an award. Next, I'll cover speaking at conventions, birthdays, anniversaries, weddings, retirements, and reunions. Finally, I'll discuss how to dedicate a building. You'll learn how to make your natural style and grace work for you in public speaking situations.

The Host with the Most: Introducing a Speaker

Brevity is always the soul of wit, but nowhere is this more true than when you're introducing a speaker. Remember: You're not the head weenie at this barbecue. Keep your remarks short so you don't steal the speaker's thunder.

What's a short introduction? A two- to three-minute speech is ideal—and certainly your speech should be no more than five minutes long. The object is to get the speaker and the audience together as quickly as possible, without making it appear too rushed.

Your introduction should include these elements:

➤ The title of the speech that the speaker will give.

➤ Why the speaker is qualified to speak on the topic.

➤ The speaker's name—preferably mentioned several times so the audience remembers it.

How can you get the answers to these questions? Ask the speaker for his or her résumé. This should provide you with more than enough information. But getting your hands on a speaker's biography also carries temptation. Should you use the résumé or vita as your speech? No. No. No.

Instead, draw what you need from the résumé. The elements should then be woven into a profile, not ticked off like an obituary. Anything that unites the speaker and the audience is fair game.

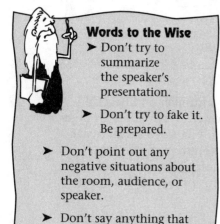

Words to the Wise

➤ Don't try to summarize the speaker's presentation.

➤ Don't try to fake it. Be prepared.

➤ Don't point out any negative situations about the room, audience, or speaker.

➤ Don't say anything that will embarrass the speaker.

Sometimes, however, the speaker will even provide you with the introduction he or she wants used. If you're lucky, you'll be all set. Other times, the canned introduction will be as stale as yesterday's news. In most situations, you're under no obligation to deliver the speaker's introduction as written. Edit it to answer the three key questions listed earlier in this section. Delete ho-hum lists of professional organizations. Fill in with lively stories that show why the speaker was invited to address the organization and why you're delighted to be making the introduction.

Use the Speaker Introduction Checklist to help you introduce a speaker with poise and self-assurance.

Speaker Introduction Checklist

❏   Be sure to pronounce the speaker's name correctly. Practice beforehand.

❏   Research the person's background and achievements.

❏   Repeat the speaker's name several times.

❏   Zero in on the speaker's qualifications to address this specific audience.

❏   Praise the speaker but don't embarrass him, her, or yourself.

❏   Use the format of the speech to inform (see Chapter 6).

❏   Speak with warmth and vitality.

❏   At the end of your speech, applaud until the speaker reaches the podium.

❏   When the speaker talks, listen closely to the opening. You might have to respond to mention of your name or thanks.

❏   Be sure to talk with the speaker ahead of time so there are no surprises.

Remember (and check off) these items as you prepare and deliver a speech to introduce another speaker.

Always-Fail Clichés

Except for death, taxes, and getting great seats at the ball game and having it rain, few things are certain in life. Well, here's something else to add to your list of certitudes: speech openings that I guarantee will always flop. Trust me. Don't try these.

1. "It is indeed a great privilege to introduce . . ."

2. "On this most ceremonial occasion . . ."

3. "Gathered here together at this memorable affair . . ."

4. "We are truly honored to have with us today . . ."

5. "Ladies and gentlemen, heeeere's . . ."

6. "Without further ado . . ."

7. "We are truly a fortunate audience because we have with us none other than . . ."

8. "Ladies and gentlemen, here's a speaker who needs no introduction . . ."

9. "As we stand at the crossroads of this momentous occasion . . ."

10. Your choice:_____

Giving a Graduation Speech

Graduation speeches are plum speaking jobs because everyone's in a good mood. Parents are finished paying obscene tuition bills; graduates have yet to start repaying their loans; professors are glad it's all over until September. Besides, everyone looks good in a graduation gown.

Don't spoil the good feelings: keep your remarks short and snappy. The most effective commencement speeches are between ten to 15 minutes long. Anything more than that and the audience starts to fidget. A wit once said: "The greatest achievement of the graduate is sitting through the commencement address." Don't let this observation apply to your speech.

If you can't be brief, at least be memorable. Craft a speech that's easy to remember and tantalizing for the press to quote. For example, in his later years, Winston Churchill was asked to give the commencement address at Oxford University. Following his introduction, he rose, went to the podium, and said, "Never, never give up." Then he took his seat. Here are some topics to consider—and some to avoid.

> **Words to the Wise**
> Have you ever heard someone go to the podium and say, "And here's Mr. Henry Huggins and his good wife Sylvia"? How about, "We're delighted to have Mr. Horatio Hornblower and his better half, Estelle"?
>
> These phrases were once accepted as the norm, but today they are considered tacky, rude, and disparaging. Instead, say, "I would like to introduce Herbert and Hortensia Huffnagle."

Good Bet Speech Topics

☺ Career issues.

☺ Political topics.

☺ Social themes.

☺ Civic subjects.

☺ Economic questions.

☺ Graduates' hopes and dreams.

Bad Bet Speech Topics

☹ Nuclear war.

☹ National disasters.

☹ Ecological cataclysms.

☹ The lousy job market for new graduates.

☹ Automotive safety defects.

☹ Possible or probable carcinogens.

☹ Anything that will result in a headache.

Hosting Toasts and Roasts

The term *toast* dates back to the 1600s and refers to a chunk of bread dipped in drinks. The term then came to refer to a drink in honor of a favorite lady and soon, a drink in honor of just about anything you could hoist one to. The custom took off so quickly that by the 18th century, Pennsylvania was fining its residents and visitors for excessive toasting.

As the custom hit the tonier joints, the toast-masters took some pains to craft their speeches. Their toasts were often printed on the dinner menu and became part of the permanent record of many organizations.

Tell Me About It
Remember that the weather in May and June is capricious. If the graduation is being held outdoors, watch for rain clouds. If you see anything threatening on the horizon, be prepared to cut your remarks short.

Today, toastmasters and roastmasters are expected to set the tone for the entire event. With toasts and roasts, the skill of the speaker is really put to the test. Toastmasters are expected to be sharp and witty, which of course you are, or you wouldn't have been asked to be the host.

But there is no rule saying that you have to spend miserable hours hunting for great jokes.

Word Power
A *toastmaster* is the chairperson, the host. The toastmaster has three important tasks: to run the program smoothly, to hold the audience's attention, and to discourage strife. A *roastmaster* is a type of toastmaster; a roastmaster presides over a roast or honorary event.

If you don't tell a joke well, you're much better off not telling any jokes at all. On the other hand, by all means display any talent you have in the joke department.

Follow these guidelines to make your toasts memorable:

➤ Make a general statement about the theme of the gathering.

➤ Introduce the head table. (Don't introduce the speaker; that will be done later.)

➤ Have the audience hold their applause until the end.

➤ Make an appropriate toast.

➤ Invite the guests to join in a toast to the honoree or honorees.

➤ Ask the designated person at the head table to introduce the speaker.

➤ When the speaker is finished, express everyone's thanks.

Here are the guidelines for hosting a successful roast:

➤ Probe what you know about the honoree to find a fresh slant on his or her life and accomplishments.

➤ Provide specific examples of your point about the honoree's character and accomplishments.

➤ Suit your remarks to the general tone of the evening.

➤ Err on the side of good taste; no matter how good a line may be, skip it if you—or the honoree—might regret it in the morning.

➤ Avoid humor if you are not comfortable with it.

The Envelope, Please: Presenting an Award

We all deserve a tip of the hat for a job well done. Saving someone's life, saving the company some money, saving customers time: they all merit public acknowledgment.

Keep your speech factual and straightforward. This is even more important if you have to present an award to someone you have never met. In this situation, don't pretend that you are the honoree's best buddy. Instead, interview the person's friends, family, or colleagues to get some information that shows why the person deserves the award. Share this information with the audience, acknowledging your sources.

Use the Award Presentation Checklist when you present an award.

Tell Me About It

It's never a good idea to reuse a speech, but it's especially important to write new material when you present an award. You want this speech tailored exactly to the person.

Never upstage the honoree by being too funny. Also avoid stealing the honoree's material, relying on memory or ad-lib, or trying try to fake a close relationship with the honoree. It's also bad form to put the honoree on the spot.

Award Presentation Checklist

- ❏ Can I be generous with my praise?

- ❏ Can I use true anecdotes from the person's life to make my speech personal?

- ❏ Can I give specific reasons why the person deserves this award?

- ❏ Can I make it clear how this person's involvement made a difference to others?

- ❏ Is my speech earnest?

- ❏ Does my speech have an uplifting, inspirational tone?

Ask yourself these questions as you prepare a speech to present someone an award.

Receiving an Award

Follow these steps to accept an award with your usual good grace and taste:

➤ Thank and praise the giver of the award.

➤ Acknowledge the help you got from others.

➤ Explain how much the award means to you, and why.

➤ Speak directly and to the point so the audience doesn't become restless.

➤ Explain the positive values you see in the award.

Speaking at Conventions

The "keynote address" is the featured speech at a convention. The "keynote" is the music on which a system of tones is based; similarly, the keynote address sets the tone for the entire convention.

To decide what to include in your keynote speech, consider the mood of the convention, the type of organization, and the kind of business being transacted. Use this checklist to make sure you include all the important elements of a keynote address:

➤ Did I summarize what has happened since the last convention?

➤ Are my remarks and tone suitable to the aims of the organization?

➤ Have I established a feeling of camaraderie?

➤ Is my speech brief?

➤ Is my speech original?

Speaking at Birthdays and Anniversaries

If you're likely to be asked to speak at an event where a large cake will be prominently featured, it's a good idea to have a few short lines memorized. There's the old story about the groom who was asked to say a few words to his bride. Everyone raised their glasses when the unprepared groom staggered to his feet and stammered: "Ladies and gentlemen, I—I don't know what to say. This thing was forced on me . . ." What the bride said is not recorded.

When You're Stuck for a Good Line . . .

Here are some lines you can use or adapt when you speak at a birthday celebration:

➤ You're not as young as you used to be
But you're not as old as you're going to be
So watch it! —Irish

➤ Another candle on your cake?
Well, that's no cause to pout,
Be glad that you have strength enough
To blow the damned thing out.

➤ May you live to be a hundred years—with one extra year to repent.

➤ Here's to a friend. He knows you well and likes you just the same.

➤ Here's to our friends—and the strength to put up with them.

➤ "The secret of staying young is to live honestly, eat slowly, and lie about your age." —Lucille Ball

➤ At age fifty-two, Lady Astor said, "I refuse to admit that I'm more than fifty-two, even if that does make my sons illegitimate."

➤ "The years between fifty and seventy are the hardest. You are always being asked to do things, and yet you are not decrepit enough to turn them down." —T. S. Eliot

Try these lines at an anniversary party:

➤ Here's to you both—
a beautiful pair,
on the birthday
of your love affair.

➤ The best way you can surprise a woman with an anniversary gift is to give her just what she wanted.

Speaking at Weddings

Weigh the nature of the nuptials and your own reputation when deciding to make your speech serious or humorous. The best speeches usually combine both elements, but this depends on your comfort zone.

Again, use only material that you can deliver comfortably. If you're at ease with comic material, you might want to offer an admonition from such respected experts on marriage as Zsa Zsa Gabor: "A man in love is incomplete until he is married. Then he is finished." Phyllis Diller has some equally trenchant advice for newlyweds: "Never go to bed mad. Stay up and fight."

But if your temperament and the tone of the wedding are more serious, use more serious material. How about this quote from Shakespeare: "Look down, you gods, and on this couple drop a blessed crown." And if you are the bride or groom, you can never go wrong with these cherished lines from *The Book of Common Prayer:* ". . . to have and to hold from this day forward, for better, for worse, for richer, for poorer, in sickness and in health, to love and to cherish, till death do us part."

Here are some other lines you may wish to weave into your wedding toast or speech:

➤ The love you give is the love you keep.

➤ Let's drink to love,
   Which is nothing—
   Unless it's divided by two.

➤ Love doesn't make the world go 'round. It's what makes the ride worthwhile.

➤ A toast to love and laughter and happily ever after.

➤ Here's to the Bride and Groom!
   May you have a happy honeymoon,
   May you lead a happy life,
   May you have a bunch of money soon,
   And live without all strife.

➤ May their joys be as deep as the ocean
   And their misfortunes as light as the foam.

➤ To keep the fire burning brightly, there's one easy rule: keep the two logs together, near enough to keep each other warm and far enough apart—about a finger's breadth—for breathing room. Good fire, good marriage, same rule.

➤ Before marriage, a man will lie awake all night thinking about something you said; after marriage, he'll fall asleep before you finish saying it.

Speaking at Retirements

Follow the directions for presenting an award. Under no circumstances have anyone sing "My Way."

Speaking at Reunions

These speeches need to focus on experiences shared by everyone in attendance. They are most successful when the speaker is able to tell stories that will help the audience recall shared events. They also need to have a central theme as a unifying element.

Cutting the Ribbon: Dedicating an Imposing Edifice

These speeches serve to pull together a community. The people who are part of the ceremony want to reaffirm their commitment to the community and help preserve the community's most important values.

As a result, emotional appeals and efforts to increase the audience's identification with the speaker win out over the use of logic in these cases. To write a boffo speech, you have to appeal to the interests and values you share with the audience. See Chapter 5, "Analyzing Your Audience," and Chapter 8, "Speaking to Entertain," for more information.

The Least You Need to Know

➤ Your purpose can be to unify the community, honor a person, or celebrate a social ritual.

➤ Speeches that mark endings and beginnings focus on common experiences.

➤ Keep it brief; you're almost never the most important person there.

Chapter 20

Nowhere to Hide: Speaking Off-the-Cuff

In This Chapter

➤ Learn why you *shouldn't* think on your feet

➤ Discover how to think on your feet when you must

➤ Plan the unplanned speech

➤ Master the tricks of the trade

In the speech biz, speaking at a gathering with very little preparation and without the use of notes is called *impromptu* speaking. In everyday life, it's often called *hell* and a few other terms we can't reprint here. But despite its terrifying reputation, impromptu speaking need not be an ordeal by fire.

Being a good impromptu speaker is very beneficial because of its everyday usefulness. Mastering this skill will help you feel more comfortable thinking—and speaking—on your feet. You will also be better able to say what you mean. And after you finish this chapter, you might even find that you enjoy being asked to speak off-the-cuff. *Really*.

Prior Experience

Believe it or not, you already know how to speak off-the-cuff. As a matter of fact, you've been doing it for years, probably since you were a toddler. Even today, when you go to the post office, nobody hands you a prepared speech. You simply go to the clerk and tell him or her what you want. When you go to the hairdresser, you're rarely at a loss for words (well, maybe after your hair is cut, but not before). You go about your daily business without writing speeches. And you do just fine at it.

So when you're asked to speak off-the-cuff at a business conference, Rotary meeting, PTA gathering, or annual convention, you're drawing on decades of experience.

Know Your Stuff

One great advantage of impromptu speaking is the fact that it sounds natural and spontaneous. But don't be fooled: that "natural and spontaneous" effect is often the result of meticulous planning. Impromptu speaking is the easiest thing in the world, as long as you follow one rule: know what you're talking about.

If you are going to any meeting where there is the slightest chance in the entire universe that someone might ask you to speak, go the Boy Scout route: be prepared. Make some notes about the topics that might come up in the discussion. Jot down ideas throughout the presentation or panel discussions. Concentrate not only on the speakers but also on the room and the conference theme.

Tell Me About It
Here are three basic Rules of Impromptu Speaking:

1. Have something important to say.

2. Want someone else to understand or believe it.

3. Say it simply, directly, and meaningfully.

There are two ways to know the territory: by research and experience. For example, even the least articulate sports figures can be taught to give an impromptu speech on some aspect of their livelihood; whereas you and I would have to gather information by reading the sports pages, listening to radio broadcasts of games, watching games on TV, reading books on the sport, interviewing players, and so on.

Some talented speakers are not above resorting to tricks to make their speeches seem less rehearsed. One such story concerns the late Mayor Jimmy Walker of New York. A journalist once saw Walker dazzle an audience by saying, "Ladies and gentlemen, I arrived here this evening with some written remarks, but I've decided to discard my prepared speech and speak to you from the heart." With that, Walker balled up the paper he had been holding and tossed it aside. He went on to deliver an electrifying speech.

After Walker and his entourage had left, the journalist picked up the discarded "speech" and looked at it. The paper was nothing more than an advertisement. Walker had spoken from memorized remarks freshened with observations he had made about the people, theme, and event. And so can you. Follow these guidelines:

➤ Keep your speech simple.

➤ Formulate one central idea.

➤ Concentrate on developing it.

➤ Practice, practice some more, and keep on practicing.

Better to write and practice a speech that you may not need than not have a speech when you do need it. Use the Impromptu Speaking Checklist to prepare for an off-the-cuff presentation.

Impromptu Speaking Checklist

❏   Who will be at the meeting?

❏   What will probably happen at this meeting?

❏   What is the likelihood that I will be asked to speak?

❏   How much do I know about the topic of the meeting?

❏   What should I prepare at home?

❏   What should I prepare at the meeting?

❏   What comments are likely to spark controversy?

❏   Should I use these comments or avoid them?

❏   How can I organize my remarks?

❏   How can I make my remarks impressive?

Check off each item to help you assess each impromptu speaking situation.

Try the following activity to help you gain experience with impromptu speaking. It will help you develop the ability to make choices through reasoning. Write your answers to the questions on paper, then draft a speech as instructed.

1. You are forced to give up the following modern conveniences:

    ➤ radio

    ➤ stereo

    ➤ CD player

    ➤ refrigerator

    ➤ telephone

    ➤ washing machine

    ➤ dishwasher

    ➤ microwave oven

    ➤ bathroom

    ➤ television

2. In what order will you sacrifice each item? Arrange them from most to least important.

3. Provide reasons for your choices.

4. Organize your speech with an introduction, body, and conclusion. (See Chapter 10 for guidelines.)

5. Give the speech.

Stay on the Topic

One of the best ways to make sure that you stay on the topic is to organize your speech. Very few speakers can resist the temptation to wander off track. In everyday speech this is not a hanging offense, but there are formal speech situations where it can be disastrous to life, limb, and reputation. For example, digressions are rarely appreciated when people are reporting serious accidents, giving testimony, or proposing marriage.

"How can I organize an impromptu speech?" you might ask. Here's how:

1. Quickly decide what you are going to talk about.

2. No second guessing with spur-of-the-moment speeches: pick the topic and stick with it.

3. Don't digress.

4. If necessary, pause for a few seconds to gather your thoughts.

5. Present only two or three facts, proofs, or supporting statements.

6. Try to wrap it up with a good punch line. People always remember a strong exit.

7. Don't drag it out; remember, you're not the main attraction here. If you were, you wouldn't be speaking off-the-cuff.

Words to the Wise
Join Toastmasters as a method of practicing and becoming more comfortable with impromptu speaking.

Question-and-Answer Sessions

Unless all questions are submitted in advance, question-and-answer sessions can also call for impromptu answers. Be sure to arrange beforehand with your hosts about whether time should be set aside for questions and answers and if so, how much time.

If questions are to be allowed, decide whether you want spoken or written queries. With a small audience, questions from the floor are relatively easy to deal with; with a large audience, questions from the floor can become very difficult to hear and to answer.

If you are answering spoken questions from a large audience, you may wish to repeat each question to make sure that everyone can hear it. But rather than simply *repeating* the questions, try *reworking* them. Deliberately revise the wording to make the question easier to answer. Keep the rewording close enough to the original to be on the topic, but remember: you're under no obligation to respond to any questions that embarrass you, your hosts, or your company.

Remember: If you tell the truth, you don't have to remember anything!

Whisper...

Tell Me About It
Here are some tricks of the trade for impromptu speaking:

➤ Open with a broad generalization to buy yourself a few extra seconds to decide what you're going to say.

➤ Stall for extra time by repeating the question.

➤ Ask yourself, "If I were in the audience, is this what I would like to hear?"

Uh, Like, Wow: Speak in Complete Sentences

A not-so-surprising number of teachers, store clerks, and telephone operators would no doubt argue that speaking in complete sentences has become a lost art in America. "Not me!" you cry out in mock alarm. Actually, you're probably as guilty of speaking in fragments as the next person. To prove my point, take a look at the following two messages:

What you *think* you're saying:

Fourscore and seven years ago our fathers brought forth on this continent a new nation, conceived in liberty, and dedicated to the proposition that all men are created equal.

Now we are engaged in a great civil war, testing whether that nation, or any nation so conceived and so dedicated, can long endure. We are met on a great battlefield of that war. We have come to dedicate a portion of that field as a final resting-place for those who here gave their lives that that nation might live. It is altogether fitting and proper that we should do this.

What you're probably *really* saying:

Like . . . uh . . . a long time ago, like maybe fourscore and seven years ago, you know. Our fathers . . . em . . . made you know on this like place like a continent a new nation . . . uh . . . conceived in you know like liberty and . . . uh . . . and dedicated to the like idea that all . . . uh . . . men but I don't want to forget like women, like they are really important too because they make up over half the population, you know, are like sort of like created equal.

Uh . . . Now we are in the middle of a really bad war. It's really bodacious. It's like testing whether our country, or any nation like . . . uh . . . so conceived and so dedicated, can long endure. I mean you know we have all gotten together on an important big battlefield of the war. Like we you know have . . . em . . . come to dedicate a portion of the field as a final grave for the men (there were no girl . . . uh women . . . soldiers then, you know) who like here gave their lives that that nation might live. I mean, you know, it is like altogether okay that we should do this. It's like an excellent idea.

Of course this is an exaggeration—but it's not as exaggerated as we'd like to think. Even the most highly trained newscasters sometimes slip into uhs, ehs, and likes.

You may be one of the very fortunate few who are able to speak lucid, well-formed sentences without any advance preparation. Trust me: you're in the minority.

Audiences will indulge you in a certain amount of incoherence, but it has to be kept to a minimum. Try these suggestions for speaking more smoothly:

1. Practice impromptu speaking until you feel more comfortable with it.

2. Repeat tricky phrases, names, and words until you have them down pat.

3. Work at eliminating distracting "throat-clearing" phrases such as "uh" and "em."

4. Get rid of intrusive words such as "like," "you see," and "you know."

5. Tape record yourself to monitor your progress.

Remember: Pauses punctuate thought. Just as commas, semicolons, and periods separate written words into thought groups, so pauses of different lengths separate spoken words into meaningful units. The haphazard use of pauses when you are speaking is as confusing to the listener as the haphazard use of punctuation in written matter is to the reader.

Be sure that your pauses come between thought units and not in the middle of them. Do not be afraid to pause whenever a break in your speech will help clarify an idea or emphasize an important point.

What If You Have Nothing to Say?

But what happens if you follow all of this great advice and you find that the well is dry—you have absolutely nothing to say?

Perhaps the most nerve-wracking situation occurs when someone at a meeting asks you for your opinion, and you're caught completely off guard. The subject/approach is virgin ground to you; you've never given it a thought. You have nothing prepared at all, neither fact nor figure anywhere near your fingertips. You're dead meat, right?

Actually, you might still be able to rescue the goose from the fire. Take a deep breath, stand up straight, look ahead, and make a rational comment. No one expects pearls from heaven, but rather logical sentences that fit the bill. If you draw a complete blank, say, "I don't know. I will look into the issue and get back to you." Then do so.

> **Words to the Wise**
> Speeches do more than fill time. They say something.

Probably the worst thing you can do is apologize for not being prepared. Never say something like, "Gee, I'm really sorry. I feel really terrible. No one ever asked me anything like that before. I don't have the slightest idea about what to say."

Stage Fright

Unfortunately, stage fright goes with impromptu speaking like caffeine and sleeplessness. I've already discussed how you speak with scores of people every day. Yet you rarely think that your daily conversation must be perfect, polished like a shiny stone. On the contrary, you and your listeners expect a few hesitations, pauses, repetitions, rephrasings, or silences.

If you approach impromptu speeches thinking that they have to be polished and perfect, of course you will be rigid with stage fright. Wake up call: Common sense tells you that your goal is impossible. Repeat the following chant:

➤ I am involved with my subject.

➤ I care about my audience.

➤ I know my subject.

➤ I recognize that impromptu speeches are not perfect.

➤ I'll do great.

The Least You Need to Know

➤ Decide what you're going to say, develop one main idea, and stick with it.

➤ Keep your speech simple.

➤ Stick to the topic; don't go off on tangents.

➤ Speak in complete sentences, without distracting "throat clearers" such as "uh" and "em."

➤ Prepare and memorize a speech if impromptu speaking terrorizes you.

Part 5
Getting Your Act Together

By this stage of the public speaking process, you're not only hearing yourself give your speech, but you're also starting to visualize yourself up on that podium. But perhaps what you see is a little scary—once again, you're facing the fear of the unknown.

Relax! As I've said before, it's a matter of preparation. That's why you have this book. Think of me as your tour guide through Public Speaking Land. On your journey, I'll point out the important points and how to get the most from them. In this section, for example, you'll learn all about preparing visual aids, rehearsing the speech, and dressing for success. So sit back and enjoy the journey as you prepare for the podium!

Chapter 21

Preparing Visual Aids, Audio-Visual Aids, and Props

In This Chapter

➤ Discover when and why to use audio-visual aids

➤ Learn how to use pictures to say a thousand words

➤ Explore different visual aids

So far, I have discussed only the *audible* aspect of your speech. Equally important—and sometimes more important—are the *visible* parts of your presentation: visual aids. Know the old saying, "A picture is worth a thousand words"? Nowhere is it more true than in a speech. The right image can convey your meaning with great effectiveness. The image can even linger in your audience's mind long after your words have faded.

This is because people process information through their eyes as well as their ears. Unfortunately, too many people don't use visual aids and props correctly. As a result, what was planned to help communication ends up harming it. It has been my experience that more speeches are ruined by audio-visual aids than are helped by them.

In this chapter, you'll learn effective ways to create and use visual aids to add a fuller dimension to your speeches. The chapter opens with a detailed explanation of when and why you should use visual aids. Then I'll take you through each visual aid, step-by-step, explaining the advantages and disadvantages of each one.

Visual Aids

Use visual aids to:

➤ Reinforce main ideas and examples.

➤ Use visual aids to give information that usually comes with a visual reference.

➤ Explain information that is difficult to visualize, such as the shape of an unfamiliar object.

➤ Introduce something your audience has never seen, such as a new invention.

➤ Explain technical or unusual terms.

➤ Help your audience compare new and previously introduced information.

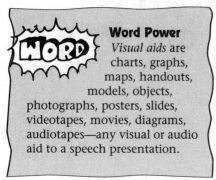

Word Power
Visual aids are charts, graphs, maps, handouts, models, objects, photographs, posters, slides, videotapes, movies, diagrams, audiotapes—any visual or audio aid to a speech presentation.

First, decide which parts of your speech you want to support with visual aids. Then consider which visual aids will most help your audience understand your ideas. Apply the following three guidelines for deciding when and how to use visual aids.

Relevance

First and most important, make sure that the visual aid is directly related to the content of your speech. No matter how attractive and beautifully designed a visual aid may be, it should be used *only* if it is relevant. Unrelated visual aids distract viewers' attention from the point you are trying to make. Inexperienced speakers often use visual aids for novelty's sake, as a crutch or distraction. You know better!

Appearance

The visual aid must be large enough to be seen by the person in the back row. If the message on the visual aid cannot be read easily by everyone, then the aid is a hindrance rather than a help.

The visual aid must also be professional looking, neat, and attractive. Keep charts, graphs, and diagrams simple and bold. I recommend a series of simple charts or graphs instead of a single complex one. By the time the audience figures out the complex diagram, your speech will be over. Listeners can process a simple visual display much more easily, which is your purpose.

However, the visual aid can't be so engaging that it distracts the audience from what you are saying. If the audience spends more time admiring your handiwork than listening to your speech, the visual aid is undercutting your purpose.

Traditionally, speakers prepared visual aids with conventional art tools such as colored pencils and markers. While these are still useful tools, computers have added a new dimension to the preparation of posters, charts, graphs, and other visual aids. Today, it's relatively simple to use computer software to create polished diagrams and charts. Color printers make it a snap to print these documents in brilliant hues. I have found that computerized clip art is another great way to prepare great looking visual aids easily and quickly.

> **Words to the Wise**
> Be sure that any computer-generated graphics are large enough to be seen by the audience. You may wish to enlarge these documents through a computer or overhead projector to be sure that everyone can see them clearly.

Nuts, Bolts, and Nitty-Gritty

Your speech is in another city. The last thing you want to pack in your overnight case is a slide projector. How can you make sure that the meeting site will have the audio-visual equipment that you need?

The easiest way is to write a letter to the hotel meeting planner or seminar planner to arrange for the equipment you need. I said "write" on purpose; this way, you can make sure that there is a written request on file. Follow this up with a telephone call to make sure that everything is in place.

But I'm a worrier. Maybe you are, too. Being a worrier is not such a bad thing in relation to public speaking, because it helps ensure that presentations go smoothly. I always call twice to double-check on all equipment I'll need. That way, I can be sure that I'll have the proper equipment, in working order, waiting for me.

What happens if you're giving your speech in a hotel that doesn't have a slide projector and you don't own one either? (How many people do?) Or say you want to show a brief video and there's no video player available? What happens if you don't have the audio-visual machines you need? Rather than dropping the visual aid from your speech, rent the machinery you need. Consider these sources:

➤ **The public library.** Very often, you can borrow audio-visual equipment free from your public library. For example, my library offers rentals on slide projectors, VCRs, and tape recorders.

➤ **Video shops.** Nearly all video shops rent video equipment at a nominal fee.

➤ **Schools and colleges.** You might be able to borrow a machine from a local school for the day. In exchange, give a brief speech for the public speaking class!

Use

Be sure that you can operate any equipment that you need. Before the speech, check to be sure that you know how to turn on the overheard projector, computer, videotape recorder, or any other equipment you plan to use. Double-check to make sure that it is working correctly. I can't tell you how many speeches I have seen marred because the speaker did not know how to operate the audio-visual aids or because the machinery was not functioning properly.

As you practice your speech, be sure to include the visual aid. Insert it exactly where it would go in your speech. If your organization is weak and you display the visual too soon or too late in the speech, the visual aid will disrupt communication rather than enhance it.

As you speak, point out each feature in the visual aid, but keep your eyes on your audience. This way, you can judge whether they understand what you're saying. In addition to making your delivery smoother and more professional, this will also help you make sure that you don't block the audience's view of the visual.

Use a pointer with graphs, charts, and diagrams. This allows you to stand well away from the display, affording your audience the clearest possible view. Display the visual aid only when it is in use. Keep it covered until you are ready to use it. Remove it when you are finished. This helps prevent audience distraction.

Get Out Those Crayons: Preparing Visual Aids

What are some of the different kinds of visual aids you can use? Which visual aid is best for your topic, audience, and purpose? And how should you prepare the charts, graphs, illustrations, and so on? Let's take a look at each visual aid, exploring how it should be prepared.

Audiotapes

Audiotapes are a superb way to present advertising slogans, short messages to focus groups, and music. They are easy to carry; even the recorder doesn't weigh much!

Blackboards

Blackboards are easy to use and easy to see. They also help keep your hands busy, which can reduce nervousness. You can use the drawing as you would a chart, map, or other completed visual aid to point out relevant and salient features.

Charts and Graphs

Charts and graphs have a number of important advantages for public speakers. First of all, if well-prepared, they show the structure of something clearly. Next, they are easy to use and easy to transport. Finally, they are inexpensive. They pack a big wallop for a little money.

There are several different types of charts that you can use. *Pie charts*, for example, show percentages by dividing a circle proportionally. Suit the type of chart to the specific kind of information that you are presenting in your speech and your audience's level of sophistication and knowledge. A general audience, for example, would expect a simple chart; an audience composed of scientists, a more complex one.

Computers

With the new software, the possibilities for computer displays seem endless. You can prepare charts, graphs, illustrations—and more. Take a tour through a computer store to see what is available in your area for your computer. Then have fun!

Diagrams

Diagrams are great because, as with some other visual aids, they can be made in advance. This makes it much easier for you to use them in your practice sessions. They are also inexpensive and easy to transport.

As with charts, there are several different types of diagrams that you can use. The diagram can be as simple as an illustration of an object or process. Or, it can be as sophisticated as a *cutaway diagram* of an object that shows its internal as well as external appearance. It can also be a *three-dimensional diagram* that shows an object completely. These are especially helpful because they allow an audience to visualize an object most fully. *Flowcharts* or *process diagrams* trace the steps in a process.

Films

Films are especially well suited for presenting a slice of real life, which makes them a great way to get an emotional appeal into a persuasive speech. They are popular and easy to use. They show action, which few other visuals can do.

You can prepare your own films or use already prepared films. Stay away from making your own films unless you are accomplished in this art; home-made films can look cheesy and spoil an otherwise polished speech presentation.

Flip Charts

Flip charts start with large pads of paper firmly mounted on an easel. To create a flip chart, you draw one stage of the process on each sheet of paper. As you deliver your speech, you flip from page 1 to page 2 to page 3, and so on. As a result, flip charts are ideally suited to showing the steps in a process.

You can prepare the entire flip chart ahead of time, as many speakers do. In fact, one of the advantages of a flip chart is that it can be prepared well ahead of time. Or, you can prepare an outline of the chart on the paper, filling in the details with a bold-colored marker as you speak.

Handouts

Handouts have a number of strong advantages. First of all, they are inexpensive and can be prepared well in advance of the speech date. Second, the audience can use them later.

Prepare handouts on a computer, if at all possible. Resist the temptation to use many computer fonts; this can make a handout difficult to read. Make the design bold and easy to read.

Maps

Maps can help you clarify the positions of countries, rivers, mountains, and other landforms and bodies of water. I recommend that most speakers mount standard maps on stiff board. This is often the easiest way to get the map you need. If you require a specialized map, you can always prepare your own maps. If you choose the latter course, use bold colors and a standard map legend.

Tell Me About It

If you point out something on a visual display, be sure that you're pointing where you want to point. Pointing to the wrong place on the display makes even the most accomplished speaker look foolish.

Models

Models can be a great way to explain the structure, function, and design of something. They are especially useful when the original is too big, too difficult, or—as in the case of a DNA molecule, for instance—simply impossible to pass around. Be sure that the model is sturdy enough to withstand handling; if not, hold it up for display instead.

Overhead Projectors

Overhead projectors are easily available and easy to use. Prepare your visual displays carefully. Use bright colors for maximum appeal, but stick to a consistent color palette. You can purchase prepared visuals to be used with an overhead projector. Look in the shop that suits your topic and audience. Good sources include scientific supply houses and school supply stores.

Photographs

Photographs can be visually stunning and provide exquisite details and descriptions. They are also relatively inexpensive to produce. Make sure that the pictures are high quality. Consider *cropping* (removing) extraneous details that would distract from your point. Your photofinisher can do this easily. Mount the picture on sturdy board to make it easier to display to an audience.

Words to the Wise

If you're planning on using a visual aid in your speech, always be ready to give your speech without it. Believe me, the number of technical and human errors possible is longer than this chapter. As a result, I advise you to be ready to carry on without any visual aids.

Posters

Posters give you a lot of bang for the buck. They're inexpensive and easy to produce. If they contain bulleted lists, include only a few main points on each. For maximum visual appeal, keep the posters simple. Sharp colors have the greatest impact, but they can be hard on the eyes.

Slides

Use only high-quality slides. If you are a skilled photographer, take the slides yourself. If you have any doubts, buy the slides you need or have someone skilled in this technique prepare the slides for you. It's worth the time and trouble: amateurish slides look tacky and can harm your presentation.

Videotapes

Videotapes provide dramatic, effective visual images and they are very easy to use. That's why they're popular with audiences and speakers alike. See my warning on films: stick with prepared videotapes unless you are a skilled with a videocamera.

Write It On, Plug It In, Turn It On: Using Visual Aids

Now that you have learned all about preparing audio and visual aids, let's turn to using these "speech enhancers" most efficiently and easily. Try the following tips:

Audiotapes

If the tape recorder runs on batteries, be sure to carry spare batteries with you. If it is to be plugged in, be sure to check ahead of time to make sure that there is an electrical outlet close to the podium. And make sure that it is functioning correctly!

Blackboards

Complete the drawing before you begin your speech or while you are speaking. If the drawing is on the board beforehand, it frees you to concentrate on your words. Drawing while you are speaking carries the advantage of immediacy, but it can be distracting and difficult to concentrate on two tasks at once.

Try not to turn your back on your audience as you write. Also, don't pull a Dan Quayle. You remember the hapless vice-president who misspelled "potato" in front of a group of school-children, right? Be sure that you can correctly spell any word that you are going to write on the chalkboard.

If your handwriting is poor, don't be afraid to print. And if your printing is that bad, have an assistant or helper write on the board for you. This also frees you up to concentrate more fully on your speech.

Tell Me About It
Use soft chalk to lessen the chance of squeaking. If possible, use a green chalkboard and yellow chalk. It's easier on the eyes than white chalk on a dark blackboard. No matter what chalk and board you use, be sure that the chalk marks are bold enough so they can be read easily, even by the people in the back rows.

Charts and Graphs

Never clutter too many statistics on a chart or graph; it will make it too difficult for the audience to follow the visual. Also, don't use more than three curves per graph. After that, the graph starts to look like an Italian dinner special, not a mathematical display. Use a bold line for your most important curve; lighter lines for less important ones. Color works especially well to differentiate lines.

In addition, use only a few type fonts and a consistent color palette to make the presentation easier to follow. This is not the time to show off all the great software your computer features!

Computers

Beware of using computer-generated art and visuals just to show that you're in the know. There's no reason to flaunt your computer skills and flashy equipment. Remember: Include the visuals only if they add something important to your speech.

Diagrams

Design and create the types of diagrams that best reinforce your topic. Sometimes the simple diagram will be most suitable; other times, a cut-away diagram, three-dimensional diagram, or flow chart will best reinforce your point.

The basic rule of thumb: keep it simple. If you're compulsive, don't worry. Bring a bold-colored marker with you. You can always add more to the diagram as you speak, if you feel that it's necessary. It rarely will be.

Films

Check all equipment before the show. Make sure the volume is properly adjusted. Be sure to watch the film before you use it in your speech.

Flip Charts

I have attended meetings on how to use a flip chart correctly, which clearly shows that speakers are concerned about using these visual aids. You don't need a meeting; just use your noggin—and my guidelines!

Flip charts work best with small groups, because they usually can't be read beyond the tenth row. Be sure that the writing is large enough to be seen clearly by all audience members. If you're right-handed, stand on the left side of the chart; if you're left-handed, stand on the right side. This will make it much easier for you to flip the pages and point out key features of the chart. Don't turn your back on the audience as you flip the pages.

> **Bet You Didn't Know**
>
> OOOOH.
>
> Here's a side benefit to using a flip chart: it's a good alternative to handouts or speaker notes. For example, if you are going to make three points in your speech, write each point on a separate sheet of the flip chart.

Handouts

Distributing handouts is a tricky business. On one hand, handouts supply a concrete example of your topic. They provide something useful that participants can take away with them. This helps them remember the key points in your presentation. On the other hand, handouts can be a distraction. Handing out papers takes up valuable time and distracts the audience. Further, people will likely read the handouts rather than listen to you speak. I recommend that you distribute any handout *after* your speech. This way, participants will have the materials to refer to later on, but still will be attentive to you during your speech.

Maps

To be effective, maps must be large enough to be easily seen. I recommend that you consider showing a zoomed-in view of a map to ensure that there's enough detail. Use them only to emphasize the points you are making in your speech.

Models

Props such as models and objects can be tricky to use. Be sure to display the object long enough for everyone to get a good look. Lift the object into the air, hold it steady for a few moments, and then move it slowly so that everyone in the audience has a chance to see it. Don't talk while people are looking at the object. This will ensure that people pay full attention to what you're saying. They also won't feel like they're missing something if they are studying the object and don't hear you.

If the object isn't fragile or valuable, pass it around *after* the speech. This way, it won't distract from what you are saying. If you are going to pass the model around, be sure to clearly specify the direction in which you want it to be handed. For example, you can say, "Please pass this from the front to the back of the auditorium." If your speech is informative, I also recommend that you supplement the object with a diagram of it. You can display the diagram on an overhead projector or slide. If you show the diagram on a handout, distribute the diagram after the speech, not during it.

Overhead Projectors

I'm a fan of the lowly overhead projector, but I also recognize that it's prone to be cranky. That's why I recommend you bring a general A-V emergency kit: spare overhead projector light bulbs, masking tape, three-pronged adapters, scissors, screwdrivers, and a small flashlight. The cost and inconvenience are minimal and are well worth it!

Photographs

Be sure the photographs are large enough to be seen clearly from all parts of the auditorium. Display the photographs on an easel for maximum impact.

Posters

Display the posters as you would a flip chart or photograph. The number-one rule: Make sure that everyone can see every part of the poster. Otherwise, it's useless.

213

Slides

Remember that slides require a darkened room. Be sure that you can adequately darken the room. Check on this *way before* your speech. Slide experts maintain that the room must be completely dark to achieve the maximum effect. Obviously, this makes it difficult—if not impossible—for people to take notes. It also moves the focus from the speaker to the slides, which is not your desired aim. I recommend that you dim the lights, but don't play East Coast blackout. It's just not necessary.

Before the speech, run through the slide show to make sure the projector works and the slides are in the proper order. Tape down the projector cord so no one trips over it. Be classy: use a screen, not the wall.

Tell Me About It

Maintain personal control of all visual aids. For instance, if you are showing a video, press the on/off switch yourself. If you're showing slides, press the control button yourself. Flip the pages of the flip chart; pass around the object you're displaying. This keeps you in control of the timing and sequence of events.

Videotapes

Be sure to check the videotape before you use it to make sure that it is in good shape. Also be sure that the television screen can be seen easily by all members of the audience—even those in the back rows.

The Least You Need to Know

➤ Use visual and audio-visual aids *only* if they enhance your speech. They are unnecessary if they don't add any new information, fail to help the audience understand your speech, or detract from your message.

➤ Suit the specific visual aid to your audience, purpose, and message.

➤ Prepare and use audio-visual aids carefully.

Rehearsing the Speech

"I don't know why you bother to rehearse," a friend once said to me. "You'll give a great speech. After all, you've certainly done it enough." I know my friend meant well, but she gave me bad advice. Rehearsing is crucial to the success of your speech delivery—no matter how many speeches you've delivered.

In this chapter, I'll explain the reasons why rehearsal is so crucial to a smooth, successful public speaking event.

In addition, you'll learn my step-by-step method for making the most of your rehearsal time. Finally, I'll discuss what you'll be rehearsing from—index cards or an actual manuscript.

Why Rehearse?

Just as actors rehearse a play, so public speakers listen to themselves deliver their speeches. Practice might not make you perfect, but it will definitely help make you a more confident and competent speaker.

My analogy was chosen deliberately: in many ways, delivering a speech is like acting. In both cases, you are giving a performance. And repeated practice is the best way to discover which parts of your speech work and which ones don't. It's also the best way to maximize your chances for success.

How to Rehearse

Knowing your speech is not enough; you also have to know how you are going to deliver it. Your delivery includes when you pause and gesture. You have to know which words get a stress and which ones don't. Follow these five steps to get the most out of your public speaking rehearsal time:

1. **Read the speech aloud.** Read the speech aloud at your normal speaking rate. Then read the speech again, this time tape-recording it. Record the time it took and see how close you are to your allotted time. Are you running short? Long?

   Make any necessary adjustments by adding or subtracting text. Don't speed up your speaking pace. Speaking faster won't fix the time problem. In fact, it will probably make it worse because the audience may not be able to understand and follow you if you speak more quickly.

   Then play the recording back and listen closely. Where do you need to pause for emphasis? Which words were hard to pronounce? Were there any words that were hard for your audience to understand? Which sentences were too long to say in one breath? Take careful notes to assess your performance.

Tell Me About It

If your assessment shows that you are speaking too softly, try putting the tape recorder across the room while you read your speech. This will force you to speak louder.

Modern technology allows for even greater refinements of this technique. If possible, videotape your rehearsal. Have you ever seen yourself on television? That fish eye lens is a merciless critic! Television ruthlessly reveals every awkward phrasing, wrong breath, stiff gesture, unnecessary sentence, and inadvertent blooper. You may be embarrassed watching yourself on tape, but you will learn a great deal about your performance. It's the quickest way I know to get rock-solid improvement.

2. **Practice the speech in front of a mirror.** Stand in front of a mirror and rehearse your speech. Focus on correcting the parts that you noticed need work. Make sure that you are putting the stress on the right words and sentences. Make sure that your gestures serve to emphasize your message. See if you are comfortable with what you see.

What happens if you make a mistake while you're rehearsing? What would you do if you made a mistake in front of an audience? Yes—you'd just keep right on going. That's how you should rehearse. Don't allow yourself to go back and reread. While you practice, try to mimic the actual public speaking conditions as closely as possible.

By this time, you should have memorized the first twenty seconds and last twenty seconds of your speech. These are the times when eye contact is most important. Having the opening and closing words of your speech down cold allows you to concentrate on other matters such as settling your nerves, making eye contact, and using effective body language.

3. **Deliver the speech for a single person. Choose a friend or family member to listen to your speech.** The success of this depends largely on the friend and your relationship. You need someone who can be honest but not cruel; forthright but not nasty. Loyal spouses and lovestricken friends are rarely good choices because they are too practical or besotted; instead, go for someone who can realistically assess your performance.

Try to match this rehearsal as closely as possible to the actual performance. Set up a stage, lectern, and chairs. Be especially sure to use all your visual aids, too. At this point, try to enjoy yourself—even just a little. Smile. Let your eyes twinkle a touch. If you look like you're having a good time, you may fool yourself into actually enjoying the experience.

> **Words to the Wise**
> Be sure that you rehearse the entire speech each time. If you don't, specific parts of the speech will be smooth; others, unprepared. For example, if you rehearse only the beginning, your body and conclusion will be weak. Or if you concentrate on the introduction and conclusion, the body just won't be as strong. Rehearse it all—every time!

4. **Rehearse the speech for a small group.** Gather together a group of buddies, family, neighbors, or coworkers. If at all possible, try to get the types of people you will actually be addressing. They will be more

apt to be interested in your subject as well as your delivery. Once again, simulate the actual speaking conditions with a lectern, table, and chairs.

Use your audience; after all, you went to so much trouble to get them there. Pay careful attention to how they react to you. There's a reason why taped television shows are recorded in front of a "live studio audience." The performers need the interaction with their viewers; the dead eye of the television monitor just won't cut the mustard. Last year, I went to a taping of the David Letterman show and saw first-hand how important the audience was to Letterman's pacing, rhythm, voice, gestures, and overall delivery. You're going to be a pro, so use the tricks that the pros do!

5. **Practice at the site.** This is the hardest part of your rehearsal because it is not always easy to get to the site ahead of time. If at all possible, visit the room. Stand at the lectern and rehearse your speech. You'll be astonished at how much more relaxed you will feel if you have practiced at the actual speaking site.

If this just isn't possible, be sure to arrive at the site a little early. Get the lay of the land. Find out where the restroom is located; check all the equipment you will need for audio-visual aids. Just scoping out the place will help improve your actual performance.

Rehearsing with Others

So far, I've been assuming that you're a solo act. As you have learned from previous chapters, this is not always the case. What should you do if you are just part of the evening's entertainment? What about being part of a panel, for example?

Tell Me About It
If you are having a difficult time getting team or panel members to rehearse together, show them the audio- or videotapes you made of your own rehearsals. After they see the progress you've made, they will be more likely to set aside some time for a group rehearsal.

The same rules that I explained earlier in this chapter still apply—except all the speakers should rehearse together. I can't emphasize that "together" strongly enough. To ensure a smooth team effort, everyone has to see what everyone else is going to say—and how. If you're the chair of the event or the group organizer, you are very likely in a position to insist that everyone gather for one or more practice sessions. If you're not the boss, use all the persuasive techniques you learned in Chapters 7 and 18 to convince your fellow speakers to rehearse en masse.

Group rehearsals allow you and all the other participants to see where each presentation should be cut or revised. For instance, one speaker may have a joke or story that strikes the other speakers as pointless or in bad taste. As gently as possible, the group should suggest alternatives. Group rehearsal has another important benefit: it allows each individual member even more quality feedback because the critics have a very real stake in the outcome.

Preparing Index Cards or a Speech Manuscript

What will you be rehearsing or delivering your speech *from*? You have two choices: index cards or an actual manuscript. The following sections talk about each in turn.

Note Cards

Good note cards meet these three requirements:

1. They contain enough material to help you remember the important points in your speech.

2. They are easy to use.

3. They do not distract the audience.

Many speakers write their notes on the smallest size index cards: 3-by-5-inch index cards. These cards have the advantage of being small enough to fit into your hand or pocket. This way, you can carry them to the podium without audience members being aware that you will be speaking from notes.

Other speakers prefer larger cards, 4-by-6-inch or 5-by-7-inch cards. These larger cards are easier to use if you have a lot of statistics to remember, if your handwriting is large, or if your vision is weak.

Unfortunately, you can't conceal these cards in your hand or pocket. But don't make secrecy your prime consideration when deciding on which size cards to use. Instead, select the cards that best serve your purpose.

Regardless of the size cards you use, be sure to fasten them securely with a rubber band or paper clip so they cannot scatter if they fall on the floor (God forbid!).

What should you write on your note cards? Include key phrases to remind you of the major sections of your speech. Also write down any statistics or quotations.

Read the following passage from a speech about the history of comic books. Then see how the speaker made notes about this passage on an index card:

> Meanwhile, over at Atlas (formerly Timely) Comics, the publisher, Martin Goodman, saw the success of his rivals and suggested to his young editor that they should start publishing super-hero comics as well. The editor, a long-time writer of comics for Timely/Atlas named Stan Lee, took a shot and created the *Fantastic Four*, *Spider-Man*, the *Incredible Hulk*, and *X-Men*.

Atlas (Timely) Comics
Martin Goodman (publisher) suggests they publish super-hero comics.
Stan Lee (editor) created the *Fantastic Four*, *Spider-Man*, *Incredible Hulk*, *X-Men*.

Here's the speaker's card for the excerpt from the comics speech.

How many cards should you use? The answer depends on your speech and your comfort level. If you are giving a simple speech and know the material well, a few cards might be enough. But if you are delivering a long speech with a lot of detail, you might have to use at least ten cards. But don't use too many note cards. They will distract you and the audience.

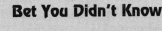

Bet You Didn't Know

Many experienced speakers shun note cards because they have to be handwritten. You can't just push a button and have them come tumbling out of your printer. Besides, the stack of cards makes an unsightly nasty lump in the smooth line of an Armani suit!

Full Text

How do you know when to write out the full speech? Consider these points:

➤ It is an important occasion.

➤ Every word of the speech counts.

➤ Time is strictly limited.

➤ Reporters might be quoting the speech.

➤ You have not had much public speaking experience.

➤ You are very nervous.

If at least four items in the preceding list apply, then writing out the full text is for you.

Follow these steps as you prepare your speech manuscript:

➤ Type or print on only one side of the paper.

➤ Use a large font, at least 12- to 14-point.

➤ Use both uppercase and lowercase letters as you normally would. Do not use all capital letters.

➤ Double- or triple-space the text.

➤ Never hyphenate words at the end of lines. Better: leave the line short.

➤ End each page with a complete sentence.

➤ Underline any words or phrases you want to stress.

➤ Number the pages clearly, preferably on the top-right corner.

Tell Me About It
Always prepare an extra copy of your speech. Keep it in a separate place. That way, even if you lose one copy, the show can still go on.

➤ Type on only the top two-thirds of the page. Leave the rest of the page blank. This will prevent you from bending your face all the way to the bottom of the page, muffling your voice.

➤ Leave margins of at least two inches on all four sides of the page.

➤ Never staple the pages of your speech together. Fasten them with a paper clip. That way, you can remove the clip when you're ready to speak.

➤ Place the speech in a folder to keep it clean and organized.

The Least You Need to Know

➤ Rehearsing your speech is a crucial step in a successful delivery.

➤ Consider tape-recording or videotaping your speech as you rehearse. Study the tape for ways to improve your performance.

➤ Prepare and read from index cards or the full text, depending on your audience and needs.

Chapter 23

Gilding the Lily: Dress for Success and Voice

In This Chapter

➤ Learn how appearance can affect performance

➤ Discover everything you always wanted to know about voice but were too shy to ask!

➤ Master the speaking style that's right for you

Demosthenes, the Athenian public speaker, is rumored to have practiced clear speaking by filling his mouth with pebbles. Fortunately, you don't have to resort to such extremes to achieve a clear speaking voice. I've got a trunkful of tastier techniques!

In this chapter, you will discover the subtle importance of dress and voice to a successful speech. You will learn how to master the secrets of presentation that can maximize your chances for success. You'll find out how an effective voice enables a speaker to make what he or she says more interesting and meaningful.

First, I'll teach you how dressing for success can help improve your overall presentation. Then, I'll explore the mechanics of voice. Let's take a look at your wardrobe first.

Dressed for Success

Shakespeare was right: clothes do make the man—and the woman. Inappropriate attire can muff your chances to win the race before you're even out of the starting gate. Put enough time into planning your clothing so that it becomes a non-issue. Follow these guidelines:

➤ **Go standard: suits or their equivalent.** What kind of suit should you wear? If you've got good taste and a good eye for color (confirmed by people who are not direct blood relatives or owe you money), follow your instincts. If fashion is not your strong point, read John Molloy's *Dress for Success* (men's clothes) and *The Women's Dress for Success Book*. These books are based on research about how people in business perceive specific clothing styles.

Perhaps the best advice in the books is to visit expensive stores and note the details on the clothing—the exact shade of blue in a suit, the width of the lapels, the number of buttons on the sleeves—and then go to stores in your price range and buy the suit that has details found in more expensive garments.

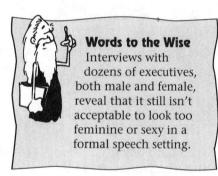

Words to the Wise
Interviews with dozens of executives, both male and female, reveal that it still isn't acceptable to look too feminine or sexy in a formal speech setting.

Traditionally, women were advised to wear suits with skirts and shoes with heels no more than two inches high. But the "dress down" explosion has blasted holes through all areas of endeavor, and less formal attire is now acceptable in some situations. Some women now wear pants suits, for example, rather than jackets and skirts. My advice? Stick to the basics. When in doubt, err on the side of conformity. In traveling around the country, I've found that most people are still most comfortable with traditionally dressed speakers.

➤ **Choose comfortable shoes.** You will be on your feet delivering your speech and fielding questions.

➤ **Take care of the details.** Check your heels to make sure that they aren't worn down. Make sure that your shoes are shined. Have your hair cut or styled conservatively; no mousse abuse. Jewelry and makeup should be understated, unless you're addressing the annual Mary Kay convention. Personal hygiene must be impeccable. Avoid cologne and perfumed aftershave lotions.

Voice

I was shocked the first time I ever heard my voice on a tape recorder. "Do I sound like that?" I wondered. After years of teaching, I've discovered that nearly everyone is discomfited when they hear their voice for the first time. "That can't possibly be me?" they gasp. "I thought my voice was deeper, lower (louder, richer, . . .)," they mutter. Doubts about your voice can make even the most self-confident speaker a little squeamish.

Some of our most noted speakers and performers have less-than-thundering voices: think of Dustin Hoffman's whine, Barbara Walter's "r" impediment, Henry Kissinger's accent, Howard Cosell's New York talk. With extensive training, most people could learn to speak with the richness of the late Sir Laurence Olivier or current Broadway superstar Patrick Stewart. But we don't have the time for years of speech training. Let me take a few minutes to help you smooth out some rough spots in your voice so you can make the best possible impression with your speech.

How can you acquire a more effective voice? As with speech delivery, one of the secrets is practice. But once again, the wrong kind of practice can do more harm than good because doing the same thing wrong over and over again just makes you better at making that mistake. To make your practice worthwhile, you should first learn something about the mechanics of voice.

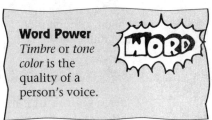

Word Power
Timbre or *tone color* is the quality of a person's voice.

Voice Quality

What people first notice about your voice is its quality. Is it harsh? Nasal? Thin? Resonant? Although a pleasing vocal quality is basic to effective communication, it does not in itself create good speech, as I said earlier. If you are to communicate your ideas and feelings to other people, your voice must meet two requirements:

➤ It must be easily understandable.

➤ It must be flexible in pitch, force, and rate.

You should try to change your voice quality if it bothers *you*. If your voice shatters your self-esteem and makes you extremely unwilling to speak in public, some time with a good speech therapist is a good idea. But I don't recommend that you learn to talk like a television newscaster otherwise. Remember: communicating your ideas is what matters.

Volume

Probably the single most important factor in making your speech understandable is the volume at which you speak.

The farther away your listener is, the louder you must talk to be heard clearly. You make these loudness adjustments without thinking when you project your voice across wide distances, as when you yell down the block to a friend.

What speakers often forget, however, is that the same principle applies over short distances. Your own voice will always seem louder to you than to your listeners because your own ears are closer to your mouth than your listeners' ears are. Beginning speakers also often forget the effect of background noise on their ability to be heard.

Word Power

The *volume* is the loudness level at which you speak related to the distance between you and the listener and the amount of noise that surrounds the listener.

Normally, your lungs take about 18 breaths a minute, providing the amount of air you normally need to breathe and speak. Protected by your ribcage, the lungs function as a bellows, pushing air in and out. At the base of your lungs is your *diaphragm*, a powerful band of muscle. You can use this knowledge to get more volume and voice projection.

Place your right hand flat on your diaphragm, just below your ribs. Without lifting your shoulders, take a deep breath. Feel your diaphragm expanding? Now hold your breath for a second and then shout, "Yes!" while exhaling. Notice how loud your voice is—without strain.

Fill your lungs with air again by expanding your diaphragm. Let the air out in little puffs, as though you were blowing out a candle. Practice these two exercises to help increase your volume without straining your throat.

How can you determine the proper strength of voice to use to compensate for the distance and background noise? There are mechanical devices that work quite well, but you've got enough stuff to carry around as it is. Instead, judge your volume by the reactions of your listeners. As you speak, look to the people in the back row. See if they appear to be hearing you clearly. If you have any doubts, *ask* them.

Pump Up the Volume: Using a Microphone

A microphone or public address system can help you communicate much more easily with a large audience. Before you use a microphone, however, you have to be prepared. Follow these guidelines:

➤ Remember that most microphone or amplification systems do not re-produce sound with high fidelity. As a result, you must speak more slowly and clearly than usual into a microphone in order to be under-stood.

➤ You should also know that a microphone system has been adjusted for a specific volume. Therefore, don't vary your volume as much as you might if you were not using a microphone. Any louder sound will very likely blast your audience; any softer sound won't be heard.

➤ Just as a microphone will amplify your voice, so it will amplify any other sounds you make: shuffling papers, coughing, scratching, and so on. Be especially careful about muttering under your breath. The audi-ence will hear that, too!

➤ The microphone is your friend. So don't tap it, whack it, blow into it, or in any other way abuse it.

➤ Be sure to test the microphone before the audience has arrived. Ask a friend or associate to stand or sit in the back of the room and tell you if the level of your voice is appropriate and if you can be heard clearly.

➤ Experiment until you find the best possible distance from your mouth to the microphone. Once you locate the distance that's best, stay there. If you turn your head away from the microphone, you will be inaudible.

➤ If you are using a "body mike," be aware of where it is attached to your clothing. Also keep in mind where the cord and battery pack are lo-cated. This will help prevent you from disconnecting the microphone or pulling on the cord.

Clarity and Articulation

Is each of your words clear? Can everything you're saying be understood? Play back those rehearsal tapes again. Look carefully at problem places. Here are some examples:

➤ **Contractions.** Do you slur "wouldn't" as "wu'nt," "could've" as "cudda," and "should've" as "shudda"? If this is a persistent problem, drop the contractions completely and say both words.

➤ **Reversed sounds.** Do you switch sounds, such as "perscription" for "prescription"? If so, take the time to practice any tricky words now so you have them letter-perfect for the speech.

➤ **Omitted letters.** Many careless speakers leave out letters, such as the "t" sound in "lists." This makes it hard for listeners to understand what you're saying. Go over any tricky words slowly and carefully.

➤ **Added letters.** Some speakers add letters to words, such as adding a "t" to "across" to make "acrost." Many of these problems are regional. Think about the language patterns in your region. Do many people add extra letters to words? If so, spend extra time combing your speech for these annoying errors.

Rate

How fast do you speak? Find out by timing yourself. Mark the beginning of a passage and read aloud for one minute. Stop and count the number of words you said. Or tape-record yourself speaking at a normal rate for one minute. Then play back the tape and count the number of words. You should be speaking at about 150 words per minute.

However, this rate is not uniform like the tick-tock of a clock. In normal speech, the rate corresponds to the thought the speaker is transmitting. Speakers in command of their material vary the rate of their delivery to reflect the content of their speech. These speakers present main ideas and difficult points at a slower pace than they summarize an argument or tell a joke. Follow these rules of thumb:

Idea	Rate of Speech
Complex	More slowly
Serious	More slowly
Humorous	More quickly
Exciting	More quickly

Remember: Public speaking isn't a competitive sport. The goal is communication, not amount.

Pitch and Inflection

Everyone has a pitch at which their voice is most comfortable. Talk in your normal pitch range. Otherwise, you might seriously strain your voice. But few things improve the overall impact of your presentation as much as a varied pitch. Beginning speakers rarely take full advantage of their full pitch and inflection; instead, they tend to hit one level and stay there.

Speech that is easily understood can still be dull. More seriously, it may fail to communicate the speaker's thoughts. This often happens when the speaker's voice is not flexible enough to express subtle shades of meaning upon which true communication often depends.

English is a multipurpose language: often, the same expressions and words can serve double-duty. This can make our Mother Tongue a killer for non-native speakers to learn, but it also gives it an unparalleled richness. Let me show you what I mean with a simple little word, *Oh!* We have about ten different ways to say it. Try it yourself. Vary your pitch and inflection to say *Oh!* to mean each of the following expressions:

➤ Now I understand.

➤ I can't wait.

➤ I'm disappointed.

➤ You expect me to believe that?

➤ That's great!

➤ That's shrewd, but devious.

➤ Look out!

➤ That hurts!

➤ How disgusting!

➤ Poor little thing.

Try the following exercise to see the powerful effect of pitch and inflection. Repeat each sentence, changing the pitch and inflection of the boldfaced word to correspond to the prompt.

> whisper...
>
> **Tell Me About It**
> Experienced public speakers mark key places in their text to help them make sure they pronounce each word correctly, emphasize key points, and slow down for emphasis. There's no magic code for marking; each speaker devises a code that suits his or her own speaking style. Create a simple code (the key word here is *simple*) that you can use to mark problem places in your script.

Sentence	Prompt
Did the company lose the new Campbell job?	It **didn't**!
Did the company lose the new Campbell job?	Or did the **rep**?
Did the company lose the new Campbell job?	Or just **delay** it?
Did the company lose the new Campbell job?	Or the **old** one?
Did the company lose the new Campbell job?	Or **another** one?
Did the company lose the new Campbell job?	Or the **contract**?

Pace and Rhythm

Pauses serve to punctuate thought. Just as punctuation such as commas and periods separate ideas in written communication, so pauses of varying lengths separate spoken words into meaningful units. Using pauses in a careless manner confuses the reader and seriously undermines your message.

Make sure that you pause between units of thought, not in the middle of them. In addition, remember that written and spoken speech are different. Not every comma calls for a pause—nor does the absence of punctuation mean that you don't have to pause.

You can also use pauses for emphasis. For example, if you pause after an important statement, you are telegraphing your audience: This is a key idea; pay close attention. In some cases, a dramatic pause can convey your meaning more effectively than words. Remember that a pause is rarely as long to an audience as it seems to the speaker. The ability to pause shows you are in control of the situation.

Bet You Didn't Know

OOOOH.

Many speakers are afraid to pause. Sometimes they think a pause will make them forget what they want to say; other times, they fear that pausing will make everyone look at them (which is what they should want, in any event). So instead of pausing, they ramble or fill the air with dead words, a string of "er-uh" sounds. Don't be afraid to pause; I have never heard of anyone ever being attacked by a pause.

Fillers

Go back to the tape recordings you made of your practice sessions. Play them back and listen to yourself carefully. Do you ruin the flow of your thoughts with annoying fillers like "uh," "ah," and "like"? If so, drop them now. They serve only to interrupt your thought and put off your audience.

Since these annoying fillers are unconscious, you will have to work on getting rid of them. As you practice, make new tape recordings. Listen to each succeeding tape and see how many "fillers" you have been able to eliminate. Keep working on it until they are all gone!

The Least You Need to Know

➤ Audiences form powerful negative and positive images of speakers based on their appearance. Dress for success.

➤ You can acquire a more effective voice through practice, but be sure to practice correctly so you don't reinforce bad habits.

➤ Speakers without a honeyed voice can make just as convincing a mark through the power of their volume, pitch, inflection, and pacing.

Part 6
The Moment of Truth

Five No-Fail Ways to Give a Terrible Speech: A Recipe for Disaster

1. **Don't prepare.** *Hey, we're all stressed for time. How can everyone expect you to find the time to write a speech? Besides, it's only a five-minute speech. You can wing that with no sweat.*

2. **Talk to your concerns.** *Drop the topic: you know what's really important. Talk about things that concern you and no one else. After all, you have the stage, so use it.*

3. **Strive to impress.** *Use a lot of big words and difficult references. That will blow everyone out of the water. They'll think you're really smart, especially if they can't understand a word you're saying.*

4. **Avoid Facts.** *Hey, who cares what the facts are? Anyway, facts are hard to find. Opinions are much better than facts any old day.*

5. **Talk as long as you want.** *Make your point, then make it a few more times. You've got that stage, so don't let it go! Try your hardest to talk until the last person's head has dropped into the mashed potatoes.*

Chapter 24

Delivering the Speech

In This Chapter

➤ Discover when your speech *really* begins

➤ Learn all about body language and how to harness it to improve your speeches

➤ Find out how to make the audience yours—and how to keep them right in the palm of your hand

The power of your speech depends both on what you say and how you say it. A speech without any real substance cannot communicate anything meaningful; but without an effective delivery, even the most thoughtfully written speech cannot be successful. Your delivery can make or break your speech.

Effective delivery depends on two main factors: your physical behavior at the lectern and your voice. People in an audience read meaning into your facial expressions, your walk, and your talk. Intentional as well as unintentional gestures assume great meaning on the speaker's platform. Listeners are quick to perceive any discrepancy between what you say and how you act.

In the previous chapter, I discussed the importance of dress and voice. Here, I'll teach you the importance of posture and mannerisms to a successful speech. You will learn how to master the secrets of presentation that can maximize your chances for success.

Preparing to Speak

When does your speech actually begin? Pick one of these answers:

➤ When you enter the room.

➤ When you approach the podium.

➤ When you start speaking.

Answer: Your speech begins when you enter the room.

Your audience will form an opinion of you the minute they see you. It's no lie: first impressions *do* count. Use this checklist to make a great start:

1. Before the speech:

   ➤ Is my hair combed?

   ➤ Are my teeth clean?

   ➤ Are my clothes straight?

   ➤ Do I look in command?

2. During the speech:

   ➤ Walk to the front of the room.

   ➤ Place your notes on the podium.

   ➤ Stand straight.

   ➤ Place your weight evenly on both feet. This not only helps you feel in control but also helps prevent you from rocking back and forth on your heels.

   ➤ Pause for a moment before beginning. Look at your audience.

I talk about what to do *after* your speech a little later in this lesson.

Attitude

Your attitude makes a tremendous difference in the success of your speech. Show your enthusiasm from the very start. Let your audience know that you are pleased to have the chance to address them. True vivacity and excitement make your speech fresh and effective—even if you have given the same address before. Make each time you speak seem like the first time. Along with enthusiasm comes audience rapport.

Establish a link with the audience as soon as possible. Your audience has already formed an opinion about you from your appearance and the host's introduction, but you need to strike a chord with the audience that immediately sets up a rapport. For example, President Kennedy once formed a bond with the French people by announcing, "I'm the gentleman who accompanied Mrs. Kennedy to Paris." I discussed ways to do this in Chapters 5 through 9. Now is the time to make sure that you do it.

Eye-to-Eye: Where to Look

From the very beginning of the speech and throughout it, you must make the people in the audience feel that you are speaking to each one of them individually. Nothing helps you establish contact with the audience as well as eye contact.

As I mentioned previously, memorize the first three sentences and last three sentences of your speech. This will let you look straight into your audience's eyes as you deliver your opening and closing.

Remember: Every public speaking event is a performance, and the most convincing performances acknowledge the audience. Look people in the eyes. Even in a large audience, if the speaker looks at people's feet instead of their faces, it registers with the rest of the audience. Each person looking at you deserves a look back. Let your eyes show that you know the audience is out there and that you care. What happens if someone is scowling at you? Don't let their frown throw you. After all, it might just be a look of intense concentration.

To achieve successful audience contact, however, you can't just look at your audience: your look must convey the feeling that you are trying to *communicate* with them. Concentrate intensively on each person you see. Make it plain to each person that you really want him or her to understand your message. Make each person feel that you are delivering the message for him or her alone.

Tell Me About It
How long should you focus on each person? One whole sentence or one whole thought per individual audience member is about right.

Body Language

Your posture helps you take charge of the situation and assert your confidence. Effective body language stresses and clarifies ideas. It also helps hold the listener's attention. People listen closely to speakers who use gestures to reinforce their words.

Move your head, shoulders, arms, and hands in ways that add to your ideas. Stand, sit, and move proudly. Let your body language convey your command of the situation. One of my favorite techniques is to rise to my full height and then settle back comfortably. I position my leg legs slightly apart for stability and power. I tilt my head back just a little. This helps my voice project and conveys the attitude of ease and assurance.

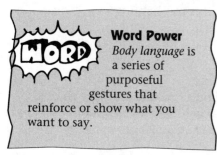

Word Power
Body language is a series of purposeful gestures that reinforce or show what you want to say.

Here are the six traditional speech gestures I recommend you use to reinforce your point and to connect with your audience. No two people make the same gestures in exactly the same way, so use the following information as guidelines, not rules.

1. **Giving and Taking.** Place your hand out with the palm turned upward to propose a new idea or ask for something. This gesture means "This idea deserves your special attention" or "I appeal to you to help me with this." This is the most widely used gesture because it is forceful without being as blunt as the pointed finger (#3).

2. **Fist.** A raised fist shows strong feelings such as anger or determination. It is an incendiary motion, so use it with care.

3. **Pointing.** Point your index finger to indicate position, to call attention to an object or idea, to show direction, or to make an accusation.

4. **Rejecting.** Show that you discard an idea by giving a sweeping gesture with your hand, palm downward. It would be used with a statement such as, "That idea simply cannot be considered."

5. **Dividing.** When you wish to show that you are separating ideas into different parts, hold your palms in a vertical position and move your hands from side to side. This cutting and separating gesture parts ideas and allows new ones to form.

6. **Warning.** You can place your hand straight out like a stop sign—palm out, heel of the hand down—to caution listeners. This gesture can also be used to calm an audience and prepare listeners to accept another idea.

But don't fake it. Don't assume gestures and mannerisms that are alien to your personality. It will show, believe me.

Qualities of Successful Body Language

As I stressed earlier, everyone varies the standard body gestures slightly, adapting them to individual speaking styles. Nonetheless, all successful body language has three qualities in common. Effective gestures are:

➤ **Relaxed.** When you are under tension, your body cannot relax. Your body language will reflect this. It will be tense, jerky, and uneven. To avoid being stiff and unnatural in front of an audience, relax before you begin your presentation. See Chapter 25, "Ways to Overcome Stage Fright," for specific suggestions.

➤ **Definite.** Effective gestures are strong and accurate. The audience should be able to read exactly what you mean. Vary the force and nature of your movements to suit your speech, but make every single movement count.

➤ **Appropriate.** The gesture must fall exactly where you want it, or it will be meaningless or even worse, it will undermine your point. Practice making the right gestures until they become a natural part of your speech presentation. Badly timed and inappropriate body language is often a result of nervousness and inadequate planning.

Dealing with Problems

An important aspect of staying in charge is dealing with problems without becoming rattled. Few speeches ever go completely as planned, no matter how meticulous your presentation. Audiences are sympathetic and receptive to speakers who admit problems as they happen and who keeps on truckin'.

Because you will know your speech thoroughly, you'll have enough time to anticipate problems: rumbling subway trains, faulty video equipment, noisy latecomers, loud waiters, burned-out slide projector bulbs. This will increase your chances of delivering a successful speech.

Here's how to handle some of the problems that arise most often during public speaking situations:

➤ Problem: The speaker before you preempts half your material.

Solution: Don't repeat the material. Instead, shorten your speech. Refer to the previous speech. Say, "As so-and-so has just pointed out . . ."

➤ Problem: The speaker before you takes up too much time. As a result, your speaking time is cut short.

Solution: Go straight to your conclusion. "Tell 'em what you told 'em."

➤ Problem: Someone asks you a question that you can't answer.

Solution: Honestly admit that you don't know the answer. Tell the individual that you'll get the answer and get back to him or her. Then do.

Reading from Full Text and Index Cards

Words to the Wise

To memorize or not to memorize? In general, I don't advise beginners to memorize their speeches because I think it creates too much pressure. Professional speakers who repeatedly deliver the same speech often memorize it, yet with each delivery they adjust the speech to suit the occasion and audience. Only a very skillful speaker can do this. So unless you are a regular on the rubber chicken circuit, avoid memorizing the entire speech.

As much as possible, you should sound like you are saying your speech, not reading it. Strive for a natural delivery by using the techniques I have already discussed. You don't have to jump right into the speech. When you arrive on-stage, it's perfectly all right—even desirable—to give the audience a few seconds to look you over while you get your bearings. Adjust the microphone, place your papers on the lectern, look around the room, smile, and take a deep breath.

Place your manuscript or cards near the top of the lectern. If you are holding your material, keep it near eye level. This shortens the distance between the words and your eye and makes it easier for you to maintain eye contact with the audience as you speak.

Don't flip the pages or lift them. Instead, smoothly slide one page or card under the next as you work your way through your speech. That's why you use a paper clip rather than staple your pages together.

Responding to Questions

The question-and-answer period is a very important part of every speech. You cannot be sure that you're getting your message across to your audience unless you get feedback from them.

Unless all questions are submitted in advance, question-and-answer sessions can also call for impromptu answers. Be sure to arrange beforehand with your hosts about whether time should be set aside for questions and answers and if so, how much time.

If questions are to be allowed, decide whether you want spoken or written queries. With a small audience, questions from the floor are relatively easy to deal with; with a large audience, questions from the floor can become very difficult to hear and to answer.

If you are answering spoken questions from a large audience, you may wish to repeat each question to make sure that everyone can hear it. But rather than simply *repeating* the questions, try *reworking* them. Deliberately revise the wording to make the question easier to answer. Keep the rewording close enough to the original to be on the topic, but remember: you're under no obligation to respond to any questions that embarrass you, your hosts, or your company.

Follow these guidelines when answering questions:

1. Be sure you understand a question before you attempt to answer it. If you aren't sure what the question means, ask for a clarification.

2. Unless you are speaking to a very small group, repeat each question before answering it.

3. If you are asked several questions at once, answer them one at a time. If your first answer is very long, ask your listener to repeat his or her other questions.

4. Answer directly.

5. If you don't know the answer to a question, don't fake it.

Embarrassing, biased, irrelevant, or otherwise inappropriate questions may be thrown at you. Someone may ask you about your personal life, for example, or broach a subject the organization you work for does not wish to discuss.

Be courteous. Never—under any circumstances—become defensive or nasty. Audiences appreciate good manners. If you stay cool, the audience will automatically reject the person who is making trouble for you and be on your side.

Being polite doesn't mean you have to be a chump, however. If the questioner is out of line, you can cut him or her off. You can always politely refuse to answer and deflect the question back to an appropriate aspect of the discussion.

Answering Trick Questions

Because it's very difficult to decipher the true motive underlying a question, I recommend that you answer every question at face value and treat it as a true request for additional information. Even if the question sounds negative, the questioner may just be expressing doubt or anxiety. The question may be the person's way of asking for reassurance. Deal with people politely and tactfully.

Stay Away from Humor

Resist the temptation to be witty or clever when you are answering questions. Audiences will think that you are not taking the matter seriously, and they will identify and sympathize with the courageous soul who asked the question that you answered flippantly. You'll be left holding the bag.

Remember: You're in Control

The better your speech and the more direction you give the audience concerning questions, the more control you retain. Start by limiting the questions you will take: "I will answer questions that deal with the subject I have explained." Don't give a set time for questions—that way you can stay flexible. If you really run into trouble, you can say, "I'm sorry; we seem to be running out of time."

It Ain't Over 'Til It's Over: Making a Graceful Exit

When you finish speaking, don't rush off; you're not done yet. Your speech isn't really finished. Give the audience a few minutes to absorb what you've said. Stay in front of the podium for a few seconds and look directly at the audience. Follow these steps:

1. Gather your notes and walk away from the podium.

2. Walk with confidence; you're still in charge.

3. Take your seat.

4. Don't start talking to the people next to you; many people in the audience will still be looking at you.

5. Look attentive and confident.

The Least You Need to Know

➤ Appropriate gestures and body language are every bit as important as the text of your speech.

➤ Your actual speech has three stages: before, after, and during. Each is equally important to the success of your overall presentation.

➤ Follow specific techniques for answering questions.

➤ Remember: You're in command.

Chapter 25

Ways to Overcome Stage Fright

In This Chapter

➤ Find out if you suffer from stage fright

➤ Discover ways to overcome performance fear

➤ Harness your fears and make them work for you

Actually, "stage fright" is the wrong name for this condition: for most people, the fear of performing begins way before they hit the stage and start the actual speech. For many public speakers, "stage fright" actually starts when they receive the invitation to speak. Fortunately, it usually recedes during the actual performance, which shows the effect of anticipation on the actual event.

In this chapter, you'll discover that fear is nothing to be frightened about. You'll learn that fear is a normal and natural emotion that can even become an asset to your public speaking events. I'll teach you sure-fire ways to master stage fright. I refuse to say that you have nothing to fear but fear itself—but it's true!

Armchair Diagnosis: Symptoms of Stage Fright

Take the Stage Fright Quiz to see how badly you suffer from stage fright. Put a check next to each symptom that applies to you when you give a speech.

Stage Fright Quiz

❑   Your stomach churns.

❑   Your palms sweat.

❑   Your forehead is beaded with perspiration.

❑   Your heart is pounding.

❑   Your mouth is dry.

❑   Your hands shake.

❑   Your legs feel wobbly.

❑   Your knees are giving way.

❑   You feel sick.

❑   You wish you were dead.

How bad is your case of stage fright? Let's find out!

If you took the Stage Fright Quiz and said "yes" for . . .

8–10 answers	How about some Prozac and a polo mallet to the side of the head?
5–7 answers	Take two aspirins and read this chapter.
1–4 answers	This isn't going to hurt a bit.

The bad news? Nervousness affects almost every speaker or performer, even the most experienced. Famous actress Helen Hayes never lost her fear of performing; comedian Red Skelton was always a complete wreck before he went on stage. Dean Martin was famous for his stage fright. Barbra Streisand, too. The list is endless.

The good news? You can learn to control your nervousness so that it actually helps you improve your performance. Your reflexes are sharpened by the nerve impulses generated by stage fright. It's working for you. Let me teach you how to channel the adrenaline pouring into your blood.

Why You're Afraid

I've already established that *all* public speakers are nervous. Why? Take a look at some of the reasons people have stage fright—and some of the best ways to overcome these fears.

Fear of the Audience

"I know the audience hates me. They're out to get me." I have actually had speakers say this to me. My response? "Your audience wants you to do well. In fact, they're delighted that you're the one up there. It means that they can sit in the audience and enjoy the speech."

How we perceive the audience definitely affects our degree of apprehension and nervousness. The more you fear the audience, the more nervous you become. Try these strategies for overcoming this source of stage fright:

➤ **Pick your subject.** The more you like your subject, the more apt you are to see your audience as friendly. You will assume your audience shares your passion and transfer your enthusiasm for the speech to the listeners.

➤ **Be enthusiastic.** If you're up-beat, your audience will be, too. If you're depressed, they're going to pick up on that, as well. You set the tone; set the tone you want. Put on a happy face.

➤ **You're the boss.** Remember: You know what you're talking about. That's why they asked you to be the speaker. You're the one in charge. Trust in your own ability. If you trust yourself, the audience will, as well.

➤ **Silly situations.** Imagine your audience in silly situations. As he faced an audience,

> **Whisper...**
>
> **Tell Me About It**
> For a day before your speech and the day of the speech, avoid drinking or eating anything with high caffeine content. Stay away from tea, cola, coffee, chocolate. Anyone prone to nervousness can be overstimulated by caffeine before a speech.

> **Words to the Wise**
> What about better living through chemistry? A little Valium to help you relax before a speech? No. Avoid tranquilizers. I have seen speakers make total fools of themselves under the influence of tranquilizers. Do it cold; stay in command of the situation.

Winston Churchill liked to imagine everyone was completely undressed. Actress Carol Burnett often imagines them in the bathroom. The situation should be absurd enough to relax you, but not so ridiculous that you dissolve into helpless laughter. This approach makes your audience less threatening.

➤ **Listener linking.** Remember all the work I had you do with audience analysis? Here's another place it pays off. The more complete your audience analysis, the more likely you are to see the audience as nonthreatening.

Fear of Failure

Stage fright arises in part from a fear of doing a bad job. "I'll make a fool of myself in front of my friends," you might think. Even worse, you may be afraid of making a jerk of yourself in front of your boss. Here are two ways to overcome stage fright that arises from this source.

➤ **Fight fear.** Yes, you're scared out of your wits, but unless you show it, no one will know it. You are under no obligation to reveal your feelings. Don't say, "I just want to tell you how nervous I am" or "You can't believe how upset I am about speaking in front of you." You may think that everyone can see the fear written on your face. In nearly all cases, they can't—unless you deliberately show it.

➤ **Visualize success.** Ever hear about self-fulfilling prophecies? They take place when you talk yourself into something. For example, if you assume that you are going to do a bad job up on the podium, you'll very likely undermine your speaking performance. Instead of talking yourself into something that will create more fear and less confidence, talk yourself into something that will create less fear and more confidence. Imagine yourself making the perfect speech.

Control your mental image of yourself; tap all your confidence. Think positively: realize that even though you may not set the room on fire with your silver-tongued orations, there is still a reason they asked you rather than the schlep sitting next to you to speak.

Fear That Your Speech Stinks

"My speech won't be good enough. I'll embarrass myself because my material is terrible." This is the easiest fear to overcome because you are in total control of the speech. You wrote it; you know it cold. Nonetheless, here are some methods you can use to overcome the fear that springs from this reason.

➤ **Write well.** The better your speech, the more confident you will be. The more confident you are, the less stage fright you'll feel. Spend the time writing and rewriting your speech. It's time well spent.

➤ **Rehearse.** As I explained in Chapter 22: practice, practice, practice. I recommend that you practice one hour for every minute of your speech. The more you practice, the more relaxed you will be. Naturally, the best kind of practice is actual public speaking; the more you do, the better you'll be.

Making Fear Work for You

Believe it or not, stage fright has its good side. Because people imagine public speaking as terribly difficult, the speaker is automatically perceived as a powerful person. This means that as the speaker, you don't have to actually do anything: just standing at the podium automatically confers a certain amount of fear in your audience.

Recognize this: once you believe that you can become a self-assured speaker, you can be. The best way to overcome stage fright? Believe in yourself.

The Ten Keys to Smashing the Fear Barrier

Keep the following steps in mind to put fear in its proper place:

➤ Admit you have some stage fright.

➤ Understand that all public speakers are nervous during most performances.

➤ Draw from the energy that fear produces.

➤ Understand that no one has to see your fear but *you*. In many situations, appearance is reality.

➤ Imagine yourself as a successful speaker.

➤ Analyze your audience completely.

➤ Speak on something that matters to you.

➤ Be fully prepared.

➤ Use whatever techniques help you allay your fears.

➤ Be confident; believe in yourself to help others believe in you.

Words to the Wise
Alcohol and public speaking don't mix. Some speakers think a drink or two will help them relax before a performance. They are correct: alcohol will indeed help you relax. Alcohol will also seriously impede your speech, no matter how high your drinking tolerance may be. Avoid all drinking. Even the smallest amount of alcohol can result in slurred words, fluffed timing, and fumbled notes.

Physical and Mental Exercises for Releasing Tension

Stage fright may not be something you actively seek, but recognize that it's normal. Try these easy techniques to master performance anxiety.

The "No Pain, No Gain" Route

➤ A few days before your performance, burn off some of your nervousness by doing some physical exercises, such as racquetball, tennis, bowling, and so on. Physical exercise is an easy and beneficial way to release tension.

➤ Just before you speak, go off by yourself to an empty room and do a few jumping jacks or run in place. Don't get all sweaty and worn out; just release that extra little bit of nervous energy.

➤ Slowly, yawn a few times. This will loosen your throat and help you clear your throat.

➤ Focus on the part of your body that feels the most nervous, such as your stomach, hands, or knees. Working slowly and carefully, tighten the muscles in this part of your body. Hold them a second, and then release. Do this two or three times, and you'll feel the area relax.

➤ Right before you enter the room to give the speech, swing your arms a few times, alternating each side.

The "Less Pain, Still Gain" Approach

➤ Conjure up a pleasant memory, such as a Caribbean vacation or a camping trip to the woods. The memory doesn't have to necessarily be real, as long as the images are vivid. Thinking about something pleasant will help you release tension.

➤ Say to yourself, "I am completely prepared. I wrote a good speech, and I know it thoroughly. I will go out there and do a wonderful job."

> **Bet You Didn't Know**
>
> OOOOH.
>
> Some speakers physically shake when they are under stress. If you're a trembler, take heart; it doesn't show half as much as you think. But here are some tips anyway to help you deal with the shake and bake syndrome:

➤ Don't hold a hand mike. Leave the mike on its stand. This helps hide your shaking.

➤ Draw attention away from your hands. Avoid holding a glass of water, for example, so everyone won't see you create tidal waves in the glass.

➤ Leave your notes on the lectern. That way, people can't see them shake in your hand.

➤ If your legs are trembling, shift your weight between them. Lean forward and grasp the lectern with both hands. If you're sitting down, keep your hands gripped on your knees. This does double-duty: it stops both your hands and legs from trembling.

Take a Test Run

Your test run can be imaginary or real. Let's take a look at how to have an imaginary test run—sort of a "virtual" speech.

Visualize yourself giving the speech and doing a fantastic job. Close your eyes and take yourself through the process, step by step. Imagine yourself walking out on the stage, standing at the lectern, delivering the speech, using your visual aids, accepting applause, answering questions, and calmly walking back to your seat. Imagine as many of the details as you can. Seeing yourself successful during this "test run" will help you give a better speech.

Your test run can also be real. Deliver the speech by yourself, in front of a mirror. As you speak, make eye contact with the "audience" by looking into the mirror. See which facial expressions and gestures work best.

You can also take a test run in front of a real audience. Gather some friends or relatives who didn't run fast enough to elude your entreaties. Deliver the speech for them and solicit their opinions. Ask them to be honest (not brutally so) and weigh their comments.

Be sure to practice the entire speech all the way through. Don't just practice the beginning or ending. If you make a mistake while you are practicing, don't go back and start all over again. Just keep on going because that's what you would have to do during the real speech.

Emergency Rx: Open Only if All Else Fails

Realize that a certain degree of nervousness can actually make you a better speaker by sharpening your edge.

The Least You Need to Know

➤ Virtually every public speaker suffers from stage fright. It's a normal reaction to a stressful situation.

➤ Recognize that the audience is on your side.

➤ There are specific techniques you can learn to make stage fright work for you—not against you.

Final Words

You're almost at the end, troopers. My main purpose in writing this book has been to teach you that writing and delivering a powerful speech is well within your abilities. You learned the basics of effective communication, what goals you should set for yourself when you give a public speech, and how to speak effectively in a wide variety of different situations. You discovered that becoming an effective speaker requires a knowledge of audience, purpose, and task. Be proud of yourself. You earned it.

To sum up, I'm going to explain all about speaker's bureaus. You'll learn how they may suit your professional speech needs. Then I'll summarize the entire public speaking process. I'll provide you with a handy reference list for a quick overview and refresher.

Using Speaker's Bureaus

How similar are the following situations to those problems you face on the job?

➤ You are the director of a manufacturing plant. People in the community are concerned that your plant is dumping industrial waste.

➤ You are an administrator at a hospital that has just opened a new clinic. You want to get the word out to the community about your services.

➤ You are employed by a telecommunications company. You want to convince people that they should switch their phone and fax service to your company.

➤ You are the manager of a supermarket and need to pursue customers more aggressively. How can you persuade people to shop at your store?

➤ You are a naturalist employed by the Environmental Protection Agency. As part of your job, you want to teach community members ways to conserve natural resources such as water, soil, and air.

Word Power

A *speaker's bureau* is an organization designed to convey the company's message to specific groups. The bureau is most often *internally* run and organized, and comprised of company members.

Many professionals in these and similar situations use a *speaker's bureau*. This is an organized effort to convey the company's message to specific groups. More and more firms are discovering that speaker's bureaus are cost-effective ways to reach people in business, social groups, schools, religious organizations, and community affairs. You set up the bureau, develop the materials, and train the speakers. The public can then call and request a speech by a member of the bureau. Here are some guidelines for establishing a speaker's bureau.

1. **Membership.** Decide who is eligible for membership in your speaker's bureau. For example, are all employees included or only full-time people? Do you want both current and retired employees? Management and union? Entry-level to upper-management? Many speaker's bureaus include a cross-section of employees to meet the widest possible needs of the organization.

2. **Size.** Your speaker's bureau should be large enough to meet your needs, but small enough to manage comfortably. It takes a great deal of time and elbow grease to run a speaker's bureau efficiently. As a result, it's best to keep the operation small when you start. It can always be expanded later.

3. **Preparation.** To be effective, your speakers must be prepared. They must be kept informed of all company policies and relevant information, especially those matters that directly impact their speech and the company's image. Here are some factors to consider:

> ➤ Booking speaking engagements.

> ➤ Matching speakers to audiences.

> ➤ Preparing speakers to meet the needs of the company and the group they are addressing.

> ➤ Checking audio-visual needs.

> ➤ Preparing and copying handouts.

> ➤ Arranging for publicity.

> ➤ Setting up substitutes for speakers who cancel.

4. **Publicity.** For a speaker's bureau to be effective, it has to get the word out to the community. Publicity is a must.

Many companies publicize their speaker's bureau through brochures. This is an inexpensive method that packs a big bang for the buck. The brochure should list the topics your speakers will discuss, the members, and their credentials. Include some jazzy graphics, snappy copy, and you're all set.

Distribute the brochure to all relevant organizations in the area. Target the groups who would be most interested in your speakers—and who can do your company the most good. Possibilities include the local Chamber of Commerce, Parent-Teacher Organizations, service groups such as Rotary International, and religious groups. Be sure to mail copies of the brochure and a press release to the news papers, as well.

Tell Me About It
Today, beautiful brochures can be prepared in-house on computers, using widely available and affordable desktop publishing applications. The affordability of color printers makes this an even more affordable option.

5. **Evaluation.** How can you tell if your speakers are effective? Consider designing an evaluation form. Speakers can distribute these to the audience at the end of their presentations.

The evaluation forms should be easy to complete. This chapter includes an illustration of a Speaker Evaluation form.

Speaker Evaluation

Speaker's Name _____

Title of Speech _____

Date _____

Circle one:

Presentation	excellent	good	fair	poor
Content	excellent	good	fair	poor
Audiovisual	excellent	good	fair	poor
Handouts	excellent	good	fair	poor

1. What was the most useful information you got from this speech?

_____

_____

2. What other topics would you like to hear in the future?

_____

_____

Optional: Name, company, address, and telephone number

_____

_____

Adapt this specific form to your company's own needs.

6. **Audiences.** At first, you might find yourself sending your speakers to just about any forum, just to get some publicity. But as the word gets out, you'll be able to more closely match the needs of your organization to the needs of your prospective audiences. Consider these questions when matching speakers to audiences:

   ➤ Is the meeting the appropriate forum for your organization's goals?

   ➤ Do your speakers meet the profile of the speakers usually sent to this organization?

➤ Does the size of the audience justify the expense of sending the speaker?

➤ Who else will be on the agenda? Do you want your speaker yoked with others on this agenda?

7. **Payment.** In most cases, members of a company's speaker's bureau are not paid for their speeches because there are too many possible areas for conflict. For example, should speakers be paid on the basis of their skill, the size of the audience, or the frequency with which they speak? Should speakers be paid more if the issue is sensitive; less if the speech is "easy"? Payment can also affect a speaker's credibility.

8. **Recognition.** Consider offering speakers other forms of recognition. Possibilities include letters of appreciation and comp time (such as two hours off in thanks for a one hour speech). Speakers can also be given tickets to the theater, concerts, or sporting events. Appropriate gifts, such as attaché cases, are also appreciated.

Regardless of compensation, speakers should be reimbursed for any out-of-pocket expenses, such as travel costs, meals on the road, and necessary overnight accommodations.

Bet You Didn't Know

OOOOH.

The rewards of effective speaking go far beyond the lectern. As an effective public speaker, you'll be more at ease with people in all situations. The sense of accomplishment and achievement will enhance your feelings of confidence. Public speaking empowers people.

Summary of the Speech-Writing Process

In previous chapters, I've given you step-by-step instructions for writing and presenting a successful speech. The following briefly summarizes the stages you complete when you write and deliver a speech:

➤ Settle on the purpose of your speech: to inform, to persuade, or to entertain.

➤ Analyze your audience.

➤ Research the information you need.

➤ Organize and outline your material.

➤ Write the introduction, body, and conclusion. I suggest that you write the body first.

➤ Revise and edit your speech.

➤ Make sure that you have used humor appropriately.

➤ Prepare visual aids, audio-visual aids, and props.

➤ Rehearse your speech.

➤ Deliver the speech.

The Least You Need to Know

➤ Speaker's bureaus may be a valuable addition to your company.

➤ The speech writing process involves several clear steps.

➤ You have learned to speak in public with confidence.

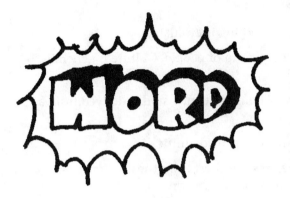

Word Power Glossary

Anecdote   A brief story, often used by speakers to illustrate their point.

Articulation   A way to form sounds. Effective articulation results in clear, crisp consonants and vowels that are easy to understand.

Audience   The people a speaker addresses; the listeners.

Body   The middle of the speech, the section that develops the main idea and supports it with suitable examples, details, and illustrations.

Body language   A series of purposeful gestures that reinforce or show what you want to say.

Chair   The person who runs a meeting.

Chronological order   A way to organize a speech. The information is arranged in the order of time, from the first to the last.

Cliché   A comparison or other phrase that has become stale through overuse.

Communication   The social process by which people in a specific situation construct meaning using symbolic behavior.

Conclusion   The last part of the speech, where the speaker's main points are summarized and reemphasized.

Connotation   A word's overtones; the special meanings that it carries within a culture.

Credibility   The speaker's believability.

Criteria   The standards by which something is evaluated.

Culture   The specialized lifestyle of a group of people. Culture is generally passed down through the generations.

Deduction   A process of reasoning whereby a conclusion is derived from a general rule.

Denotation   A word's dictionary meaning; its definition.

Diaphragm   The muscle that separates the chest from the abdomen. Controlling the diaphragm results in good breath control.

Empathic listening   A type of listening that strives to provide the speaker with emotional support.

Eulogy   A speech given in praise of a person. Eulogies are often delivered at funerals, although they can also be given at testimonial dinners.

Evaluative listening   A type of listening that strives to assist in decision-making.

Evidence   Details, examples, facts, statistics, and other data that supports the speaker's thesis.

Eye contact   Making direct visual contact with members of the audience.

Feedback   The reaction that the audience gives to the speaker.

Figures of speech (or Figurative language)   Language that is not meant to be taken in a literal sense. Figures of speech enrich ideas by making them more vivid and easier to visualize.

Goodwill   The audience's perception that the speaker shares their concerns and interests.

Identification   The audience's perception that the speaker is similar to them and can be trusted.

Impromptu speaking   Speaking at a gathering with very little preparation and without the use of notes.

Induction   A process of reasoning that arrives at a general conclusion from specific examples.

Inferring   Making generalizations; "reading between the lines."

Informational listening   Listening to gather information and facts.

Informative speeches   Clarifying a concept or process for your audience, defining terms and relationships, or in any way expanding the audience's knowledge. The object of your speech is to *inform.*

Introduction   The beginning of the speech. In the introduction, the speaker gets the audience's attention, states the topic and purpose, and may preview the main ideas.

Narrative   A story or anecdote meant to inform or entertain.

Oral interpretation   The art of reading a selection aloud to communicate emotion or ideas.

Perception   The process we use to derive meaning from sensory data.

Persuasive speech   A type of speech that attempts to move the audience to action or belief.

Pitch   The highness or lowness of a sound. It is determined by the frequency of vocal waves.

Post hoc ergo hoc   The mistaken belief that one thing was caused by another. It is a type of logical fallacy.

Prejudice   A preconceived judgment or opinion about a person or a group.

Public communication   Communication with a large group; one member talks while the rest of the group listens.

Rate   The speed of speech.

Reasoning backward   A logical fallacy whereby people assume that since members of a particular group share common qualities, anyone with those qualities must belong to the group.

Rehearsal   Practicing your speech.

Spatial organization   A pattern of speech organization that presents information in terms of its position.

Speech communication   Sending and receiving oral messages to create meaning.

Speaker's bureau   An organized effort to convey the company's message to specific groups.

Testimonial   Having a celebrity endorse a person, place, or thing.

Theme or Thesis   A speech's one main idea.

Timbre, Tone, or Color   The quality of a person's voice.

Topic   The subject of a speech.

Topical organization   A pattern of speech organization in which details are arranged according to subdivisions of the topic.

Transitions   Words that link ideas.

Visual aids   Charts, graphs, maps, handouts, models, objects, photographs, posters, slides, videotapes, movies, diagrams, audiotapes—any visual or audio aid to a speech presentation.

Volume   The loudness level at which you speak related to the distance between you and the listener and the amount of noise that surrounds the listener.

Sample Speeches

In this section of the book, you'll find three sample speeches: an informative speech, an entertaining speech, and a persuasive speech. Each illustrates a series of different speech techniques covered in this book. Study these examples to see how everything you learned fits together.

Sample Informative Speech

This speech was delivered before a group of community leaders and business people at a luncheon meeting of Rotary International. The purpose of the speech was to inform the audience about comic books; the speaker is the Executive Director of Production for DC Comics and *MAD* Magazine with more than twenty years experience in the industry. The speech took about fifteen minutes to deliver, including the use of visual aids. It is presented here to illustrate a contemporary example of the type of informative speech you would be likely to deliver in similar situations.

The History of Comic Books

Good afternoon, ladies and gentlemen. I've been asked to give you a short history of the world of comic books. As some of you already know, I'm the executive director for production at DC Comics. I also wrote comic books for about ten years. In my speech today, I'll hit the high points in the history of comic books and maybe have time for questions at the end.

The comic book industry began in the mid-1930s. A man named M. C. Gaines, known as "Max" to his friends, had the idea that compiling a collection of newspaper comic strips in a magazine form would work well as a premium giveaway. So the first comic book was just that—reprints—and it was given away to people who bought Ivory Soap. Other companies also saw the popularity of such magazines and very soon, all the usable strips were being reprinted.

In stepped Major Malcolm Wheeler-Nicholson, a man with a hefty paper supply and a solid printing contract. Nicholson started his company by printing *New Comics* and *New Fun Comics*, using all new material. And he hired Max Gaines to be in charge. In 1936, they started another new title, *Detective Comics*, the first comic book devoted to a single theme. It was this title that gave the company its name: DC Comics.

In 1938, looking for a lead feature to launch another new title, Gaines and his editors settled on a strip that had been created five years earlier. It had been unsuccessfully offered as a newspaper strip by two teenagers from Cleveland. The character could lift cars, leap over buildings, and bounce bullets off his chest. The young writer-artist duo were Jerry Seigel and Joe Shuster. The new magazine was named *Action Comics*. The character was called Superman.

Superman proved to be an overnight success. As quickly as they could, other publishers (and DC itself) sought to make economic lightning strike again and again. Costumed heroes arrived by the busload, including Batman, The Flash, Green Lantern, and Wonder Woman from DC; Captain America, the Human Torch, and Sub-Mariner from Timely; Captain Marvel and the Marvel Family from Fawcett; and Plastic Man and The Spirit from Quality. It was an age of heroes that lasted through the second World War and into the late 40s.

By the end of World War II, interest in the heroes was waning. Publishers started looking for new kinds of magazines that would sell. Crime comics, Western comics, war comics, and romance comics all started appearing. MLJ Publications, for example, started a back-up feature about "America's Typical Teenager" . . . Archie! And at EC Publications, which Max Gaines had started after leaving DC and which was now being run by his son Bill, there was the dawn of the horror comics.

With such titles as *Tales from the Crypt* and *Weird Science*, Bill Gaines and his crew sent the industry scrambling in a new direction, one that eventually spawned a parental uproar and a Congressional investigation. With each new rival publisher going for more and more gory material, it was an easy task for psychologist Fredric Wertham to gain notoriety and generate sales of his book *Seduction of the Innocent,* which blamed all the ills of society on comic books.

In an attempt to forestall Congressional action and public backlash, the larger comics publishers banded together and formed the Comics Magazine Association, with a Comics Code for appropriate comic book material. Virtually overnight, Gaines and his schlockmeister competitors were forced to abandon comics. Gaines continued on the fringe of the business, publishing a highly successful comic-book-turned-magazine: *MAD.*

Comics languished throughout the early- and mid-50's until Julius Schwartz, an editor at DC, proposed bringing the superheroes back for another try. The year was 1956. He revised and revamped The Flash to an enthusiastic response, then followed with Green Lantern, Hawkman, The Atom, and the Justice League of America.

Meanwhile, over at Atlas (formerly Timely) Comics, publisher Martin Goodman saw the success of his rivals and suggested to his young editor that they should start publishing superhero comics as well. The editor, a longtime writer of comics for Timely/Atlas named Stan Lee, took a shot and created the Fantastic Four, Spider-Man, the Incredible Hulk, and the X-Men. It was not long before a new age of superheroes was upon us. The early 60s saw almost as many new characters as the 40s had, products of a frenzy fueled by the *Batman* TV series in 1966.

In the early 70s, the comic book industry became aware that their audience was changing. Instead of readers losing interest at age 14, they were staying on, looking for more diverse and challenging material. This was coupled with the utilization of new printing technologies and the growth of a direct market, in which the publishers could supply books directly to comic book shops. As a result, the industry went through its largest expansion ever, with record numbers of titles being produced every month.

A new generation of horror comics, many produced by fans-turned-professionals from England, began to appear, aimed at an adult audience. Far more graphic than those of the 50s, but also with far more complex storylines, these books in particular have led former readers back into the comic book fold.

In leaps and bounds, led by DC Comics and its incredibly foresighted Production Director, the comic book industry dove into computerized color and art, bringing it up to techno-speed . . . and in some cases ahead of the curve. New printing techniques were utilized. Paper was reformulated to best show off the subtleties of the artwork.

Which brings us to the present . . . when it would cost over $2,000 to buy a month's worth of titles. Superheroes still rule the day, but there is room for much, much more. There is something for every taste . . . for every reader.

Now, since I think we have a few moments left, are there any questions?

Entertaining Speech

The following entertaining speech is by Mark Twain (1835–1910), one of the most captivating writers and speakers to ever grace a podium. Mark Twain, the pen name of Samuel Langhorne Clemens, rocketed to fame with humorous local-color tales of the West; he became a media darling by transforming stories of his childhood into American myth. Twain was extraordinarily popular on the lecture circuit, a popular venue for public entertainment before movies, television, radio, and Ross Perot.

Mark Twain Reveals Stage Fright

My heart goes out in sympathy to anyone who is making his first appearance before an audience of human beings. By a direct process of memory I go back forty years, less one month—for I'm older than I look.

I recall the occasion of my first appearance. San Francisco knew me then only as a reporter, and I was to make my bow to San Francisco as a lecturer. I knew that nothing short of compulsion would get me to the theater. So I bound myself by a hard-and-fast contract so that I could not escape. I got to the theater forty-five minutes before the hour set for the lecture. My knees were shaking so that I didn't know whether I could stand up. If there is an awful, horrible malady in the world, it is stage fright—and seasickness. They are a pair. I had stage fright then for the first and last time. I was only seasick once, too. I was on a little ship on which there were two hundred other passengers. I—was—sick. I was so sick that there wasn't any left for those other two hundred passengers.

It was dark and lonely behind the scenes in that theater, and I peeked through the little peek holes they have in theater curtains and looked into the big auditorium. That was dark and empty, too. By and by it lighted up, and the audience began to arrive.

I had a number of friends of mine, stalwart men, to sprinkle themselves throughout the audience armed with clubs. Every time I said anything they could possibly guess I intended to be funny, they were to pound those clubs on the floor. Then there was a kind lady in a box up there, also a good friend of mine, the wife of the governor. She was to watch me intently, and whenever I glanced toward her she was going to deliver a gubernatorial laugh that would lead the whole audience into applause.

At last I began. I had the manuscript tucked under a United States flag in front of me where I could get at in case of need. But I managed to get started without it. I walked up and down—I was young in those days and needed the exercise—and talked and talked.

Right in the middle of the speech I had placed a gem. I had put in a moving, pathetic part which was to get at the hearts and souls of my hearers. When I delivered it, they did just what I hoped and expected. They sat silent and awed. I had touched them. Then I happened to glance up at the box where the governor's wife was—you know what happened.

Well, after the first agonizing five minutes, my stage fright left me, never to return. I know if I was going to be hanged I could get up and make a good showing, and I intend to. But I shall never forget my feelings just before the agony left me, and I got up here to thank you for helping my daughter, by your kindness, to live through her first appearance. And I want to thank you for your appreciation of her singing, which is, by the way, hereditary.

Persuasive Speech

Abraham Lincoln (1809–56) served as president during one of the most difficult periods in American history. But even if Lincoln had not been president, he would have been remembered for his words and speeches. Lincoln was renowned as an exquisite stylist. It has been computed that his printed speeches and writings contain over a million words. These words are more important for their quality than their quantity, however. Lincoln delivered the Gettysburg Address in 1863. The reporter for the *Providence Journal* asked, "Could the more elaborate and splendid oration be more beautiful, more touching, more inspiring, than those thrilling words of the President?" *The Chicago Tribune*, however, understood the speech's true importance: "The dedicatory remarks of President Lincoln will live among the annals of man," it wrote. And so it has been.

The Gettysburg Address

Fourscore and seven years ago our fathers brought forth on this continent a new nation, conceived in liberty, and dedicated to the proposition that all men are created equal.

Now we are engaged in a great civil war, testing whether that nation, or any nation so conceived and so dedicated, can long endure. We are met on a great battlefield of that war. We have come to dedicate a portion of that field as a final resting-place for those who here gave their lives that that nation might live. It is altogether fitting and proper that we should do this.

But in a larger sense, we cannot dedicate—we cannot consecrate—we cannot hallow—this ground. The brave men, living and dead, who struggled here, have consecrated it, far above our poor power to add or detract. The world will little note, nor long remember what we say here, but it can never forget what they did here. It is for us the living, rather, to be dedicated here to the unfinished work which they who fought here have thus far nobly advanced. It is rather for us to be here dedicated to the great task remaining before us— that from those honored dead we take increased devotion to that cause for which they gave the last full measure of devotion—that we here highly re-solve that these dead shall not have died in vain—that this nation, under God, shall have a birth of freedom—and that government of the people, by the people, for the people, shall not perish from the earth.

Seven Speeches to Study and Remember (or: Only Crib from the Best)

1. **George Washington's farewell address (1796)**

   Washington stressed the importance of national unity as the "main pillar" of the nation's independence, peace, and prosperity.

2. **Thomas Jefferson's first inaugural address (1801)**

   Jefferson is revered as one of the finest prose stylists America has ever produced. This speech contains his famous reference to the United States as "the word's best hope" and his praise of "wise and frugal government which shall restrain men from injuring one another, [and] shall leave them otherwise free to regulate their own pursuits." At the time, the fact that Jefferson's election marked the first real change of the party control of the government made his promise to respect the rights of the Federalist minority seem the most important point in the address.

3. **Daniel Webster's second reply to Hayne (1830)**

   In this speech, the silver-tongued Webster called the American flag "the gorgeous ensign of the republic" and concluded the speech with this sentence: "Liberty and Union, now and forever, one and inseparable."

4. **Abraham Lincoln's "House Divided" speech (1858)**

   Lincoln delivered this speech on the occasion of his nomination as the Republican candidate for senator from Illinois. It was probably Lincoln's most radical statement about the implications of the slavery issue, the one he predicted that "this government cannot endure permanently half slave and half free."

5. **William Jennings Bryan's "Cross of Gold" speech (1896)**

   Bryan made the speech at the 1896 Democratic National Convention. Bryan, arguing for a plank in the party platform calling for the free coinage of silver, ended his speech with this sentence: "You shall not press down upon the brow of labor this crown of thorns, you shall not crucify mankind upon a cross of gold." "You" were the Gold Democrats, the supporters of the incumbent President, Grover Cleveland, who opposed the unlimited coinage of silver. The speech made Bryan a national figure and led to his nomination for the Presidency.

6. **Woodrow Wilson's call for declaration of war against Germany (1917)**

   This speech contains the famous line: "The world must be made safe for democracy." The speech is also remarkable for Wilson's insistence that "we have no quarrel with the German people . . . We fight without rancor and without selfish object." Such self-restraint and Wilson's promise that victory would result in "a universal dominion of right" helped win liberal support for the war effort.

7. **Franklin Delano Roosevelt's first inaugural address (1933)**

   This is remembered for its ringing line: "The only thing we have to fear is fear itself" and Roosevelt's promise to "put people to work." Although it was a very effective speech, it was also padded and full of doubtful advice. For example, Roosevelt felt compelled to point out that "happiness lies not in the mere possession of money."

Index

Symbols